Expat Life
Slice by Slice

APPLE GIDLEY

First published Great Britain 2012 by Summertime Publishing

ISBN 978-1-904881-71-1

Book Design by Creationbooth – creationbooth.com

For JKG

who has my heart

Table of Contents

Expat Life: **SLICE BY SLICE**

Glossary of Abbreviations
Timeline
Prologue

First Slice: An Itinerant Early Life 1
Second Slice: STARS 17
Third Slice: A TCK and Didn't Know It 59
Fourth Slice: Customs, Culture and Calypso 91
Fifth Slice: Service with a Smile 111
Sixth Slice: Education, a Conundrum 137
Seventh Slice: Volunteering is Work................................ 155
Eighth Slice: Staying Connected 197
Ninth Slice: Death at a Distance 215
Tenth Slice: Empty Nests and New Chicks 237
Eleventh Slice: Home is Where 249
Twelfth Slice: R 'n' R: Repatriation and Retirement 279
Last Slice 295

About the Author 297

To Delia,

Enjoy your time in Trinidad – it's about the journey,

Apple Cidder

The future is nothing, but the past is myself,
my own history, the seed of my present thoughts,
the mould of my present disposition.

Essays of the Road
Robert Louis Stevenson

Glossary of Abbreviations

ANZAC	Australian and New Zealand Army Corps
BAMBI	Babies and Mothers Bangkok International
BOAC	British Overseas Airways Corporation
BWG	British Women's Group
CCK	Cross Cultural Kid
EG	Equatorial Guinea
FIGT	Families in Global Transition, an international organisation dedicated to helping people (and those who support them) from all sectors, diplomatic, corporate, military, ngo, missionary, and the arts, relocate around the world.
ICH	International Connections of Houston, a group for expatriates and repatriates
KL	Kuala Lumpur, capital of Malaysia
MK	Military Kid
NEGS	New England Girls School, Armidale, NSW, Australia
NGO	Non Governmental Organisation
PNG	Papua New Guinea
STARS	Spouses Travelling and Relocating Successfully
TCD	Third Culture Dog (see TCK below)
TCK	Third Culture Kid: A person who has spent a significant part of his or her developmental years outside their parents' culture.
TSU	Texas Southern University, Houston
VSO	Volunteer Services Overseas, started in the United Kingdom in1958. The US Peace Corps, established in 1961, is a similar organisation.
WI	Woman's Institute, a network of women's groups in the UK, famous for, among many things, making jam!

Timeline

Relocation dates are never precise, rarely taking place on 1 January, so the following is a rough guideline. As advance warning, *Expat Life: SLICE BY SLICE*, by the very nature of the timeline, tends to jump around in time and place.

1958	Born London, England, moved to Nigeria
1963	England, sailed to Malaysia
1964	Singapore
1966	Malaysia
1969	Based in Malaysia, went to boarding school in .. Australia until 1975
1973	Australia, moved Papua New Guinea
1975	Left Australia when school finished
1976	England
1977	Papua New Guinea
1978	England
1980	The Netherlands
1984	Trinidad and Tobago
1985	Thailand
1986	Singapore
1987	Thailand
1989	Singapore, then Scotland
1997	USA
2002	Equatorial Guinea, West Africa
2005	USA

Prologue

Until the explosion of the Internet and the subsequent proliferation of blogs, expatriates were a rather silent subspecies. People have been expatriating since records began, for agriculture, for land, for freedom from persecution, for riches, for adventure. Whatever the reason most expatriates, whether willing or not, whether man or woman, will at some stage get the blues. Whatever the reason, no global entrepreneur should be denigrated for having the courage to leave everything they hold dear, for taking a giant leap into the unknown.

A lot less is unknown now. The Internet allows us to thoroughly research a country, to make cyber contacts, to meet friends of friends, to get a pretty good idea of what awaits when disembarking the plane. But there is no preparation for the momentary panic as you hit the tarmac, not running but staggering from travel fatigue and jetlag and the last frenetic months. The sense of loss of, "What-have-I-done?" is overwhelming. For some that feeling lasts a few minutes, for others it lasts weeks or months. For a very few it lasts the length of time abroad, but often on repatriation this minority realises just how much time they wasted on regrets.

I truly believe to know a country we have to become involved in that country. We cannot be a mere bystander if we wish to pierce the psyche of a nation, to become more than a paying guest, to come to love her culture and her people without necessarily being enamoured by all her behaviours. But when we have our honesty hat on, we realise there are a variety of customs and rites of passage, which do not appeal from our own country.

I do not claim real citizenship of any country, though I am eligible to vote in two. I claim kinship with many. I have extraordinary memories from all those I have lived in, and some from others merely visited. I love a few. I am the epitome of a global nomad. I am happy wherever I am, though naturally happier in some places than others. There are a few I have no yen to return to. There are a couple I would leap on a plane for at a moment's notice, and some unknown for which I would do the same. Some I regret not having seen in their heyday, before corruption and politics ruined them. But that is subjective.

I grew up in the last days of colonialism. As a child I seemed to go from emerging country to newly independent country and back – Nigeria, Malaysia, Papua New Guinea. I believe every country has the right to run its own affairs, I really do. But often, for all the anti-colonial feelings of many, both in the ex-colonial power and in-country, the man on the street can still be heard to say, "Ahh we were left with policies, with education, with electricity and clean water, now we have none of that." It is a sad indictment for self-government. I get very cross with the apologists. On the whole, countries once colonised were run with justness, with the welfare of the people in mind. Granted land riches were plundered, the Congo under Leopold of the Belgians could be classified as one of the worst examples. All colonialists are guilty of sending riches back to base.

But isn't that what expatriates do now? Send monetary rewards to offshore accounts?

This little book is the culmination of over fifty years as an expatriate. Lessons learned along the way from many people: my parents, John and Ida Girling, who showed me how it's done with, on the whole, humour and compassion; those people in all the countries who graciously allowed me a glimpse of their culture and steered me away from *faux pas* in a foreign land.

My thanks go to my husband John, who has encouraged me on whatever tangential path I chose; my children, now grown, for surviving my parenting shortfalls but who somehow turned out to be good and true global citizens; my old friend through many countries and years, Kay Chapman, for being my first reader of all things and always gentle in her comments; my new friend, Sandy Lease, who graciously agreed to also read; my publisher Jo Parfitt for making me sit down and write this book; my editor Jane Dean for making my words more readable, and finally to all of you out there who have lived this life as an expatriate, many miles from where you grew up.

We have all become richer in our knowledge of the world, richer from friendships made in the strangest of places, but many of us still don't know *where home is?*

And really does it matter? Home is where you are happy, whether Honduras or Houston or Hungary, home is where you are.

First Slice: An Itinerant Early Life

"Dat piccaninny, she dun be bad Madum! She dun tek mon-kee 'gin."

I don't think I was a particularly naughty child but flitting across the misty rim of my mind I can hear those words, and so I can only suppose they were used quite frequently. I do remember I was only called 'dat piccaninny' when I was in trouble.

The 'mon-kee' referred to was Munnings, who, unless closely shadowed by my mother, was kept on a long chain staked at the back of the house. I felt, at age four, quite capable of providing the same supervision and would, when the mood took me, unchain him and we would play.

Munnings was always gentle with me, but could be very easily tempted by any hapless woman wandering down the dusty lane outside our fence, carrying her precious cargo of bananas to market on her head. He would lollop away, scramble over the gate, and terrorise the fruit carrier until, in desperation, and amid frantic screamings from both sides of the fence, he would be pacified with a banana, caught and retethered. My mother would in turn calm the poor woman, offer her a cool drink and of course buy her load. Peace would return, but for 'dat piccaninny' a scolding would be forthcoming. And we ate a lot of fruit.

I was almost born in Africa. I suppose you could say Africa gave me my name. *Tinkling Stream over Rolling Pebbles* or *Running Fox Fast as the Wind* are charming, evocative names if you happen to be of Chinese or American Indian birth. Celestial Apple, the name my father chose for me, is an unreasonable name to live up to if you are born a hefty eight-pound Anglo-Australian baby with red hair. Fortunately my mother, the down-to-earth Australian part of my lineage, told him, "Not bloody likely!"

In the interests of marital harmony my parents agreed to call the daughter of their union, me, Apple, although for bookkeeping purposes I was to be known as Frances Alison Havelock.

Celestial Apple came about when my father, safely out-of-the-way in Nigeria, awaited my birth in London, England, and was being hounded by the resident expatriate busybody.

"What," she kept asking him, "Are you going to call the baby if it's a girl?"

In desperation and because letters to and from Britain and Africa discussing the life-long decision of their baby's name took rather a long time fifty or so years ago, he finally blurted in all his pomposity, "I shall call her Celestial Apple." It was the name of the main character, a beautiful and sympathetic soul by all accounts, in a book set in 19th Century China.

Not satisfied with his flippant response, she wandered the cocktail circuit of Kano, pink gin in one hand and cigarette in the other, asking all and sundry, "I say, have you heard the extraordinary name John Girling, you know the new manager of L&K, is giving his daughter?"

"Oh I didn't know the baby had arrived."

"No, no, it hasn't. But if it's a girl he's going to call her Celestial Apple! What do you think of that?"

"Good Lord, rather a strange name for an English child. Is his wife foreign?"

I am eternally grateful 'Celestial' was relegated to the bad idea pile.

Mum and I joined my father a month after my birth. I don't remember the flight or much of the ensuing six years during which we moved five times within Nigeria. I do have grainy memories of incidents; being the Virgin Mary in the nursery school nativity play, tea parties on the verandah with my mother, all the animals, stuffed and real, the house next door burning in the middle of the night, and Pamela Smith wetting her pants.

I don't remember my nannies, I am told I had two, Adelaide and Demetu, who cared for me when Mum started nursing in the various local hospitals. I do, though, remember very well Ali Wadai, our cook, who traveled with us throughout our moves around the country and provided an element of continuity in an itinerant early life. Ali was a Sudanese who had served in the Nigerian Regiment during the war and, whenever we had guests, wore pinned across his white *buba* his full set of medals.

"Apu, yu no tuch!" was a constant admonishment.

Sam, who worked closely with Ali, was our houseboy. When I was hounded out of the kitchen and away from Munnings, it was Sam I would tag along after. It was he I sat with on the kitchen steps leading back to their quarters, cleaning the silver before a Sunday lunch party, and he who taught me to set a table.

I shadowed him as he walked around the table first placing the forks, small and large, in perfect alignment. Next we walked around with the knives, small and large. We counted as we went around and around the table because I can still hear him saying, "Two fok, two 'nif, two spon, two fok, two 'nif, two spon" as a kind of mantra, possibly instilled by my mother when she taught him the same task. We would wander out into the garden where brilliant red and orange ixora and hibiscus bloomed in profusion and Sam would help me pick flowers for the table.

"I do it."

"No, missy Apu, I do. Yu no cut," he'd say waving me away from the secateurs.

Sam taught me well. One of my favourite jobs before a dinner party is to set and decorate the table and mutter my own mantra of, "Two fok, two 'nif, two spon".

We moved a lot in Nigeria. From Kano to Zaria, to Lagos and Port Harcout and finally to Aba. I don't remember the turmoil I'm sure surrounded each relocation. I only remember Ali and all the animals came too. My father used to disappear to Ontur for weeks on end. He would return with a sunburnt right arm, which had rested on the open window of his car as he travelled. It was a long time before I understood he was actually going 'on tour' visiting the towns and villages, all in the name of trade and gas distribution. I missed him but enjoyed having my mother, with her endless patience with my imaginary friends and animals, to myself. One such friend was Ginjiraf, who everyone had to be careful not to tread on, close the car door on, or forget to kiss goodnight.

"Did Gingiraf enjoy school as well?" Mum asked, as I returned from my first day at kindergarten.

"He's dead." I replied, and apparently never mentioned him again. Ali, Sam and my parents missed him more than I. I had real friends now.

Piccaninny, Chil' Missy and Apu were all names I grew up with and I think it rather depended on the level of my transgression as to what I was called. I don't ever recall being teased for having a slightly unusual name at school though. Some of that was quite possibly because I was strange anyway.

When we returned to England for home leave, which in those days was six months every three years, I was enrolled in the local village school. The whole deal was arduous as far as I was concerned. I did not like wearing lots of clothes, and lace-up shoes and socks were horribly restricting.

"It'll be fun, sweetie-pie, meeting lots of new friends," Mum said, as I trailed along to school that first morning, huddled deep into a scarf that tugged my hair, along pavements slick with fallen leaves and drizzle.

"How do you know they'll be my friends?"

"Well, isn't it nicer thinking everyone you meet will be a friend?" she replied. She always worked under that assumption – each new move, each new school, each new country was a treasure trove of possibility.

My first day was uncomfortable. I was an oddity, in class for only a term, a pudgy little girl with pigtails who did not like wearing shoes and hated custard. My fellow students found me very strange, and I found them even stranger.

"Where are you from?"

"Africa," I said.

"No you're not."

"I am so."

"You're a liar. You're not black."

Lunch was grim, filled with high-pitched voices that swirled around the dining hall, which doubled as an assembly room, bland food glooped onto my plate. Curry would've been my choice.

But life settled down and Rosie and the Twins were my best friends, for a term. And then it was home to Ali, Sam and all the animals.

We had a menagerie of common, and not so common, animals. Villagers, Dad's employees and random strangers who had heard of 'de lady she like mon-kee' would appear at the gate with a furry creature. Sometimes a baby whose mother had been shot - that was how Munnings became part of the family, sometimes an injured squirrel or bush baby. They all joined Cottage, our mutt.

Dad put up with the animals, but photos show a rather strained face as a squirrel runs along his rigid arm. Mum had a steady correspondence with Gerald Durrell, the author and zookeeper, about one particular bush baby, but before arrangements could be made for shipping to his Jersey zoo it disappeared and presumably ended up in the cooking pot. That was the first time I remember seeing my mother cry, she had nursed the shivering, almost hairless handful to a cheeky bug-eyed bundle of fur. She loved babies and animals and was far more affectionate and tactile with them than older humans.

It is rather strange writing this because, as I write, I start to appreciate how much an influence my mother has had on my attitude to moving, on my parenting, and on how I live my life in general. None of my transfers as an adult have come close to encompassing those my mother faced, and I suppose I never felt I had much to moan about. Mum rarely talked about her childhood, her mother died of diptheria when she was eight, but for all that she was close to her seven siblings, four the progeny of her father's second marriage. As I came to appreciate her strength I also came to understand her sometimes prickly demeanour, though not soon enough to avoid the constant antagonism of my late teens.

Mum was a pragmatic woman. She'd had to be. She was in Singapore as it fell to the Japanese during the war; the *Empire Star*, the ship she and other Australian Army Nurses were being evacuated on, was bombed and strafed as they ducked around the islands on their way to Batavia. On their arrival in Perth, Australia, they were met at the dock by people waving white feathers, angry Mum's ship had escaped and the *Vyner Brook*, also carrying nurses, had not. She was then posted to Alexishafen in New Guinea where more horrors of war awaited. As the war ended she nursed in a repatriation hospital for a couple of years just north of Sydney before heading to Europe, where she worked in Denmark and England. Tired of reporting to harridan-like matrons, she applied to the British Red Cross and was posted to a one-woman clinic in the jungles of Pahang in Malaya, then in the midst of the euphemistically called 'Emergency' – in reality a Communist uprising that lasted ten years.

Her adventures were never discussed. A snippet might surface in an overheard conversation now and then when I'd hear her say, "Yes, I was here then," or "Yes, I remember him. He was with the 3 Malay," or some such other tantalizing comment and I'd quiz her later.

"Oh, sweetie, it was all such a long time ago, I really can't remember," would be her stock response, but her experiences obviously coloured her ability to upsticks and move on as my father's job dictated. I really don't ever remember there being dramas or any real fuss made about saying goodbye to friends. We were lucky and privileged to be able to lead an exciting life and if it meant we had to move, well we had to move. It was part of our life and that was that. Her method only backfired once.

"Apple?" I heard my name bellowed up the spiral staircase from the ground floor of the dormitory building at NEGS, New England Girls School, my boarding school in Armidale, New South Wales, Australia.

"Yeah," I shouted back helpfully.

"Phone!"

"Okay, coming."

I barreled down the stairs, against all regulations, wondering who could be calling. I was not in the midst of a teen romance, which was normally announced to the world by the sudden flurry of phone calls.

"G'day?" I said.

"Hello? Sweetie-pie? "

"Oh wow, hi Mum," I responded warily. Phone calls from home were very rare.

"Hello? Hello?" she repeated, the signal screeching and echoing under the ocean. I heard her say to my father, "The bloody line's down, I can't hear her!"

"Mum," I shouted, "I'm here! Don't hang up!"

"Oh, that's better. I can hear you now. How are you?"

"Okay, why are you calling?" Three minutes on an international call went very quickly.

"Some news actually. We're leaving KL. Isn't that exciting?"

"Why? When?" I asked, not believing KL would no longer be home.

"In July. We're coming to Australia for a while. Won't that be fun?" I could hear the phone changing hands all the way across the countries.

"Hello, sweetie," my father's voice came over deep and very English to my ears once again accustomed to an Australian twang. "I've decided to leave James Warren. Time for a change. We're going to live in Brisbane while I look around for something."

"But what about home?" I asked. "What about Ah Moi, Ah Yong and Peck Yoke? What about the animals?"

"Don't worry Apple, everything'll be sorted out. It'll be fine. Won't it be fun to live in Australia for a while? Everything all right? Oh damn, there are the pips."

"Yes, Daddy," I said, and hung up as he said goodbye.

I was in the office that doubled as a cocoa and biscuit station just before lights out. The normal occupants at that time of evening were prefects and other 6th formers lounging around and in charge of doling out the fare.

"You okay, Apple? What's happened?" one asked, waving a shushing hand to someone asking for more cocoa at the counter.

"Yeah," I said, and climbed the stairs to my dorm.

Word travels fast along the corridors of a boarding school. The door burst open and my dorm-mate threw herself on my bed next to me.

"We're leaving KL in July," I sobbed, "I won't get to say goodbye."

"Oh no," Fi said. "Can't you go home for the May holiday?"

"I never do that," I hiccupped, tears and snot mingling on my pillow as I scrubbed my eyes.

"Where are you moving to?"

"Here. Brisbane."

"Oh. That'll be strange for you. Can't you ask to go first?"

"I don't think so. Dad didn't mention it. And it's expensive."

It was the start of a horrid couple of months. Letters came from home giving more details but no mention of me going home to say goodbye. I started sleepwalking. I couldn't stay awake in class. I had headaches. I cried a lot. I was sent to Hosie, the school hospital, who sent me to the doctor. "Buck up," I was told. Eventually, I imagine after calls between the school and my parents in three-minute increments where, "What shall we do about Apple?" was the topic of discussion, it was decided I would become a day pupil and live in town with my beloved aunt, Patricia, for the remainder of term, about three weeks.

I felt as though my cornerstone was being wrenched from me. My identity was being changed and I had no say in it. I was no longer 'Apple, who was a little different, who lived in Malaysia and who always spoke like a Pommie when she returned from holidays there.' Instead I would be 'Apple who lived in Brisbane with an English father who everyone loved because he sounded so posh, Apple who no longer flew around the world on her own, just plain Apple.' And I couldn't even go home before my life was packed up for me.

It was I believe, Patricia, one of Mum's sisters, who finally said, "She has to go home. She has to say goodbye."

I went home for two weeks. I said my goodbyes; to Ah Moi and Ah Yong, the two women who had been with us for eight years, who had looked after me, scolded and loved me, to Mak Peck Yoke, Ah Moi's daughter and my companion on many escapades, most of which we thought were undercover, to Ebi, our driver, and keeper of my secret teenage dalliances and to the animals, four dogs and one cat, who could not come to Australia because of the strict quarantine laws and the expense. Friends were not an issue. My primary school friends had mostly left, or dispersed to boarding schools mainly in England and those who stayed in KLwere no longer on my radar.

It was a tear-filled time. Hugging Ah Moi, the dogs clustered around sensing drama, as my parents waited by the car, ready to take me back to the airport to return to school. I thought I'd never be happy again.

"Time to go, sweetie-pie," Mum said, and hustled me into the back seat.

At the airport Ebi, who had driven me to and from parties, firstly children's parties and then later teenage ones; Ebi who made sure I didn't break my curfew; Ebi who never told my father about the time I threw up out the car window after experimenting with gin one night; Ebi, whose third marriage was the first Malay wedding I attended, bowed and wishing me goodbye and safe travels said, *"Selamat tinggal Ahpu, nasib baik!"*

My father's hand on my arm stopped me from hugging him and instead I bowed back, shook hands and replied, *"Terima kasih Ebi, tuah kepada anda juga,"* thanking him and returning his good wishes before walking into the airport through a veil of new tears with my parents.

"Everything will be fine, sweetie," they said, as they waved me off and away from my home.

And it was. I'd been able to say my goodbyes. I adjusted to my holidays being spent in Australia and not Asia. There were advantages, even though Brisbane in those days could not really decide if it were a large country town or the more serious state capital of Queensland. I saw more of my parents. My school friends could come and stay instead of me always staying with them. Financial woes were more easily rectified with a penitent phone call rather than the old three-week wait for the mail.

Nine months later my axis tipped again, but this time happily. We moved to Papua New Guinea and it was around this time that home, for me, became a *concept* and no longer a *place*. Life started to be compartmentalised. Home and school were two completely separate parts of my life that rarely converged.

It was rice that took us to Papua New Guinea, a mandated territory under the protection of Australia, which was heading toward independence.

If Brisbane had not been to my liking, PNG certainly was. The excitement of a new country and a people very different to those already experienced, was heady. My self-perceived aura of 'different' returned and I was able to determine my place in the world once again.

I loved Lae. On the northern shores of the Huon Peninsular and the commercial capital of the country, it was a slightly ramshackle town of mostly unpaved roads, imaginatively numbered, First, Second, Third, Fourth Street and so on. But the colours of the country were spectacular. The sky and sea blended together at the edge of the world in a haze of cerulean. In the Highlands the deep heather-like hues of purple and blue drew a defining line between sky and land, but only when the heavy clouds allowed the sky to show through. On the coast hedges of red, tangerine and yellow hibiscus bloomed with jaunty abandon, purple and magenta bougainvillea rioted on sunny walls, and the stately bird of paradise flowered in regimental order along the roads. The more brazen cannas clumped in masses of yellow, orange and red all under the intense glow of the sun. The vines and undergrowth violated any breach of fence or paving whenever possible, and the razor-sharp kunai grass lashed back at anyone attempting to tame its passage.

Added to the physical beauty was the fun to be had with the lingua franca, *Tok Pisin*. For a country with over seven hundred tongues Pidgin English was the most effective way to communicate, not just between expatriate and local but also between villages. One of the words that caused the most amusement to our facile young minds was the word for finish, *pinis*. The evening news on the radio, there was no television, would end with announcer saying *"ebenin nius i bagarapim pinis"*, which translated as "the evening news is now over" or more coarsely, "the evening news is buggered." The language was derived from English with strong Australian influences, indigenous Melanesian languages and German. As well as amusing it could also sound rather beautiful. *The Lord's Prayer* in *Tok Pisin* starts like this:

> *"Papa bilong mipela*
> *Yu stap long heven.*
> *Nem bilong yu i mas i stap holi.*
> *Kingdom bilong yu mas i kam..."*

There was symmetry to some of the words, 'we' becomes *mipela*, 'you' or 'you all' becomes *yupela*. Old-time New Guinea hands spoke pidgin fluently, but many newcomers merely added *'im'* to the end of words, which rather made a mockery of the poetry of the real language. Our adolescent sniggering didn't, of course, count but I was envious of friends who did speak it properly.

Papua New Guinea brought many ghosts to the surface for my mother who had been posted there in the Australian Army Nursing Service in 1943. She rarely talked about her experiences, but every now and then a snippet would emerge of how grim life had been until the arrival of penicillin, used to treat not only wounds but tropical ulcers. She had been moved by many of the young injured or sick soldiers, who would apologise for their filth as they were stretchered into the tent hospitals after weeks in the jungle, carried by the resilient and strong 'fuzzy wuzzy' angels, the local guides and stretcher bearers. Or of the excitement when some current entertainer appeared to perform for the troops, and of turning a dirty yellow from too much quinine taken to prevent malaria.

For a fifteen-year-old, however, in 1973 it was an idyllic place to spend school holidays. There were rafts of kids up from boarding school though I was once again different, not really fitting in with the rough and tumble of the Australian kids.

"Mum, can I go over to Salamua this weekend, with Jenfa?" I asked. Salamua was the site of some of the worst fighting between Australian and Japanese troops during the war. About an hour's boat ride from Lae it was a small isthmus where we would swim, water-ski, and generally hang out. Sarongs and swimming cozzies were the dress code and beach life was easy.

"Is it for something special?" she asked.

"No, but everyone's going."

"What about revision?"

"I'll take books with me," I said, knowing, as I'm sure she did too, the lure of the sea and beach would be far too great. I convinced myself history would be revised with a poke amongst the rusted remains of the guns at the top of the hill behind Salamua. Imagining what it must have been like as battles raged back and forth right under my sandy feet was far more evocative than reading about it in books.

Holidays in PNG were also a little unnerving. Many of my peers seemed to live without boundaries, and the rules in my home appeared to be alien to most, maybe because most had grown up together and gone to primary school in Lae. Their parents knew each other and so curfews were non-existent. Often I would rather not bother going through the rigmarole of questioning before being allowed to go out. I could always get a lift to a party but often not home in time to beat my curfew so it was easier not going. And to have my parents come and collect me would have been the height of 'uncool'.

But I also enjoyed my parents' company and did not feel hard done by. Dinner was always an event at home, conversation was broad, often political, sometimes fiery but always interesting. I was more sophisticated than most, which sounds rather pompous now, but many of my peers had only known New Guinea, small country towns in Australia, and then boarding school. My travels set me apart, and the expectations of my parents did as well.

"Do you have any wine?" I asked, when a stubbie was pushed into my hand.

"Beer, Coke or water," I was told when I rejected the luke warm bottle of beer.

"Where dja think you are?"

"Water then," I said, finding my way to the sink.

I did not smoke grass, finding it singularly lacking after my one attempt, which also set me apart. At the back of my mind was the thought that if caught, my parent's disappointment in me would have been unbearable. They were very liberal in many ways in that I was allowed wine, or Dad's favourite tipple for young women, Dubonnet. Though not encouraged to smoke, I was allowed to. Conversation was an important part of my growing-up, and geo-political awareness was encouraged, as were opinions. Though I don't think I ever won an argument with my father, who would stymie me with a Greek or Latin quote that left me uncomprehending and therefore speechless.

I found my peers lack of interest in the country frustrating.

"What do you think will happen after Independence?" I remember asking at one of the first parties I went to.

"Dunno, if it gets too bad here we'll just go finish," was the average response.

'Going finish' was the term used by expatriates in PNG to mean repatriating to Australia. The lack of interest in the affairs of the country they lived in surprised me. But there were some parties, the occasional holiday romance with, of course, the accompanying broken heart, and an ample supply of grass for those interested. Our suitcases were always rigorously searched on re-entry to Australia, usually at Brisbane.

It was a wonderful childhood, though I think I tried to be a little more empathetic with my children. Moves have always been looked on as a new adventure, but goodbyes have also been encouraged, no doubt a direct result of the initial plans in place for our departure from Malaysia.

Take-Away Slice: Does it really matter where children grow up as long as they feel secure, loved and listened to? The opportunity for young children to benefit linguistically from early exposure to different languages is surely of huge benefit in later life, as is early exposure to different cultures.

Second Slice:
STARS – Spouses Travelling
And Relocating Successfully

I didn't plan on becoming one of the STARS.

"I don't want to go to university," I said for the hundredth time, as the rumbling argument with my father about my future continued over dinner one sultry evening of my penultimate school holiday in Lae, sounds of the jungle filtering in through the open windows.

"It would be such an opportunity for you Apple," my father said, for the hundredth time.

"I do not want to be a teacher. And that's what most people who read English end up doing. And you despised my suggestion of going into social work."

"That isn't a job. Why on earth would you want to do that? Only do-gooders and left-wing intellectuals make a career out of interfering in other people's lives. There are other options you know," he said, lighting another cigarette in frustration.

"I have been institutionalised for seven years. I don't want another four of them."

"I would hardly call NEGS being institutionalised," my mother commented.

"It's an institution isn't it?" I asked rounding on her, ready for battle.

"What do you want to do then?" my father finally asked, after the conversation had jolted back and forth across the *bobotie*, one of Mum's standby recipes.

"Earn some money," I said.

"Well, you'd better go and learn to be a secretary."

"Okay."

"That's it?" he asked.

"Yeah, I can do a quick course, get a job and then see what happens."

"Where?" he asked.

"Sydney I suppose," I said.

"No. If that is your decision you can go to London and do it properly."

Out of the corner of my eye I caught Mum's left eyebrow doing its leap up her brow and waited for fireworks along the lines of, "And just why would Sydney not be suitable?" But they never came, no doubt due to her relief that the impasse seemed to have been broken, and the conversation at the dinner table could move on.

"Okay," I said again.

And that was it. My future decided. St Godric's was the last of the Miss Moneypenny colleges that turned out secretaries with a thin veneer of polish. Proper finishing could be applied at a cost, but I railed at that suggestion when tentatively broached by Dad over dinner another night.

I spent a year in London learning my craft and then flew home, my swansong as a limpet. From then on I would be my own woman.

Wandering around the edge of a cocktail reception at the Australian Consulate in Lae, a gin gimlet in hand, I gazed out into the darkness behind the Residence, the sound of cicadas strumming their night song vying with other jungle noises drifting in.

"Hello," a voice actually aimed at me brought me back to attention. "I've been looking for you. I've got a proposition."

"Hello Chris. Okay. Sounds intriguing," I smiled at the tall Englishman with a beer in one hand and a cigarette in the other. He was quite old, early thirties to my late teens, but always charming.

"My secretary's going finish. She heads back to Brisbane at the end of the month. Would you be interested? I need someone who knows what she's doing and I know St Godric's turns out good secretaries."

"Umm," I said.

"I've spoken to your father and I must tell you he is not keen."

"I can imagine," I replied, irritated the subject had been broached with him first, though knowing of Dad's diligence in trying to persuade expatriate executives to employ New Guinea staff. His secretary was one of the first to graduate from the local college.

"I don't even know if we'd be able to get a work visa, but would you be interested?"

"Yes. I think I would," I told Chris.

"Good. Come and see me tomorrow at about noon and we can thrash out details."

I sipped my gimlet wondering if all job interviews would be that easy.

My father was not keen and I could see his point, he was trying to set an example and then his daughter takes a job a local girl could do.

"I might not get a visa, Dad," I comforted him. "But if I did it would be a good opportunity to get some money behind me before I go back to London." I had no idea where I wanted to go, but I knew saying 'London' would please him.

A visa for fifteen months was granted on the proviso I train local staff to take over all administrative duties in the office at the end of that time.

Working for a coffee and cocoa trading company was interesting and I was diligent, but also played hard. Chris was a patient boss and forgiving with my mistakes. He knew I had his back and my facility with words allowed occasional avoidance of people he would rather not see.

It was a strange kind of time. Not having lived at home for eight years, with the previous one spent in London on my own, although in halls of residence, it was difficult for my mother and I to reach an amicable settlement on rules. My poor father was very much the go-between a lot of the time.

Lae had only a handful of single expatriate girls in town and we were in demand by the plethora of Australian accountants in PNG, who were getting overseas experience before heading back to base to settle down. It was all very heady, but none really appealed.

Jenfa, a friend from school holidays up for a break from nurses' training in Brisbane, and I had been invited to a party. We had not been that interested but wanted to show support for our host and his Papuan girlfriend. A precautionary stipulation from both Jenfa and my parents involved taking one or other of our dogs with us on all evening outings, as a deterent to 'rascals'. A dog in the car was also a good excuse to leave early should the entertainment factor be slim. It had appeared to be that night, but whilst thanking our host, an Englishman interrupted.

"Hello, I didn't think there were any English girls in Lae," said a slightly slurred voice.

"Well, you're looking at two of them," Jenfa replied.

"Are you leaving?"

"Yes we are," I replied nudging Jenfa towards the door, not impressed by his opening salvo.

"It's only early. Stay a bit longer. I'm Richard. I'm here with a friend, come on over and meet him."

Jenfa, a gorgeous brunette with a wide smile and brown eyes that truly glowed, was intrigued and plainly wanted to stay. With bad grace I followed them back, through the throng to the edge of the garage, festooned with fishing nets and fairy lights, to meet the friend.

"This is John," Richard announced.

The first glance was not propitious. Tall, with dark shaggy hair, a stubble before stubble was fashionable and red-rimmed blue eyes, he was propping the wall up, beer in hand. He levered himself away from the wall long enough to shake our hands and then relaxed back into it.

"He's had a rough day," Richard said, "He almost got killed."

"Oh?" I asked.

"Wow, what happened?" Jenfa, far more forgiving than I, asked.

"We were gummying," Richard explained, determined to keep the conversation going.

"On the Busu?" I asked in spite of myself. White-water rafting on inner tubes down the fourth fastest flowing river in the world was not something to be undertaken lightly. "What happened?"

"Hit a rock," John said, finally speaking. "Couldn't figure out which way was up. Was running out of breath."

"We thought he'd had it. Eventually found him miles down river."

"Are you alright?" Jenfa asked.

"Bit bruised."

As the party trickled to a close we piled into the car, Jenfa's dog Footsak being delighted to finally see us, and went back to my parents' house, closely followed by Richard and John. I breathed a prayer Mum and Dad would not still be challenging each other over the Backgammon board and had gone to bed. My prayers went unanswered as I saw the lights blazing upstairs in the sitting room.

"Hello sweetie, lovely to see you Jennifer," my father greeted us. "Pour yourselves a drink."

"Did you have a nice time?" Mum asked.

"Not bad. A couple of the blokes are coming for a swim," I said, edging back down the stairs.

"Well bring them up," Dad said stubbing his newly lit cigarette out.

Richard came up first, saying as he made his way up the stairs and looking around him, "Gosh I thought all houses here were jerry built."

"Not all," Dad said.

"Good evening, sir," John introduced himself. Dad beamed and shook his hand, the first of the men I'd brought home to call him 'sir'. After what seemed an agonising amount of chat we went down to the pool for the promised swim.

Later when Jenfa called to say she was safely home, another ironclad rule between us all, she said they had followed her home before heading off to sober up in time for the wedding they were both in town for.

Through the course of that first evening I learned John was a VSO from Devon on two years voluntary assignment building bridges, roads, wharves, hospitals and schools, anything that the Morobe Provincial Government had funds for. He lived, when he was in town, with a fellow volunteer in a tiny one-room house they shared with an army of red ants and clutch of cockroaches, on the edge of Lae.

The next day as Jenfa and I lounged again in the pool, John's jeep screeched to the gates and amidst frantic barking from Negrita, our sort of spaniel, we were invited to gatecrash the wedding reception.

"I don't know them," I demurred.

"Doesn't matter, they said it was okay," Richard said.

"I've met the bride once or twice," Jenfa added, "It'll be fine."

At the end of the week Richard went back to Mendi, in the New Guinea Highlands and Jenfa to Brisbane. And John came back to town more often than before from the head of the Slate Creek road, which he was surveying and building, and which would eventually reach the Kokoda Trail, north east of Port Moresby, across the Owen Stanley Range.

Luckily for John, the choice of places to wine and dine me in Lae was limited, as being a VSO, he was on a local subsistence salary. My parents, always hospitable, opened the house to my boyfriend and as I got to know him, so did they. I kept the beer fridge stocked and Mum fed him, and any other stray VSOs who happened our way.

Picnics became a weekend treat as he introduced me to the rugged beauty of the jungle, rivers and hills around the Markham Valley, areas he knew well from his work but where I had never been. From travelling with my parents in the comfort of an airconditioned car with good suspension whenever we left Lae, I went to being lurched from pothole to verge in a canvas-doored jeep.

Forging water courses where bridges had been washed away, or where culvets were just not man enough to handle the rains falling in the Highlands was always fun. We would remove the doors to allow the water to flow through, and around the sealed Suzuki engine. Invariably people would appear from the jungle happy to provide ballast in exchange for a hitch across the river and possibly a cigarette, sometimes wearing only a penis sheath or sometimes a Trukai tee-shirt, produced by my father's company. John spoke fluent Pidgin English and there was always much laughter and never any edge, or concern for our safety.

It was a romantic and exciting courtship. More used to being taken out to dinner, or in London, the theatre or the symphony and dinner, John was very different to previous men I had dated, and at only five years older than me he was also the youngest, which pleased my father.

"Gees Apple, what'd'ya see in that bloke from the jungle?" A spurned suitor asked. I didn't know where to start, so I laughed and kept quiet knowing he would never risk his life on a tyre.

After flirting briefly with the idea of joining the Australian Foreign Service I decided I did not want to live in Canberra for the next few years, owing to having met John, and so returned to London.

The city in April was dreary, cold and wet, and after the lush exuberance of Lae, thirty-six hours flying time and a heavy heart did not auger well for the challenges of job and flat hunting. I had floor space for five nights in a flat in Maida Vale before a friend from St Godric's days flew to Haifa to become a kibbutznik.

Finding a job proved remarkably easy due to the glowing reference Chris had written, kindly glossing over the many errors I'd made in my first position as a P&C secretary. I started working for an American on secondment from New York, at a large advertising agency. We understood each other, both being outsiders, and I could empathise with his children's feelings at being away from family and friends.

Finding somewhere to live was a great deal more difficult.

"Do you mind sharing a room?" asked the girl at the flat-share agency on Bond Street, bringing my attention back from the rain drizzling down the windowpanes to the dingy room.

"Yes I do," I replied.

"Do you mind co-ed sharing?"

"No I don't."

As back up I sat in a dank café, ringing 'possibles' from the advertisements in the Evening Express. Phoning from the pay phone in the corner of the grimey little place for appointments late into the night was a depressing exercise. Neither did traipsing around London armed with an A-Z map of the city, references and an umbrella do anything for my spirits.

"How far are you from the Tube?" I asked.

"Not far," I was assured by the tinny voice at the other end of the line. Our definitions of distance differed as I struggled to find addresses in the dark. It was scary. No one knew where I was; hell, I didn't know where I was most of the time and I certainly didn't know who I was meeting.

Rejections were theirs or mine until in desperation, with only one more night on the floor available, I found a place in Wembley, a ten-minute walk and a bus ride from the Tube station and then thirty minutes to The Embankment, close to my soon-to-be office. But the flat was new and clean, and whilst I didn't take to the owner, I figured I wouldn't be sleeping with him so it would do.

"Honey," said my new boss over coffee and cigarettes about a month after I started working for him, and as we planned the day in his office overlooking the Embankment, "How would you like house sitting for us when we go on vacation next week?"

"I would like very much Tim, thank you," I replied, thinking of their stately townhouse in Holland Park, a stone's throw from the Tube. It was extraordinarily generous of them and I lived in luxury for a month, pretending I belonged in the four-storey mansion with access to the private garden opposite. It gave me breathing space to find somewhere more suitable than with the oily man in Wembley and a changing conga line of women in the bathroom each morning.

London was lonely. I was in love with a man on the other side of the world, checking the mail every evening for an aerogramme that meant he still thought of me. My college friends had dispersed around the country, and I had very little in common with the girls in the office. With the exception of Fiona, who was great fun and whose family were very generous in their hospitality. Tim was the one who, after a few months of ticking along, challenged me to do more and it was due to him I started writing, though just for myself.

By then I was living in a bedsit with orange walls and coin-operated electricity, 20p pieces were worth their weight in gold in winter, and the little three bar heater moved with me as I moved around the two room flat. Fiona helped me repaint.

I did not miss a television, never having had one, but I wallowed in music. I read a lot, I probably drank too much and I certainly smoked too much. I occasionally went out, but my dates did not live up to the man I was waiting for and to whom I wrote a lot of letters. It was a strange, and strangely lonely time, but one I have never regretted. It was the first, and only, time I have ever done anything entirely on my own. No parental help in getting established, though over the eighteen months Dad did help financially a couple of times when London overstretched me. I learnt, though, that I could be on my own and be happy.

John left PNG three months after me and spent five months hitchhiking most of the way back to England with Malcolm, another VSO. The agony of wondering whether my letters were reaching him at the *Poste Restante* addresses along the way was lessened, for a short while, whenever I received a letter from him telling me of the next post office to write to.

We spoke only once in those eight months. Working myself into a frenzy over the thought the British mail strike would mean he did not receive a letter in Kathmandu, I sent a telegram, *Poste Restante*. John got the letter but missed the cable. Fellow travellers caught up with them saying a cable had arrived for John, from London.

"Good afternoon, Tim Sickinger's office," I answered the phone as I always did.

"It's me. What the hell are you doing there?" asked a voice made scratchy across the wires.

"Oh my God, John? I'm at work. Where are you?" His voice sounding more Devonian than I remembered.

"Delhi. Are you okay?"

"Yes of course. Why?"

"I heard I'd missed a telegram from London. For Christ's sake Apple! We have raced through India to get to an international phone and now I've spent four days worth of food money on a three-minute call. Don't do that again. Okay?"

"Okay," I replied tearfully.

"Right. I've got to go. Bye."

"Bye," I said and put the phone down, convincing myself he wouldn't have called if he hadn't cared.

"Frau Schmidt?" I said to the eye peering through the crack in the door, wary at the unwanted intrusion. We shared the same front door and bathroom, but were only on nodding terms normally.

"*Ja.* You vant vhat?"

"I'm going away this weekend. If my boyfriend rings the door bell, would you please give him this letter?" I asked, handing her an envelope with the key to my flat.

"I vill know him how?"

"His name is John."

She took the envelope and pushed the door shut with a non-committal humph. Upon my return late on Sunday evening, after a weekend spent with my parents visiting from PNG, I found a note from John on the hall table.

"Frau Schmidt, you didn't give him the letter," I shouted to the cracked door.

"*Nein.*"

"Why not?"

"Not good in dis hows," she said, and firmly clicked the latch.

Having been delivered to my front door by a friendly trucker, it was not the homecoming either of us imagined. His long hair and raggedy jeans did not fit her profile of a suitable young man. After a chilly night spent in the Gents at Paddington Station John caught the milk train home to Gloucester.

His parents not having a phone in those days, I risked another telegram. He came back to London, using up precious pennies, the next day. Tim gave me the rest of the week off and we spent the time exploring London and getting to know each other again. He lived an unsettled repatriate existence, working for a friend's landscape gardening business and playing rugby on the weekends he was not in London, before joining the oilfield a year later.

"Where do you think you'll be sent?" I asked, over a glass of wine at Liverpool Street Station as we waited for his train to Great Yarmouth for offshore training.

"Probably the Middle East or Holland."

"It'll be exciting going abroad again. You'll love it." I comforted myself that both places were closer than Lesotho in southern Africa, where there had been a chance of a job a month or so earlier. Rather like the night I met him and I prayed for my parents to be in bed, I spent all my thoughts on the European option. This time they were answered.

Six months later I joined John in Holland. Six months after that we married on a brilliant but icy day in St Bartholomew's Church at the top of Chosen Hill, in Gloucestershire. Early December coinciding with meetings my father had in London.

The wedding was organised long distance with the minimum of fuss. I spent three weeks before the day living with my prospective in-laws to fulfil marriage licence requirements. My dress was bought the week before the wedding when Mum arrived in the country, that having been her only request. My groom arrived a few days before, in time to be fitted for a morning suit and to buy my ring.

The night before our vows I had dinner with Mum, Dad and his sister Sally, my godmother as well as aunt, at the Greenway Hotel where the reception was to be held. As Mum and Sally headed upstairs, Dad held me back.

"Sweetie, if you have any doubts at all it's not too late to cancel everything," he said, through the fug of smoke that hung between us.

"Not a single one Dad, but thank you," I said.

It was a day of sunshine, champagne and laughter with people who cared about us. It was also the start of my life as an expatriate wife.

I had to learn to do it my way and not the way my parents had done it, in the cooling embers of colonialism. When I look back I realise how pompous I must have been, but it was the only way I knew how to operate. I expected men to wear a tie to dinner when they came to our house, and God love 'em they all did, without a murmur. Even our single friends in Holland, back in Emmen for a few days between rig jobs, would scurry home, shower and tie up. I loved them for it, and for their acceptance of me.

Emmen was also lonely sometimes. John was on the bottom rung of the ladder and away a great deal. Never on rotation but rather in town a few days, away a few weeks, home a day then gone a month, but my training in London stood me in good stead. I could function on my own, which has probably helped our marriage. A lot of our thirty or so years have been spent alone or as a single mother.

Never having liked sports very much, apart from swimming, John taught me to play squash, which I loved, and we taught ourselves how to windsurf. Only being able to afford one wetsuit between us, I was always the one to shimmy into a damp wetsuit whose shoulders reached my ears, and whose knees runkled and swelled as the cold water pooled into the excess creases. But I'd get my own back when, exhausted from an exhilerating sail across the lake, I'd be too tired to fight against the wind on the return leg. I'd sit on the board, water sloshing over the sail and wave feebly, the sign for John to jog a couple of miles around to the far shore to save me. It would be his turn to haul on the wet neoprene and tack his way across to the beach in the time it would take me to saunter around to meet him, easing the tension out of my back as I walked.

Our daughter, Kate, was born in the Emmen *Ziekenhuis* in 1983. John was on hand for the delivery and around for five days after her birth. Thank goodness, because although his experience with babies was as limited as mine, he was a natural and eased me through panicked moments. And then he had to go offshore.

"Goedemiddag. Hoe is de baby?" asked our stern-faced neighbour after banging on the back door. She had seen John depart earlier in the day and came to check up on me. She stood on the doorway with her gentle old black poodle, her face softening and the lines seeming to disappear as she smiled at Kate. *"Ben je oke?"* she continued, seeing my weepy eyes.

No, I wasn't okay. I was a gibbering wreck. Vrouw Gert took Kate and with remarkable ease stopped her fretting, changed her nappy and put her down for a nap. Then she sat with me a while. We had, until that afternoon, only exchanged pleasantries in the little lane that ran between the houses.

"Thank you so much, Vrouw Gert," I said, blowing on the coffee I'd made for us both. "I'm sorry. I can't stop crying this afternoon."

"It is normal. You vill cry more eh!"

"Do you have children?" I asked, thinking I'd never seen many people visiting.

"No, God did not send them."

"Gosh, you're good with them though," I said.

"Ach, I was a midwife for many years," she said. Even her tightly curled hair seemed to relax as she thought of all the babies she'd delivered and cared for.

Such kindnesses come from unexpected places all over the world and that is what has made life fun and interesting. It was later that same day I called my mother-in-law in Gloucester, again in tears.

Eight months later Kate and I flew to Trinidad to join John in his new role as country manager, the day after she learnt to crawl. Ten hours was a long time to follow her joyous passage, a crab-like scuttle up and down the aisles. Towards the end of my stamina she passed out in exhaustion as we crossed from ocean to land. A Chinese whisper could be heard trickling to the back of the plane.

"We can't land," said one.

"Why not?" asked another.

"What's happened?" queried a third.

"Did they say cows?" I asked my neighbour across the aisle, who had been remarkably patient with Kate's clumsy attempts to haul herself up on his armrest.

"Yeah man. Dey on de ronway 'gain," he replied.

"Again? Aren't there fences?"

"Yeah, bu' dey brek. De grass always greener yu know. She sleep nuh," he said, smiling at Kate curled in my arms.

I was naïve when we arrived in Trinidad, a classic case of expectations not being managed. My expatriate childhood had, as far back as I could remember, been well organised with housing available on arrival, basic amenities and services connected and a welcoming atmosphere. It was not like that for us but when complaining to Mum via airletters, she put me right with stories of the managerial incompetence from head office she had faced in Nigeria and Malaysia. Twenty years later it had not changed.

I slowly figured out my place in a new expatriate environment with a few ups and downs. It took a couple of months and more than a couple of false starts to find somewhere to live and then I was ready to take on the role I'd watched my mother play for many years, that of hostess.

In some countries the manager is expected to accommodate visiting people from head office and it can be difficult. For all parties. Your spouse gets no down time from the pressure, you are in entertaining mode every evening preparing meals while trying to get children to bed, not to mention having to appear bright and chirpy over the breakfast table, and children are well aware of the tensions and inevitably try it on.

Until I met John my sole attempt at cooking a meal was for a former boyfriend, neither the meal nor the man was a resounding success, for which I take full blame, I was ready for neither. But by the time we got to Trinidad my culinary skills had improved somewhat, and I found I actually enjoyed spending time in the kitchen and became evermore confident and adventurous. It helped I had a willing tester.

My first attempt at socialising in San Fernando did not go well. Six guests were invited, I having decided that cooking for eight was just as easy as cooking for six, and allowed more individual conversations around the table. I spent two days preparing and cooking a Chinese feast. I had an active helper in Kate who enjoyed standing on a chair and helping prepare the dough for dim sum.

"Mumum," Kate gurgled from her perch, on hearing a knock at the door.

"Hello. Good morning. You have no phone?"

"Er no, hi, come in," I said to the woman standing on the doorstep, about my age, and one of the intended guests. British born, she had been on the island since childhood and was married to a Trini who managed another oilfield company, and who John had met at a business function. He thought we would connect.

"No, no. I just want to say we will not come this evening. My mother cannot babysit."

"Oh? Well would you like to bring the children, they can go down here," I asked.

"No, that is not a good thing. What you offer?"

"Chinese," I said, realising what she meant.

"Good. That is easy. So, no problem. I see you soon, okay. Bye."

"Okay. Bye," I said, a little miffed, thinking Chinese cuisine might not be hard to cook, but it was time consuming to prepare.

Next, John dashed home at lunchtime to tell me another couple had cried off. And then we had a no-show. We ate Chinese dishes and rice for the rest of the week. It was not an auspicious start to entertaining in the Caribbean. I later learned at least four of our guests had assumed we were sending out for the food. A concept I had not come across before when asking people to dinner.

On the whole there haven't been too many disasters and as my confidence grew so too did my ability to laugh off the odd mishap. An Irish friend with a wicked sense of blonde humour, Grainne, who we met in Bangkok and have subsequently crossed paths with in many countries, has a limitless memory for *faux pas*, egged on by her husband Nick.

"*Bon appetit*," I said, realising it was a little strange inviting our ten guests, a mix of British, Irish and Australian friends and business aquaintances, to dig in to a Malay curry with French words when we all lived in Thailand.

The normal confusion of curries, dahl and gado gado ensued, as they changed hands along the table and I complimented myself on the choice of a yellow cloth as a foil to spills, decorated with single orchids that could be strategically replaced if necessary. As we settled, I noticed John gesticulating and mouthing something from the other end of the table. I shrugged and ignored him.

"Apple?" Grainne called down from her place next to her host, "John is trying to tell you there appears to be no rice."

"Bloody hell," I said, glancing along the groaning table, bare of rice. "Alright here's the deal, with or without? With means cold curry, without means hot!" I leapt down the stairs to the kitchen to find Bo, our *amah*, in the throes of boiling the staple.

"Sorree madam, I dink betta hab rice."

"Oh Bo, *kobkhunkah*," I thanked her.

Nick and Grainne weren't present when a platter filled with nests of potatoes *dauphinois* exploded one sultry night in West Africa many years later. Our guests were again a mixture of work and pleasure, a combination, which I think lessens any formality. In a country where occasional gunshots were heard from our terrace, the bang made a number of heads duck and me run to the serving table in horror. Creamy potato ejected at a high velocity from a dish placed on a warming tray makes a hell of a mess, but created much hilarity.

They were, however, in attendance at probably my worst culinary mishap for many years. Christmas lunch for ten with no turkey. In my defence I have successfully stuffed and roasted said bird for over thirty years, in ovens of varying efficiency but whose quirks I was aware of. A family and friends reunion on the West Coast of Ireland put an end to my successes when the bird, obtained with great expense from the local butcher and paid for by my brother-in-law, after five hours in the oven resulted in juices running clear from one drumstick, red from the other. Ham and salmon with bread and cranberry sauce saved the day, with copious amounts of champagne for the cook. The coronation turkey on Boxing Day was well received, the bird having roasted another three hours.

Maybe it was a hangover from my parents' days of business entertaining, nearly always done at home whether a cocktail party for sixty or a dinner for twenty, but we have chosen to do the same. It takes the stiffness out of an occasion and allows business acquaintances a glimpse of a different side to the people they are dealing with, and of course their spouses. It can make for complicated catering when a variety of faiths are involved and on one or two occasions I have called in outside help.

On the whole the mishaps have been mine alone, but so too have the triumphs, those odd times when absolutely everything gets to the table on time and tastes as it should and nothing is left in the fridge. I know John has appreciated the effort and it makes for good stories when we bump into people on the other side of the world who remember the time when…

But on that first true expatriate posting as an adult, to the Caribbean, I was a little lost. Trinidad was challenging. Holland was Europe and my expectations had been different when I moved there. I thought 'T 'n' T' as I called Trinidad and Tobago, would be like Malaysia, or even PNG, but it wasn't. I had read up about it as much as possible and had quizzed John's boss who travelled there often. I went full of enthusiasm. Not being able to buy certain things didn't bother me in the least, but the overt aggression on the streets was something I had never come across before.

"Apple, you must lock the veranda grill when you are at the back of the house," John reminded me one day as he sauntered in from work. "Anyone could've come in."

"I hate being locked in," I moaned.

"I know, but you have to," he said hugging his daughter, grubby from crawling on floors covered in a fine soot from the burning cane fields, "There are too many burglaries around here to risk it."

I did not like not having a phone, which I finally learnt was my fault. I had not been paying, something apparently expected by the engineer charged with switching us on. I felt unsafe when John was away and lived in fear there would be a fire at the front of the house, and Kate and I would be trapped because of the locked grid across the hall leading to the bedrooms, as all the windows were also barred.

There was no support group to call upon but our neighbours made life more bearable, their May/September marriage had produced two beautiful little girls, both imps.

"Hello you two," John said on a Saturday morning, not long after moving in. They were at the fence, fingers curled around the wire, noses pressed through the links, chatting away like flitting finches as we had our breakfast. "Would you like to come and play with Kate? Go and ask your parents and I'll walk over and get you."

"Oh no, we can't ask them," they replied in unison, "We're locked out. Mummy and Daddy are busy in the bedroom on Saturday mornings."

There was not a lot we could say to that. Our conversation continued through the wire. It was the same each weekend. Their father became our doctor and I had always to clear my mind of his daughters chatting to us whenever I saw him.

"Apple, you must recognise that if any of you get seriously ill, especially Kate, you must leave the island." His first words did not fill me with comfort. Luckily we didn't, but he did teach me coconut milk was the best remedy for a baby, or anyone, with an upset tummy.

Another kind and welcoming couple lived on their family compound a few doors along from us, also Indian, though Khalil's wife was Canadian.

It wasn't all grim, and we did have some light relief. Some of which came from the language, Trinidad Vernacular English, a mix of French, Spanish, Hindi, Creole and African dialects all around an English base. It's colourful and lilting and sometimes impossible to understand, unless you had time to go away and think about what had just been said. *Doan vex me* was self-explanatory. *Back back* was not, meaning to change your mind or reverse your car, and once understood seemed reasonable. *Now fuh now* is much more fun than 'while you wait'.

We've all heard the slurred, bellicose voice of the expat propping up a bar of some club around the world expounding to anyone who would listen, "When I am reincarnated I'm coming back as an expat wife."

It is usually met with a guffawed agreement from the sot by his side, and polite titters from others in the room. I too was one of the titterers until two facts dawned on me, that most men would not get past the reincarnation door, and that most men could not do what we do.

It is a snide comment. From stories, fact and fiction, of India's Raj to Somerset Maugham's Malaya to Robin Moore's *Dubai*, the theme that fascinates most is the difficulty women face as expatriate wives. The tales of infidelities and imperious demands usually covering an underlying unhappiness and frustration, often aimed not only at their physical surrounds, but at the men they thought they knew, their husbands.

It is not just women whose heads are turned by the increased salaries, the large house, the servants, the company car, the business-class travel and the rest of the frippery that goes into many expatriate salaries. Men who may have held mid-level positions in the home country find themselves fêted by local businesses and dignitaries, men of average looks fawned over by local women eager to find a route out of poverty. The acronym FILTH – *failed in London try Hong Kong* applies to all corners of the world – an undefined and less than stellar career at home may be an outstanding success in another environment.

That, of course, does not apply to all expatriate men, or women. Many would have had just as successful a career at home, but wanted the adventure and the challenges of overseas living, but it is worth thinking about sometimes. The same applies equally to the spouses who follow them around the world.

Catapulted into a life of relative luxury, in most instances, can be a heady experience. Fortunately, most adapt remarkably quickly. Unfortunately, there will always be those who become rather grander than they should be and sometimes those who cannot adapt to a life away from what they know.

Some choose not to adapt and spend their overseas experience bemoaning the lack of Oreos, or baked beans, or a particular shampoo. Others put their own careers on hold, knowing full well the chances of re-entering the job market will be difficult on their return.

The vast majority, however, make a concerted effort to make the most of wherever they end up. Expat woman is a hardy beast, adaptable, resourceful, resilient and open to new ideas and challenges. An entrepreneurial spirit flies in as the packing cases are removed from her new living room, as the children settle in school and as she finds her feet not only in the supermarket, but the street market as well.

But actually on the ground, in situ wherever that happens to be, one of the most valuable resources is other women in similar circumstances. I firmly believe international women's groups around the world, whether a luncheon group, a tennis club or a sewing group are expatriate man's best ally.

"Ladies, ladies, please, we must start."

How many times have we heard that entreaty? It doesn't matter if the group meets in a village hall, a lavish ballroom or a marquee. It doesn't matter what the subject is. It doesn't matter if it's in Bangkok or Bangalore, Singapore or Stockholm, and it really doesn't matter what language it's said in. It is the same worldwide. Women, when gathered, support and talk.

It is this sisterhood that has proved to be a lifeline for me in posting after posting. As an adult there have been twelve moves and the only one that proved difficult was in Trinidad, where there was no ladies' group to prop me up in San Fernando, the town we lived in on the south of the island. No friendly face and wise voice to say, "It's okay, your baby will be just fine," after a night awake with a fevered tot, no older voice to reassure me it does get easier, as I waved goodbye to my husband leaving for a six-week stint on the other side of the world. I was left holding the baby and the bath, but with no water, on a Caribbean island that did not fit the picture of tropical paradise in the guidebooks.

I took my first foray into the realms of women's clubs in Bangkok, our next posting, thanks in part to a woman I met at a hospital.

"Are you alright?" a friendly voice asked.

"Kate, my daughter, is under a general anaesthetic."

"Oh my dear, how old is she?"

"Eighteen months," I said, tears trickling down the sides of my nose.

"They are wonderful here. Can I ask what the problem is?" She sat beside me on the sagging sofa on the verandah of the Bangkok Nursing Home, open to the breeze and the steady hum of traffic from Silom Road.

"She has about forty little white spots, like hard boils on her tummy and back. It's a waterborne virus she got from a pool in Trinidad. They took a few out there, just in the surgery with no anesthetic which was awful, and more keep coming back."

"How long have you been here?"

"Just over a month."

"Is your husband around?" she asked.

"He's upcountry," I sniveled.

Before I realised, thirty minutes had passed thanks to the distracting tactics of the woman chatting to me. The door to the operating theatre opened and out came Dr Britton, holding my drowsy daughter in his arms and smiling.

"Here's Kate, Mrs Gidley. She is absolutely fine, a bit dopey. Give her a little supper and then let her sleep it off. No bath tonight or swimming for a few days. Come and see me next week. Call if you're worried about anything."

"Okay, thank you," I said, as fresh tears welled up.

"She really is fine," he said, handing my precious bundle over to me.

"When she's in bed I suggest you have a quiet glass of wine, eh?" He smiled and turned back into the theatre. I turned to thank the kind woman, whose name I didn't know.

"I'm so glad everything's okay," she said. "Look, we're leaving Bangkok in a couple of weeks and I am far to old to be involved, but there is a group that supports young mums. It's called BAMBI. They meet at the British Club. Why not give them a call?"

I never saw her again, but I never forgot her kindness to a lost young woman.

Babies and Mothers Bangkok International were in their fledgling days and just happened to need a secretary. I volunteered and, as in most voluntary endeavours, gained far more than I gave. As well as supporting expatriate women from all over the world living in the city, it also offered short-term assistance to women arriving in Thailand to have their babies, from neighbouring countries whose healthcare might not have been as good. BAMBI, started by Dr Tanit Habananda and his English wife Mel, is about to celebrate 30 years of helping young women cope with the demands of motherhood far from home, wherever that was.

From those baby steps I progressed to the British Women's Group, fondly known as the Bitches and Witches, also in Bangkok. It was my first exposure to a group of ladies all from the same country. The members were caring and supportive, but I have found that a coterie of women from one country, whichever it is, tends to bring out the worst in each other. Instead of celebrating the differences they tend to moan about them, whereas international groups are more forgiving. There have been women's clubs in every other country I've lived in since, though in Scotland life was so busy with working and caring for children I didn't have time to join one. But where I have, all have supported me with friendships formed, new cultures learned and recipes exchanged.

On our return to Houston, Texas after an absence of nearly three years, and to a different part of town I again joined a group.

"Apple, I introduce you to ICH," said Lucy, a Bolivian friend from Equatorial Guinea who happened to be in Houston visiting her daughter. "You will meet many people. You will come?"

"Okay, I'd love to," I replied. International Connections of Houston was my entry into the expat/repat world here and I immediately felt welcome, as has been the case in so many places.

"This is Apple, my friend from Africa," Lucy introduced me to a woman at the newcomer's table.

"Hi, welcome," a friendly woman greeted me. "I'm Chris."

"I know this sounds familiar, but I have a feeling we've met before," I said. It took us a few minutes of figuring out times and places, but we found the connection.

"I've got it. Bangkok. I was Mary-Ann's next door neighbour," Chris said.

"Of course. That's it. She and I met at the Hilton when we had both just arrived. Edward and her daughter are days apart in age."

And so ICH really did connect.

Women who may not have been seen dead at a Women's Institute meeting in the village in England, come to realise it doesn't matter where you are in the world, a friendly face and voice are sometimes the difference between a successful transition to a new life and a total fiasco.

Expatriate living sounds wonderfully glamorous to sisters left behind with the soapsuds and the ironing. But leaving that sister behind can be one of the biggest wrenches. Who else will put up with your moaning? Who else can you ask the most probing of questions when life plays tricks on you?

Living a global life makes women sisters very quickly. With no family within a twelve-hour flight we learn to accept with alacrity an offer of help, a hand outstretched. And friendships mature rapidly. There is no time for slow early pleasantries to become deep and intimate conversations. We might not be in the same city, the same country for very long. We have to make the most of our time together.

In hardship postings, I think sometimes it is more difficult to adapt because with the generous leave allowances every three months, there isn't time to settle. It is hard to feel at home anywhere when you have feet in two, and sometimes three, camps. In non-hardship postings it is easier to acclimatise if you commit to the place and the people. The sooner we become engaged the sooner we start to feel at home.

"Aah'll be right back in six weeks," Janine said at her goodbye lunch with the gals, all friends from a Houston volunteer organisation. "You can't get ridda me that easily."

"Why are you coming back so soon?" I asked.

"Aah promised aah'd help Alison move apartments. Aah know it's justa coupla blocks, but aah'm gonna miss her so much, aah can't bearda think about it."

"Does she expect you to fly over and help her move?" I harried.

"No, of course not," Janine said. "But she's ma daughter an' ahh promised."

"Oh ducky, you promised before you knew you were moving across an ocean and a few countries. Sometimes, 'specially when the kids are grown, we have to put ourselves first," I said. "What does Philip say?" I asked, wondering how her husband was coping with his wife's reluctance to leave a grown daughter.

"That aah can do whatever aah want. He's just so dang excited abouda chance to go overseas at this stage, he just can't wait to git goin'. But you're tryin' ta tell me it'll be harder for me to settle if aah keep flyin' back, right?"

"Yes, I suppose I am. It'll be harder to get through those early stages of missing 'back home' if you don't stick it out for at least six months, you end up going through the same phase of the cycle time and time again."

"Oh honey, you've done this so many tymes. It's easy for youda say."

"I know, but it's the same no matter how many times we go through it. You could get Alison over to see you at Easter," I suggested. "Showing her around your new place would be exciting for you both, and give you a sense of ownership."

"Aah'll think about it! Aah know you're just tryin' to help," Janine said with a hug.

Goodbyes are hard. Whether to a place you've called home all your life, or a place you've called home for a short while. And they are doubly hard when we leave behind our children, no matter how old they are.

Goodbyes to friends, old and not so old, are equally hard. Promises to write regularly fall by the wayside as the chaos of packing, unpacking and making new friends while keeping children on track, and supporting a husband, takes over life. The intensity of the relationship lessens over the miles and the years, but the memories don't. And if by chance you happen to bump into one another again in some distant country, at some other women's club, you will pick up just where you left off. A few more grey hairs, a few more hard-earned lifelines, and a trunkful of experiences you have to share before one of you moves on again.

Occasionally, though, that sisterhood has let me down. Arriving in Singapore with a six-week-old baby, a three-year-old, and a desperately unhappy 75-year old mother at midnight was a pretty low point. Mum travelled with me under the guise of helping. My father had bought her a first class ticket, the children and I did not travel that way. John was in Houston for six weeks and I was spearheading our relocation. We were met by a cab and taken to our two-room service apartment to find the beds unmade and nothing in the fridge.

"Mum, you sit here while we go and find some basics," I said, pouring her a slug of whisky from the duty-free bottle, and propelling her into a chair by the window overlooking the lights of Orchard Road. She was exhausted.

The children and I went searching for a corner store, which fortunately we found and returned a little later laden with milk, bread, butter, coffee and juice, enough to start the day a few hours later. I struggled to forgive my husband's company for that welcome, or indeed any of the company wives.

Struggling again a few months later to get a baby, and a now three and half-year old, off a plane at Dubai airport in the middle of the night is when self-doubt really walloped me. Lugging one and hauling the other up and down the halls during a mandatory walk about, as the plane was readied for the next leg of the journey to England, I saw myself in a shop window and wondered where the jaunty young woman I had thought myself had gone.

"Mummy, why are those men wearing drethes?" Kate asked, waving her arms at Arabs wandering the halls. Her lispy question brought me back to my current reality.

"Shhh, possum, don't point," I said. "You've seen men wearing sarongs at home, in the Middle East they wear *dish dashes*. Isn't that a great name?"

"Yeth," she said. "Ith funny." Edward, heavy on my hip, gurgled.

I was rushing from Singapore to England to help sort out a messy separation between my parents after a frantic call from my father a day earlier.

"Your mother needs you. She's throwing things at me."

"Well, Dad, if I were her I'd throw things at you too."

He sighed down the 'phone; I knew I had to go.

John was somewhere in China. I left a message for him in Hong Kong with Malcolm of PNG days, and another with the office in Singapore. And then I flew.

As the kids settled back into our flight routine, Kate on the floor below Edward's suspended basinet, I spent the rest of the long flight wondering if life was always going to be this disconnected. The kids and I in one place, their father in another.

And then as we landed, and life took over again, I did what so many do, I coped. Helped hugely by my in-laws, who happily had their lives turned upside down when they took Kate for a week while I went down to my parents with Edward, still too young to understand the turmoil around him. I was too anxious to leave him with anyone for any length of time in case he had an attack of bronchiolitis, which came on normally in the middle of the night with a wicked vengeance.

"Mummy, guess what?" Kate asked on the phone one evening, just before her bedtime.

"What sweetheart?"

"I drink tea with Gran and Grandad. In their bed. Every morning."

"Oh wow, that's a nice way to start the day isn't it? I'll bet Gran lets you have a biccie too!"

"She does. She says I can have Grandad's too an' he gets cross. But it's okay, it's only pretend cross."

"I'm sure it is, possum," I said, smiling at the thought of my father-in-law ever being cross with her.

"Mummy are you coming soon?" Kate's little voice suddenly quietened.

"Yes sweetheart, in two more days I'll be there," I said, my throat hurting from missing her. It was the first time I'd left her and I missed her constant chatter and observations. "Two days is really soon and after we talk tomorrow night it'll only be one more day. Now you give Gran a big hug from me, and I'm sending you one too. Sleep tight sweetheart."

"Night, night, Mummy," my daughter said.

A few months later, and back in Thailand after an eight-month stint in Singapore, the realisation I couldn't always cope came as a great shock.

"Apple, you have got to see the doctor," John said one Sunday evening, after we'd put the children to bed and after yet another bout of tantrums and tears, not the normal *modus operandi* of the previous six years of our marriage. "This has gone on too long. I'll come with you."

I have never been a particularly patient person but even I was getting scared at the shortness of my temper. Kate was bearing the brunt of my impatience and her forays into stretching the boundaries, a natural part of any child growing up, were being squashed with an anger not commensurate with the deed.

John, who normally could always get me to laugh and calm down was, I am sure, getting more and more concerned about leaving the children with me whenever he went away.

We were lucky to have Bo, our *amah*, who lived with us and who could step in when I fell into a crying jag. She was kind and caring of me, and took care of my babies when I couldn't.

It was a horrible time, but it took John's patience to snap to make me admit I was a mess.

And so the next day we went to see Dr Britton. He could be a dour man, and did not brook self-pity, but I thought very highly of him due to his care of Kate, and he knew me.

"What's the problem, Apple?" he asked, shaking John's hand and ushering us to chairs in his little office on Sukhumvit Road.

That was all it took. I started sobbing and couldn't stop. It was John who explained the previous twelve months. A new baby, who had stopped breathing at a month old, and subsequently had been in and out of hospital with bronchiolitis, two international relocations done on my own with two infants, the vitriol surrounding the breakdown of my parents' marriage, guilt at liking my father's new partner whom I'd known for ten years, houseguests for the previous month and the ongoing need to support a devastated mother from long distance, all with the added pressure of an often absent husband.

It was the first time I could not control any situation, and I did not handle it well.

"Listen to me, Apple," Dr Britton said, "You are exhausted. You need to sleep. If John isn't here let your maid do the night shifts with Edward for a while."

"I can't do that. It's not fair to her. He's my baby," I hiccupped.

"If you don't let someone else help I will put you into hospital for a week. No visitors. Just sleep. Your choice."

"I'm home for the next week," John said. "She'll do it."

I was prescribed various drugs to calm me down and make me sleep.

"I want to see you every day for the rest of this week," the doctor said. "No ifs or buts. I can still put you in hospital."

I hated being out of control and not being able to manage the various situations, but it taught me the lesson that I couldn't do it all, it was okay to ask for help and some things can't be controlled. It took a few months and quite a lot of medication, a lot of sessions in that dusty upstairs consulting room and amazing patience from John, but I got there. When Dr Britton died a couple of years later from cancer, I cried again.

Those doubts that nag and rag your mind, *Who am I? What shall I do now?* resurfaced when the children became more independent and were ready to explore the world without constant supervision. The answer is obvious to all except those going through that phase. You are you first, then a wife, mother, general factotum and all the myriad roles you cover as an accompanying spouse.

It is easy to only write about the accompanying spouse, whether male or female, and the trials inevitably faced living in a foreign country; trials, it has to be added, which occur wherever you happen to live but are exacerbated by being away from base. Those of us doing the trailing have to remember the spouse we have followed also goes through mixed emotions with a new job, a new country and often many days away from home.

John missed a lot of our children's growing up moments, those precious ones you hope you don't ever forget. The first tooth, the first words, the first steps, and then the school plays, the recitals, the matches, never because he couldn't make the time but because he was in some other country. The nature of his job meant planning was not something that could be done, certainly in the early days of their childhood. Christmases and birthdays were hit or miss affairs and though we of course missed him, at least we had each other. He was stuck on a rig somewhere, not only working but knowing he was missing a special moment with his family.

Early in our marriage I was laughingly told a story that sent shock waves through me.

"My children are so used to Henry being away they forget about him," she said.

"Oh God how awful," I said.

"Well, it makes it easier for me in a way."

"How?" I asked.

"I don't have to keep explaining why he's not at home, where he is and when he's coming back."

"What about when he gets back?"

"They won't go to him. Jacob cried last time Henry came home, took him a couple of days to get used to him again." She laughed again.

I saw nothing funny about the story and vowed to myself that if we ever had children I would talk constantly to them about their father when he was away. And I did.

"Look, I made one for Daddy," Kate said one lunchtime in Bangkok.

"Oh, possum, that looks yummy," I said, eyeing the squidgy sandwich with cheese and peanut butter oozing out from the crusts. "But remember he's in Phitsanulok and won't be back for a couple of days. It might get a bit stale."

"I 'member Mummy," she said. "I put in the fridge."

"Okay, that's a good idea," I replied.

And so the pile of things we had to remember to tell John, or show him when he returned, would grow. He was always patient, no matter how tired he was, and would spend the time with them both, and me, listening to all our stories, often long-winded and with many interruptions.

Great inroads have been made with the support offered to the accompanying spouse, and by extension the family, by the sponsoring organisations whatever the sector. Specialists in relocation, counsellors, inter-culturalists and educationalists have all entered into the fray. An organisation called Families in Global Transition has been a great catalyst for much of that improvement.

One of the simplest, yet often least discussed parts of relocation is that expectations need to be managed from the outset and from both sides of the equation. The sponsoring organisation is keen for their chosen employee to go on assignment, and sometimes a rosier than honest outlook may be presented.

A family from rural mid-Western America relocating to the crowded poverty of an Asian city will find it disorienting. The reverse is equally true. Delhi to Duncan, Oklahoma provides quite a contrast. A bustling hustling Indian city to a small rural town in middle America, and culture shock is a real phenomenon as is the reverse, often experienced on repatriation.

In my early married life, negligible consideration was given to family adjustment issues. The deer-in-the-headlights gaze of women dropped into cultures different to their own, with little or no intercultural preparation, often lead to great unhappiness, floundering marriages and failed assignments. I find it surprising it has taken so long for companies to put more energy into ensuring a smooth transition, before, during and after the relocation. Moving a family across the world is an expensive undertaking, moving them back before their assignment is officially finished, more so.

Many sectors have made tremendous strides. Some take great care of their international assignees, with an eye to both the well-being of the family and their Return On Investment. However, there are still too many international organisations, whether public or private, that have a long way to go in assisting those accompanying their partners to new and strange pockets of the globe.

Language, and the tenor of discussions, not just with the sponsoring organisation but within the family, takes on a whole new meaning. Ambiguities can lead to huge disappointments, and for those relocating with children it can be even harder. Already an emotionally charged time, children pick up any negative vibes in a heartbeat. A tired word at the end of a day of packing can be misinterpreted very easily by a teen eager to lay blame for their unhappiness, and what was a throw away comment becomes a platform for anger.

There have always been independent adventurers. In colonial days it was often the black sheep of the family. Now, with the ease of virtual working, many people upsticks and head for a country far away from home to start a new life on their own dime. I have nothing but admiration for them. They do not have the safety net of a corporation, government, NGO or mission behind them, or often even a regular income to support themselves, a home to move into, medical assistance or the many other things those of us who relocate with an organisation sometimes take for granted. Even if in our minds that entity is not doing all we feel it should.

For working women it is often hard to meet other expatriate women, those not working and who tend to gather during the day. For men, who do not appear to need the same brotherly support that us women do, sport or the local bar is often an entry into both the expatriate and local side of life. No matter how much one hopes to assimilate into a foreign country, there are days when a friendly face from one's own culture is welcome.

Moving with children, whatever age, is a wonderful door opener for us, the parents. One huge part of the equation is hurdled within days, as we get involved with the business of getting schools sorted out and meeting other parents. Moving as a young woman without children can be difficult because we are programmed to work and our identity is suddenly whisked out from under us, particularly when we know we won't be able to get visas. And at the other end of the spectrum, leaving children behind is difficult because a little piece of our soul is always with them. Moving is sometimes, just plain difficult!

"What can we call the plenary panel?" asked the program director of FIGT, the organisation that supports both the families from all the different sectors, and also the individuals and groups who support them. "There'll be a facilitator and three or four panellists using their experiences to highlight the resilience of the accompanying spouse."

"Who have you got lined up?" I asked, the phone tucked under my chin as I scribbled various acronyms and words on the pad in front of me.

"No one yet, but I want at least one man on it," she said.

"We don't want *woman* in the title then," I muttered.

"No, but trailing spouse is such a limp expression, I really don't like."

"I don't either. I'd rather be a camp follower. At least that sounds a little more fun than a clinging vine!" I said. Words were filling the page, "How about STARS?"

"Stars?" she asked.

"Yeah, Spouses Travelling And Relocating Successfully. It covers men and women, and sounds kind of fun."

"Yes. I like it. It's certainly better than the State Department's acronym."

"What's that?" I asked.

"EFMs," she laughed.

"EFMs? What the hell does that stand for? Sounds like a disease."

"Eligible Family Members! Okay, STARS it is."

And so STARS came into the FIGT lexicon. The annual conference is the place where global friends reconnect and make new friends as they listen, learn and share new research and best practice ideas that help the global nomad cross cultures. It is also an organisation that has done much to consolidate my thoughts about expatriate living.

No matter how wonderfully we cope as STARS, and manage our expectations, we also need to think about contingency planning. There will sadly be times when situations are entirely out of our hands. The death of the working spouse while on location, quite apart from the ghastliness of the actual circumstances, can be made even more terrible by the sudden realisation that you, the accompanying spouse and your children, have a limited time to stay in the country due to visa issues. You are in the country under the aegis of the company and your spouse, not your own merit, and 45 days is not long to completely reorient your life while helping your children come to terms with their grief, not to mention your own.

It is a thought that would occasionally flit across my mind, particularly when we lived in Thailand, which was prone to attempted *coups d'etat*. Where, I wondered, would I go if we had to be evacuated or, far worse, something happened to John? My parents lived in Papua New Guinea with no base anywhere, and my in-laws, who I cared for deeply, could only house us a short time. Would I go to Australia where I had no right of residency anymore but did have a good support system, or would I go to England in the knowledge my in-laws were there, and my parents would eventually end up there?

It was something I fortunately never had to face, but I have known women who have had to deal with the enormity of the issue. I suppose the lesson I learned from their tragedies was to have a plan, but it was a lesson I never put into practice.

Something I have also not had to face is spousal abuse, which in any society in any country is unforgivable but it does happen, sometimes in the most unlikely couples. Terrible things can happen in any marriage, but an abused woman, or man, in a country far away from the familiar, and familial support, is in a horribly vulnerable position and any attempt to expose the problem can bring all manner of invective, from the sponsoring company or organisation, and sadly also from other expatriates. Practical issues of interim housing, or help leaving the country can be difficult to find, not to mention bringing the protagonist to court. There are people who can help though, and can often be found through the network of women's groups around the world.

Marriages do fail on assignment for a variety of reasons, but then marriages fail wherever you happen to live. Sometimes the stressors of continual relocations are too much for a partnership but other times they deepen the bonds of co-dependency and care. Occasionally temptations are too great to resist, from either partner, and if the will is not there to get through the bad times, or to be able to forgive if not wholly forget, then separation and divorce can follow.

If children are involved, custody issues raise an ugly spectre when families are divided across land and sea. Many of the countries we get sent to have different laws to our home country and it's important that professional advice is sought before any rash moves made. Particularly with regard to both dividing the assets and childcare and even more so if one party is from that host country.

The fun of new horizons, new peoples and cultures has been the carrot whenever the bad days threaten to overwhelm me. Days when you can't make yourself understood by the electrician unfazed by loose wires in a child's bedroom, or the plumber who doesn't think it a problem to have a leak in a maid's bathroom.

It has of course helped that John, whilst not always around, has always supported any decision I might have made without his input. Nothing life changing, but important at the time and normally under a time restraint, like flying to Helsinki to get to London because I was going through an, "I hate BA" phase.

Take-Away Slice: Remembering to make, and take, time for ourselves in between supporting the family is, I think, vital in keeping a sense of proportion and fun. Focusing on the important issues of relocation and bridging cultural divides while allowing the minutiae to flow by, rather than getting caught in the eddy of negative energy, and boxes, is what we need to remember. That ability to be resilient and empathetic enables us to traipse around the world with our spouses and children, and for the whole family to become true and engaged global nomads.

Third Slice: A TCK and didn't know it

"Oh, you're an expat brat," the hunky-looking man sitting next to me on the plane said, as I left Sydney on my flight to London to start my secretarial training.

"I don't think so," I replied, resenting the implication and wanting to impress him with my *sangfroid*. I wish I'd known the term Third Culture Kid.

Third Culture Kid was coined in the early 1950s by sociologist Ruth Hill Useem after her second yearlong visit to India with her three children. She defined TCKs as, "Children who accompany their parents into another society." Later David C. Pollock interpreted it as, "A person who has spent a significant part of his or her developmental years outside the parents' culture". Pollock went on to define the early global experience as having, "… elements from each culture (are) assimilated into the TCK's life experience, the sense of belonging is in the relationship to others of a similar background."

Maybe because I'd never had a base, even though my father referred to England as home, and my mother referred to Australia, I never felt a gut-deep connection to either place except as somewhere to visit or go to school. Both held wonderful memories for me, both were home to family and dear friends, but as a place I felt rooted to they meant nothing, though I loved the different geographical features of both.

At NEGS, my boarding school, except for the brief Brisbane interlude, home was either KL or Lae. Holidays spent in either place were weeks of either intense activity or loneliness. There was no television and so entertainment was homemade, especially in Lae, which was and still is a small town compared to KL.

With my parents' decision to send me to an Australian boarding school, my mother's old school and in the same town as much of her family, came the severing of close ties with my English friends from school days in KL. Time spent at home was vastly different with my long summer holiday being at Christmas and theirs in the English summertime. Their summers were spent rekindling childhood friendships and forging new ones with newcomers to the city, most of whom flew out from their British boarding schools. Mine were spent in a flurry of activity for an overlapping week and then nothing. It was in many ways a forced gaiety on my part, trying hard to fit in with their accents, their friends, their activities. Christmas was the reverse, with a pell-mell three weeks of parties over the actual festive season with teens hardly known, and then five weeks of solitary time with the exception of Mak Peck Yoke.

Three weeks though can be time enough.

"Where the hell have you been?" my father raged at me. "You are three hours late. I have telephoned everyone we could think of."

"Oh no," I muttered. What possessed me to think my parents wouldn't know when I broke curfew, I don't know. What possessed me to think I could sneak in with four dogs guarding the house?

"Well?" Dad demanded. Mum hovered behind him, with Ah Moi behind her, both glowering.

"I lost track of the time Dad, I'm sorry," I mumbled, hiding my face in Charlie's fur as I bent to pet him.

"Where have you been?"

"Just around," I said, grateful I wasn't drunk as well as late.

"Around? It's two in the morning Apple. I imagine you've been at a nightclub?"

"Yes," I admitted. "But there was a group of us so it was okay."

"No, it was not okay. Do you recall a conversation we had a few weeks ago? The one about nightclubs? The one wherein I said you were not to go to them?"

For a first nightclub it was fantastic, and very few have lived up to it since. The waitresses, all wearing silver minis and tank-tops, silver wigs and glittery six-inch platforms shimmied around the futuristic version of a Malay tin mine. It had all been very heady and grown-up, until I got home, but I never really regretted it.

Dad was livid. A rare occurrence with me, and which was far worse than Mum's fairly frequent diatribes. Soundly reprimanded, I was shamed out of existence as the calls started coming in once daylight arrived, and my fellow partygoers, all older than me, asked what had happened. They having been ripped into by their parents whose slumber had been disturbed by my father's anxious phone calls.

Life as a teenager in KL was sometimes fun, sometimes lonely but always privileged. It was before the days of home swimming pools, afternoons were spent lounging around the pool at one of the clubs. Most of us were allowed to sign the drinks chits that ended up on our parent's desk at the end of each month.

"Apple, the Lake Club bill arrived today," my father mentioned one evening, as we sat, napkins on our lap, in our normal formation around the dining table, Dad at the head of the table, Mum to his right and me to his left.

"Oh?" I squirmed, and gazed over my mother's shoulder wishing I could escape through the open French doors and into the inky Asian night, scented by the night-flowering cirrus strategically placed by the doors.

"Yes. Rather a lot of gin was signed for the night of the Summer Ball. I don't believe your mother or I were there. You were, it seems, from the signature scrawled on the chits. Thank you," he continued as Ah Moi served him.

She glanced at me from behind his chair and raised an eyebrow.

"Sorry Dad," I said, "It was the night Susan and I went together, and she couldn't sign because they're not members. And she signed for me at the Golf Club the other evening in return," I rushed on.

"Is that so?" he asked. "It would still seem to be rather a lot of gin to be consumed by two young ladies, don't you think? I thought we agreed on an occasional Dubonnet."

"Yes Daddy," I said, "I'm sorry."

"I will pay this one, but if it happens again you pay out of your allowance. Understood?"

"Yes Daddy, thank you."

As I took the coffee cups out to the kitchen a little later Ah Moi glared at me.

"You no tell him about car, huh?"

"No, Ah Moi. Please don't tell – I hosed it down and Ebi said it was okay," I begged, knowing she was referring to the time I chundered out the window.

"You bad girl sumtime Aphu."

"I know. But you love me huh?" I hugged her and she shoved me out of the kitchen with a snort.

Public transport was safe in KL if a willing mother, Ebi, or someone else's driver was not available to take us on our outings when holidays overlapped. Bowling alleys, shopping in markets and the newly built mall, and cinemas were our entertainment with occasional forays to the hills or the seaside.

I was tall, relatively worldly and got on well with adults, or maybe they were just being kind to a lonely teenager, but I was often included in invitations to cocktail parties on the expatriate circuit where my hours of conversation at our dinner table paid off. For all the solitary time I still loved going home. I spent hours reading, often wholly unsuitable, risqué books that I'd found on my father's shelves, and I was spoilt, particularly by him.

My privileged feet were nevertheless kept firmly grounded by both parents, especially Mum. She volunteered for the Red Cross the whole time in we lived in KL and Singapore, and was awarded their highest medal, rarely given to foreigners.

On twice-yearly holidays home to KL from NEGS, some portion of most days would be spent helping Mum at whatever she happened to be doing at the time. Checking in medical supplies sent from other countries was something bound to bring her to apoplexy.

"For God's sake," she'd splutter, "Why do people in Europe think it okay to send us out of date drugs? Do they think we don't carry the same risks here?"

"Can't they be used if they are just a little out of date?" I asked.

"How little is little?" she countered. "It's a bit like being a little pregnant – you either are or you aren't. In this case you either can or you can't." And she'd storm off to write a stinging letter to the hapless fool who had sent them.

She ran weekly clinics in outlying villages, normally in the local community hall, where she would persuade doctors to come on a rotating roster and give their services for free. Scabies was prevalent and I would be assigned the sluice room, more often than not a single cold-water tap with a length of hose in a little room out the back. Rubbing the infants down with some concoction Mum had the aides make up in batches, and then rinsing them off, was a soggy, unpleasant task made more so by an army of indignant mosquitoes hell bent on attacking the interlopers, and the squeals of the kids. Once home I too hosed down, trying to get the sticky ungent out from under my nails and the antiseptic smell from my hair.

A more appealing task was being assigned to play jacks with kids waiting for a parent being examined. Their dexterity invariably beat me as we tossed pebbles on the concrete floor.

"Sista Ida," I would hear a nurse say, "This lady not be good. She no take medicine." And so Mum would sit down and patiently explain again why the weeping tropical ulcer had to be cleaned every day and had to be treated with both ointment and pills.

Mum's Malay, even after years of living there on and off, was never very good but she had translators and always got her instructions across, and they loved her though were also a little wary. She could be ferocious if she felt a husband was stopping his wife or children from following her instructions. She would haul the hapless man in and explain that if he didn't stop hindering his wife's progress she would put her in hospital, and then who would look after the children.

Her voluntary work was a big part of her life, along with the Mah Jong mornings and lunches, the receptions and foreign trips with my father.

Dad also volunteered, though in a more cerebral manner, being active on local school boards, government committees as well as acting as an advisor /mentor to government, organizations and individuals.

There was never any ambivalence in their roles, we were lucky and therefore it was our duty, and a privilege, to give back no matter where we lived. And so I never questioned the expectation that I also paid my dues.

But just sometimes things do go awry for the TCK.

"What's the matter with Diana's sister?" I asked Mum. It was my first holiday home to Kuala Lumpur, which happened to overlap with an old primary school friend who was at boarding school in England. "She says she's going to be in hospital for ages but doesn't really know what the matter is."

"The poor girl has lost a lot of weight and is now very sick."

"Shall we go and see her? We could take her some of those chocolates she likes."

"I think we should let her Mum tell us when it's okay to visit her, don't you?" mine said.

"Okay," I agreed, and put my nose back in the book I was reading.

Just before I went back to school a couple of weeks later, we visited Diana's sister. It frightened me. A pencil thin girl, only four years older than us, lay on a padded hospital bed with dull eyes and straggly hair that looked as if it were falling out. I thought she was dying. She didn't, thank goodness, but neither did her illness prevent Diana from going the same route. It was my first encounter with anorexia nervosa.

A year or so later I recognised the signs in a classmate at NEGS.

"Whaddya doing?" I asked, watching her surreptitiously stuff her gloves with food under the rim of the dining table at lunchtime, one eye on the prefect at the far end.

"I'm not hungry."

"Well just leave it on the side of your plate and tell her."

"No."

The same thing happened at supper, and breakfast, and every meal after that. We tried talking to her, but she would not listen. In the end a couple of us went to the school nurse and explained the situation, which was then taken out of our hands but not before she became very sick and eventually left NEGS.

Eating disorders are not just the realm of young women, though they do tend to be the main sufferers, boys can also suffer from them. They do however seem to be relatively common amongst TCKs. I have no hard facts but many, both close and second hand, anecdotal tales of the mental issues that manifest themselves in anorexia and/or bulimia.

Teenagers are a peculiarly sensitive breed, throughout the years their brains are refiling earlier knowledge, memories and habits, and sometimes despite the best intentions of all around them, they go through the agonies of an eating disorder. And it is agony for all the family, all of whom need to be engaged in the rehabilitation.

Forty years later, though, it is better understood but still rears up and creates anger and despair at the helplessness it provokes in everyone involved.

"How is Olivia?" I asked a friend who'd returned to England from Houston six months earlier.

"Terrible. She's been diagnosed with anorexia and bulimia."

"Oh God, I'm so sorry. She seemed fine about leaving here."

"I know. It's all come about since we rented a house in the same village as her school. We thought we'd rent there and buy in the north once she finished 6th form."

"Is she still boarding?"

"Yes. She didn't want to become a daygirl. We thought she'd like us to be close by."

Neither Olivia's parents had been to boarding school, and so I tried to explain the strange blend of vulnerability and defiance kids get at boarding school. I know because I went through a similar loss of identity when my parents left KL and moved to Australia, albeit not in the same town.

Suddenly, particularly if your school is predominantly TCKs, you no longer fit the same mould, and on the whole teenagers do not want to be different to their peers. Bad enough you will not be flying off to foreign climes at the end of each term, but even worse to have your parents living on the school doorstep. Your sense of independence, the one you have nurtured since your first day as a boarder, is taken away from you and you are no longer quite sure where you fit in. It is disturbing. You do not want to upset your parents, and you don't really have the words to explain how you feel.

Thankfully Olivia received consideration, counseling and care and is now a healthy and happy young woman. Others are not always so fortunate. Not so much now, thank goodness and because the illnesses are better understood, stories of teenage girls, all TCKS, and all in the same class, suffering different levels of eating disorders, are hopefully not so prevalent.

In many ways holidays were easier in PNG because we all had the same dates, but there I had the exact opposite of KL in that I, to most Australian ears, sounded English and so I didn't quite fit in. NEGS was where I was most at home, apart from with my parents.

In Lae our entertainment consisted of two cinemas, both with tin roofs. If it rained hard the film would be turned off until the worst of the storm moved out into the Huon Gulf. When the power went off, or the projector jammed, locals and expats would gather outside until someone shouted, *"Emi orright nau"* or "Okay, it's back on." If a play was showing in the Niall theatre some of us would be in it.

All of us TCKs, though we didn't know that's what we were, met, played and partied, and then dispersed at the various airports at the end of each holiday and met again the next time school broke up – often at the airport departure lounge. None of us were special, or different, it was just our life.

The main difference for me in PNG was that most of my playmates and partners in crime were Australian, whereas in Malaysia at primary school they had been multi-national and then British. Strangely, and only on reflection as I write this, do I realise my closest friend in PNG, Jenfa, was an Anglo-Australian brought up in Kenya.

Even by the time our children were born in the 1980s the term TCK had not crossed my path. I had been an 'expat brat' and my children were fated to be the same. Did I give any great thought to them being born outside their parents' passport country? Absolutely not. Did I have any concerns? Absolutely not.

I can remember being vaguely piqued listening to a couple of expatriate women I knew in the Netherlands, discussing the pros and cons of raising children whilst living abroad. I could honestly see no down sides and so when our daughter Kate was born a few years later, my only concern was that she have her own passport rather than appear on mine. Our son Edward was born three years later in Bangkok, Thailand, again to no reservations about their proposed international upbringing.

John did not have an expatriate childhood but was, and is still, a man of *laissez-faire* disposition. We both felt that the home environment was what would imbue the children with their moral compass, with, of course, influences from around them. And what better way to instill an empathetic, compassionate and open mind than to live in other people's countries? Not necessarily adopting all the local mores and customs but being aware of them, and to a certain extent accepting them, though naturally blatant cruelty and corruption do not fall into that acceptance pile.

I was reminded of the moral compass a few years ago when Miss Meg, our wonderful Third Culture Dog, and I happened to bump into Atticus, a rather handsome Standard Poodle, and his owners at our local coffee shop and mid-way resting point on our morning ambles. It brought to mind Harper Lee's American classic, *To Kill a Mockingbird*, Atticus being neither a common name for man nor dog.

The book is relevant because Atticus Finch was one of the main characters, an honest-to-God good man, a white lawyer defending a black man for allegedly raping a white woman. A repulsive crime at any time in any society but deemed even more heinous in 1930s Alabama. Reading the book as a teenager, narrated by Atticus' daughter Scout, but not having been exposed to segregation I didn't really understand the racial significance, though I think I was shocked, and probably a little titillated, by the story. But as an adult, discussing the book over lattes on a sunny Saturday morning, I realized why, in my youth, whilst I found the book shocking because of the supposed rape, I did not appreciate the horror felt by many readers in the US at the time of its publication, the 1960s, a black man daring, allegedly, to touch a white woman.

Atticus the dog, ironically black, talking about *To Kill A Mocking Bird* and the mocking bird nipping red berries off the asparagus fern on my terrace, all contributed to me joining the dots and appreciating that my upbringing was so free of the entanglements of colour prejudice. Growing up, particularly in Asia, multi-racial marriages, whilst not ten-a-penny, where not despised and parties my parents threw were a mingling of many races. Such were and are, I think, the benefits of growing up a TCK.

"TCKs will become the proto-type citizen of the world," said Ted Ward in 1989, then a professor of sociology at Michigan State University. His words are starting to ring true with Cross Cultural Kids (CCKs) as defined by Ruth Van Reken, co-author of *Third Culture Kids: Growing up Among Worlds*, as children who have lived in several cultural environments while growing up; for example, children of bi or multi racial parents, children of refugees as well as traditional TCKs, and so on, becoming a defined demographic.

For those children brought up as TCKs or CCKs, a nonjudgmental and accepting attitude to different customs, colours and cultures is the norm. As this demographic grows, let's hope for an even greater understanding of cultural differences for all our children, because ultimately we could all still learn from Atticus Finch's response to his daughter's comment that, "People are normally nice", with the words, "Most people are, Scout, when you finally see them."

"I don't want my daughter playing with the locals," said one mother. I had been asked to lead two Brownie troops in Lae, at the advanced age of nineteen and just after I had started working there. I refused the role unless both were amalgamated. The edict was initially wrought with racial tension even though the head of PNG Guiding favoured the idea.

"Why not?" I asked.

"Well, they have different ideas to us. They do things differently."

"Wouldn't it be a good time for the girls to understand the differences?"

"Not really. No."

And so the conversation went on. For about a month. But as no one else was prepared to lead either troop I fortunately had the upper hand. After the first few weeks of frosty drop-offs and collections, feelings thawed with only one brief revolt.

"Next week I want you to bring whatever you clean your teeth with," I said, as the little girls, all wearing brown and sporting yellow ties, dispersed.

The following week we discussed dental hygiene. Along with the expected toothbrushes came a few sticks.

"How come Shuri's teeth are white?" asked one little girl. "An' she doesn't have fillings," she continued, after they'd peered in each others' mouths.

"Shuri, you tell Susie," I suggested, as she viewed the amalgam curiously.

"I use stick ebery day. Else my mumi shout me," Shuri explained. "Why yogat silber?"

"'Coz she got holes," answered another helpfully.

"Why?"

"'Coz she eats too many sweets," announced another little cherub.

The outrage came the week after.

"Apple," said an irate mother, some of whom understandably struggled to call me Brown Owl. "Susie refused to use her toothbrush all week. She has been putting toothpaste on a stick she picked up from the garden."

"Does she like it?" I asked, my laughter not helping defuse the situation.

"Of course not. But she won't stop."

"Well maybe if you ignore it she will stop on her own. It's not much fun spitting out bits of bark."

"That is not the point!"

"No, but at least she now knows that not everyone has a toothbrush but they can still have healthy teeth."

Fortunately the mother did not bring up the subject of *buia,* the disgusting mixture of betel nut and lime, chewed by many New Guineas who start to use it as teens. As well as rotting the teeth, the combination produces a spew of blood red spittle freely expectorated onto pavements and cars with impunity. I am also pretty sure it contributes to mouth ulcers and other oral complaints in many older people.

It was the last time there was dissent among the parental ranks and our troop had a lot of fun, even if I didn't exactly stick to the manual. When, later in the year, we held a hygiene drive asking for toiletries to be dispersed at a nearby village, toothbrushes and toothpaste were high on most mothers' lists.

Finding out our blood was the same colour after a scraped knee produced both blood and tears while on a scavenge hunt in the botanical gardens, was another 'mockingbird' moment for many of my Brownies.

I was sometimes a restless as well as impatient mother to my TCKs. John was away a great deal and I loved the spur of the moment adventures I had with Kate, and when Edward was born, with them both. On a whim we would decide to go somewhere for a few days, by car, train or plane, it didn't matter.

What mattered was the fun and excitement of new places, new smells, being anonymous.

"Shall we go and find Daddy?" I asked Kate one day.

"He's in Pisanananalo," she told me, her name for Phitsanulok, an old town in central Thailand where a lot of the onshore drilling took place.

"Let's surprise him!"

"'Kay," she said. "In the car?"

"No, let's go by train. You've never been on one. It'll be fun."

"'Kay," Kate said. "Tessie come?"

"Of course," I said, looking at my daughter, thumb in mouth, holding Tessie her lemur hand puppet, a much favoured toy given to her by her godmother, Jane.

And so, much to our driver Ay's dismay, he dropped us off at Hua Lompong Station.

"Madam, Cake too small for train," he warned me.

Why it was okay for Thai children to travel by train and not Kate I never quite got to the bottom of, though at one stage, unable to find the right train, I was beginning to regret my rashness. Thankfully we traveled light, one rucksack and her little one filled with a colouring book, pencils, Tessie and Lion, another constant in her life, so didn't have to cart anything heavy along the platforms bristling with people all able to read Thai ticker tape. A skill set I did not have.

"Sawahdeekrap," a gentleman, bowed with age and luggage, greeted us. "I assist you?"

"Kobkhunkha," I thanked him.

"I'm going to see my daddy in Pisanananalo," Kate informed him importantly before I could ask for direction.

"Phitsanulok," I translated for the smiling man.

"Come, I show you the precise train."

He wove his way, still bowed by luggage, through the

throngs with us close behind him, and ushered us onto the correct platform, bowed and waved away my thanks before continuing on his journey. I don't know where he was going.

Kate was a precocious two-year old and expected the world to love her, and it did. She spent most of the five-hour trip up the spine of Thailand, eating sticky rice, mangoes and sweets given by entranced passengers.

I'd left a message with the rig telling John where we were staying and that we'd be around for a couple of days if he could get a few hours off.

"Daddy, Daddy, I thurplized you!" Kate lisped, as he joined us for breakfast the next morning.

"You certainly did, sweetheart, it's a lovely surprise! Shall we go exploring today?" he asked, giving her and Tessie a hug before he sat down.

"Yeth, you too?" she asked.

"All day," he answered to our delight. We wandered the ruins at Ramkamhaeng, the old Sukhothai and original capital of Thailand. Wat Mahathat, considered 'the magical and spiritual center of the kingdom' and famous for the stucco frieze of walking Buddha images sculpted by the Sukhothai artisans, was part of an idyllic day where Kate showed her knowledge of Thai protocol. Whether kicking off her sandals before entering a *wat* and never pointing her feet at a Buddha image, to happily *wai*ing any passing saffron-clad monk, she was at ease with the culture surrounding her.

Another lovely jaunt, again wholly unplanned, occurred when living in Singapore and I got island fever. I think John was in New Zealand. The three of us, Edward by that time having joined the family, bundled onto another train and headed up the Malay peninsula to Malacca where we wandered for four days, returning tired each afternoon to a little local-run hotel on the beach about ten miles north of the city. We were the only foreigners there and had a lovely time in the evenings playing on the sand and under the palms, rinsing off later, with a smorgasbord of other children who squealed with delight as I took turns tossing them in the pool.

"*Selamat datang mem*, let me take you and chilrens," the Malay trishaw driver said, as we disembarked from the bus the first morning, "I show much."

"*Terimah kasi,*" I thanked him as we clambered in.

"You spik *bahasa melayu?*" he asked, pedaling off to Cheong Houn Temple, first on our list because the kids wanted to look at the fanciful creatures on the walls that they'd seen in the guidebook.

"*Tidak,*" I replied. "I lived in KL as a child, but I don't remember very much. I'm sorry." When I told him my parents had met in the jungles of Pahang in the 1950s he was delighted.

"You papa he army?" Faiz asked.

"Malay Regiment, based in Port Dickson."

"I same. Fight communists. Bad time but British good."

Faiz became our guide for the duration.

"*Selamat pagi mem, selamat pagi Cake and kechi Ed,*" he said every morning, as he met the bus before taking us to his favourite stalls, shops and of course the sites. Poor Kate was called 'Cake' wherever we lived in Asia, and Edward at three and a half could hardly be called little, but that was Faiz's name for him, Little Ed.

"You try dis," Faiz said one hot afternoon when we all needed a break.

"I don't want to eat that," Kate objected.

"Eat. Is good," he persuaded.

"Yuk, green worms," Edward said looking at the *cendol*,

bits of pea flour layered with sweet red beans dunked in coconut milk and presented over shaved ice.

"You'll like it, it's very sweet," I told the kids, tasting a spoonful of what really did look like green grubs. Too sweet even for them, we bought a lime juice as well.

Apart from Faiz, the highlight of our little escapade was a lovely afternoon lazing along the Malacca River in a boat that only operated at high tide. Kate was fascinated by the long shop houses, sometimes only ten or twelve feet across but stretching back 200 feet to foil the Portuguese policy that taxed buildings on their width. Edward liked the 'godowns' with all the hustle and bustle around them. They reminded me of when I was a child in Singapore.

"Where's Daddy gone?" I'd ask my mother.

"He's gone down to the godown," she'd answer. It always seemed mysterious and a little sinister.

Faiz delighted in the children and I was quite happy to leave the three of them under a tree while I popped into a shop or museum. They thought he was wonderful and he'd let them take turns sitting up front with him on the bike. Edward even put up with the chin chucking without demur.

"*Selamat jalan*," Faiz said, as we boarded the train home, wishing us a safe journey.

"*Trimakasi Faiz*," the children chirped, as he gave one final cheek pinch to them both.

"*Selamat tinggal*," I said, wishing him safety and promising to send photos of a magical few days in Malacca. He would not accept the extra *ringgit* I offered for all his guidance and care, but I did send some when I sent the photos to his *kampong*. I wondered if I offended him because I never heard back.

School, once the children started, was a horrid shock to me, the rigidity and lack of freedom stopped our impromptu trips and I missed being able to take off with the kids on a whim. I was that mother who loved the lazy days of school holidays, and the sudden trips to somewhere. At least until the teen years when life became more complicated with sensitivities and hormones, and in order for peace to reign I often needed John's rational and calming influence on Kate and I.

We all have TCK stories, and one of my favourites is told by Kay, a friend of twenty-five years who saw me through some dark days, both in hospital and at home after back surgery, and who I first met in Singapore; it came from her time spent there. Her daughter, Katherine, came home from school one day full of chatter about a little boy in her class.

"He sounds nice," Kay said. "I don't think I've met Mark, have I?"

"Yes you have Mummy," her daughter replied, "He's got sparkly eyes."

Kay, none the wiser, nodded but made a mental note to look out for the boy with the shiny eyes. She finally met him and yes he did have sparkling eyes, but what Katherine had failed to mention and which most adults would have used as a first descriptor, was that he was extraordinarily black, a Tamil from Southern India. Katherine had not seen his colour, just his eyes. How wonderful to grow up 'colour blind'. What a gift we give our children.

A lot is written now about the TCK. We are a sub-genre of the global world and we come in many forms. The *classic* – the kid moved from his birth or passport country to another thereby forming his own individual culture. The *immigrant* kid, under which must fall the *illegal immigrant* child, and the attendant issues relating to attempting assimilation into a way of life that could be snatched away at any time, the *refugee*, the *adoptee*, and so the list goes on.

Sadly there is another. The arrogant and therefore *ugly* TCK, the true expat brat.

Much is spoken about the adaptability and self-confidence of the child brought up in often multiple countries. Both are born of necessity. That sink or swim state of mind on walking into yet another new school breeds a natural stiffening of shoulders that, "I don't really care if you speak to me or not" attitude. The glazed look in the corridor that says, "Beware, don't approach" really means, "If you say something nice my defences will crumble and I might cry and then I'll never make friends". That is not arrogance. That is fear. Fear no one will understand. I know. I've felt it.

But you do care. Of course you desperately want someone to say something welcoming. Matter of fact is the best way to approach that off-hand, distant face. "Hi, where've you moved from?" works much better than, "Hi, where are you from?" We don't always know where we're from.

That other type of TCK, the *ugly* one, comes across as brash, which I know can initially be a form of nervousness, but rather than dissipating at the approach of a friendly face it tends to increase the, "I've been everywhere" kind of kid with a swagger wholly unbecoming. My immediate reaction is invariably, "How sad to be so jaded so early in life'. Followed quickly by irritation.

A typical scenario might be that of a young man introducing the girl at his side. "This is my girlfriend," he says holding her hand. "She's only just got her first passport. She hasn't been anywhere."

"Hello," you say to the slim young woman looking a little deflated, wondering at his arrogance and the relevance of the statement. "It's hard to define 'anywhere' isn't it?" you ask, attempting to defuse the lack of manners.

"I'm a TCK," the young man says before she can respond, "I've lived all over the world."

"Is that so?" you ask, trying desperately not to turn your back on him and say to the woman standing at his side, "Dump him before he undermines you anymore" but instead ask her where home is.

"Littlerock, Arkansas," she replies.

"I haven't been there," you say, "But it's quite somewhere to a lot of people I'm sure! Arkansas is on my list of places to visit."

The young man with his *braggadero* is fortunately not a common breed but they do exist. Most TCKs go about their business, quietly confident they can surmount most issues encountered with a mixture of empathy, compromise and yes, cultural intuition. Most are aware they have been privileged to be long-term guests in other people's countries. Something that does not give boasting rights, but a responsibility. And an inherent understanding, for the most part, that to tread lightly through the quagmire of growing up a global nomad is a wonderful preparatory lesson for the multi-cultural world we all live in. Seeing the person before the colour or creed is, I think, a cultural radar in balance.

As a counterbalance to the obnoxious TCK there is the child, sometimes very young, who, particularly in immigrant families but also in some expatriate locations, takes on the role of translator. It is the child or teen, being educated in the host country's education system who is able to understand and decipher official letters that come through the door, who is the designated form filler in all things legal or medical, who is the bridge between cultures and language. It is an onus they take on willingly, but it is a burden that can shorten their childhood, the awareness of issues that parents attempt to keep from their children for fear of worrying them. In immigrant families from third world countries these same children are often the only ones in the family educated in computing skills, and they take on the added role of researcher.

No wonder clashes occur between cultures within households, these children walk a fine line in both worlds they live in. Wanting to be part of their adopted culture while not wishing to offend their familial culture, or disrespect their parents.

Children do not ask to take part in a life of perpetual motion, of packing and unpacking, of making new friends and saying goodbyes to new schools every couple of years, so it is up to us, the parents, to ease their transitions, to let them know this new move is not being done without thinking of their happiness. However, at the end of the day they also have to realise, particularly as they get older, that the bonuses of a global childhood do come at a price sometimes. The price being continuity.

"Will I be able to dance?" Kate asked each time we moved.

"Yes, sweetheart," was always the answer. We would not have gone somewhere she could not practice her passion. Edward, being a generalist as far as sport was concerned, was easier to accommodate.

How we speak tells such a lot about us, geographically, both within our own borders and internationally, socially, despite protestations that we are a one-class society, and educationally and economically.

It was after we moved to Lae that my accent became more steadfastly Australian – much to my father's chagrin – rather than switching back and forth, which I had apparently been doing each time I went back home on holiday. My mother, having lived away from Australia for many years, spoke with a very soft accent, unless riled.

For TCKs particularly, I think moving between English-speaking countries, the accent with which English is spoken speaks volumes. For some children the quicker they sound like everyone else in the playground or the classroom, the quicker they feel they will be accepted. Sometimes, as I think was my case, we don't realise we are adapting our accent. For others it is a deliberate effort to blend in, to become in essence a chameleon.

Kay tells the story of how, when they moved to Houston, Texas, her eldest daughter slunk out the school doors and into the waiting car, imploring her mother not to say a word until they'd moved away from the kerb.

"You sound too English and I don't want anyone to know I'm not American," she muttered by way of explanation to her confused mother.

Sometimes it is a survival mechanism, like a toddler swatting away a hand that grabs a chunk of cheek, that habit so common in Asian countries.

"If I have to repeat everything I say twice I'm not going to bother talking," Edward exploded one hot afternoon, swinging his knee-buckling rucksack onto the kitchen table, not long after our arrival in the same American city.

"Why do you have to say everything twice?" I asked, putting a slab of cake in front of him. He was always hungry after school and the sugar boost helped everyone prepare for the homework phase, always my least favourite part of term time.

"Because," explained my son as if to a child, "They like my Scottish accent."

And therein lay one of the greatest ironies of all our moves. When we first arrived in Scotland fresh from Singapore shores, both my children were hounded in their school playground for sounding English. Neither of them had ever lived in England, but their tormentors, and tormentors they were, had immediately labeled them and treated them accordingly. Both children left Scotland with an Aberdonian accent!

The PolVan Cultural Identity Model, developed by David C Pollock and Ruth van Reken in 1996 defined "cultural identity in relationship to surrounding culture" by categorising and defining the four predominant TCK types:

> Foreigner: Look *different*, Think *different*
> Hidden Immigrant: Look alike, Think *different*
> Adopted: Look *different*, Think alike
> Mirror: Look alike, Think alike

Kay's daughter, and to a certain extent ours, were both a classic case of 'hidden immigrants' in that they looked similar but thought differently, and yet both desperately wanted to mirror their peers, wanted to be seen as the same, with the same accents, same hairstyles, same clothes, same likes and dislikes. Was that a teenage girl's response? I don't know. Our son, also a 'hidden immigrant', didn't care about thinking differently, he just wanted to sound the same to avoid constant repetition.

If a child or teenager arrives fresh from India or Sweden and looks the part, either Indian or Swedish, they do not, to a certain extent, seem to be ribbed quite so much in that they are obviously a 'foreigner'.

On going to boarding school in England two years later, Edward was instantly known as Tex. Did that make him a 'reverse hidden immigrant'? He spoke with a Texan accent, was of Anglo parentage but had never lived in England. He now speaks with an English accent dotted with Scottish and American colloquialisms and Thai words. My daughter having spent the last ten years in England speaks in a similar vein but with added Trinidadian overtones, her partner being from the Islands.

Maybe TCKs are even more like a sponge than most children, what Maria Montessori described as 'the absorbent mind'. They seem to excel in the arts and music perhaps more than any other medium, allowing for true integration of a global soul. The heartbeat of the music, whether reggae, R&B, gospel, punk rock, chutney, gamelan, pop, classical or any other kind, might not be liked by all, but they have a rhythm that transcends race and religion.

"Who's that you're listening to?" Dad asked one evening on my goodbye trip home to KL.

"John Denver," I replied, with teary eyes.

"A bit whiney isn't he?"

"No. I think he's great," I defended the singer who seemed to understand just what I was feeling.

"Well when that side is finished why don't you put on some Ella Fitzgerald? She'll cheer you up," he said, on his way to the decanter to pour drinks for he and Mum.

"Not if she's singing *Stormy Weather*," I muttered to back.

Leaving on a Jet Plane epitomised my life as a teenager leaving Malaysia with the words, "Don't know when I'll be back again" and still remind me of my most painful dislocation.

It was only later I learned Denver had been an MK shuttled between stations in Japan and the US.

According to the PolVan Model, Jason Hershey, a singer known as O-Shen, is an Adopted TCK in that he looked different but thought alike. Born to American medical missionary parents he was raised in Butaweng in Papua New Guinea. Growing up, a white boy among the Yabim, he learned the same language and customs of any other young man in the village and did not speak English as his first language until moving to the US at fifteen. It is through his lyrics that he addresses the issues of the Pacific Islanders and attempts to instil a pride in their cultures and languages.

Listening to Gerald De Palmas, a French *Reunionnaise* sing *Je Suis Un Homme Sans Racines* makes me wonder if our TCK *racines,* roots, lie in the music we listen to, the art we view and the theatre and dance we choose to watch rather than to a specific place.

Music is such a fusion of styles and sounds that we don't realise it is also a merging of cultures and colours. It doesn't matter if we don't always understand the words; the spirit of the rhythm moves us, allows boundaries to be crossed and helps lessen the immediate need to burrow for answers, which I think allows a slower pace of understanding to occur. Sometimes we try too hard to understand a new place, a new culture, rather than just going with the beat and letting ourselves assimilate at a leisurely pace, not forcing acceptance either on ourselves or our hosts. It's a bit like trying to make a shy child like you. If you ignore them they are intrigued and will come to you.

For all my blasé attitude at producing and raising children abroad, we as parents, owe them a responsibility to ease their way through what is, certainly for teenagers, already a stew of emotions.

One such time is when the expatriate, who is not a TCK herself, starts making the lists for a summer spent 'at home'. Swarms of expatriate wives and children from all over the globe descend on clogged airports intent on 'going home' for the summer. Plans are made for Dad to join the fray, for a couple of weeks, in the middle of this madness of visiting grandparents and living out of suitcases. The initial pleasure of seeing family and friends, the latter you actually don't have much in common with anymore, begins to pall when the laundry piles up and the rain lashes down.

And why do we put ourselves through this supposed pleasure year after year? We tell ourselves it is so our children get 'a sense of home, a sense of place, a sense of where they are from.' But is that for them or for us? For most children home is where their parents are, no matter their nationality or where they might be living.

"I don't know why Paul is so crabby," Elaine, a young mum, said. "He keeps on about wanting to go to summer camp with our next door neighbour's son."

"Well, Houston is home to him now," I said. "His friends are here and not there."

"Yes I know that. But he needs to know where home really is."

"Perhaps he already does," I suggested. "And it's hard being on good behaviour for the whole summer."

"It's different for you. You've always done this. You've never known about home."

It is a comment that has been tossed my way many times.

If children choose to call their current location 'home' and want to stay home for the summer, maybe we should let them. Most parenting is compromise anyway. Perhaps by agreeing to spend a couple of weeks seeing the grandparents and your old haunts, then letting them go back to where they call 'home', that place you moved them to, will help avoid conflict. Or better yet, fly the grandparents out to you. Let them face the queues and lightning strikes by air-traffic controllers or luggage handlers, but more importantly it allows them the chance to see you and their grandchildren in your environment, and let them become part of your lives.

The long summer holidays bring a lot of emotions.

"Er, Mum?" Edward said, over the crackly line from his boarding school in Devon, England to Malabo, Equatorial Guinea.

"Yes?"

"I think, er, I'll stay in England most of the summer holidays this year. Is that okay?" he finished in a rush.

"Oh," I said blindsided, "Why? Where will you stay?"

"So I can get a summer job. I've spoken to Mrs Finch. She says I can have her basement flat for free if I repaint it for her."

"But what about cooking, and stuff?" I asked, scrabbling for a reason his plan would not work, so he had to come home.

"I'll eat with them. We'd just have to pay a little for food. I'd really like to stay here, Mum. I can pick up a bit of work and get some studying done."

"Okay. I understand. Do you want to come out at all?" I asked, gazing out the kitchen window at the shanties and clearings transforming the once verdant hillside opposite our house. Frustration at not being able to work due to visa restrictions, being reliant on parents for handouts, which invariably is never enough, is understandable though a loss for the parents.

"Yeah, I thought the last couple of weeks. Would that be okay?"

"Yes of course. Let me talk to Dad and we'll sort something out."

"Great, thanks, Mum," he said. "Got cricket now so gotta go. Speak to you soon."

I put the 'phone down and cried, thinking how hard it was sometimes to be a global parent. It's difficult to accept that for our children, on the threshold of young adulthood, expatriate life can sometimes be very cloistered, particularly if living on a compound. The added restrictions laid down either by the company, or the country, can seem too claustrophobic for teens already railing against parental confines.

For American kids abroad the inability to drive at sixteen sits poorly on their shoulders, in comparison to the perceived freedom of their cousins back home when wheels become the most important thing in their lives.

So too the pressure to behave becomes omnipresent. The risk of a teen's behaviour on a parent's job is another issue we sometimes forget, particularly in some countries where the risk of deportation looms large for what, in another country, might be a slap on the wrist. Safety can also be an increased issue.

"Mum?" Kate asked, as we attempted to rinse seawater off Miss Meg after a dip in the Gulf of Guinea, West Africa, a two-man chore that necessitated swimwear due to her trembling dislike of water out of a tap.

"Yes?" I answered, trying to angle the hose under the dog's legs. "Don't let her go Kate, we'll never get her back here!"

"I've got her, quick rinse her tummy, it's still soapy," she said. "Stop shaking Meg, how come you'll swim for hours but won't let us rinse your coat? You're a silly dog," she cooed, rubbing the velvet ears and kissing her muzzle.

"Mum?" She started again.

"Yes Kate?"

"Sally and I've been asked to go to the *fiesta* tonight."

"The Christmas one? Down behind N'bili? Who with?"

"Yeah. A couple of the guys from Sally's dad's company. I met them the other night, they're okay. American. They'd look after us."

"Kate, you've driven past there, you know what it's like. Are you sure?"

"Yeah, it'd be different."

"It certainly would," I agreed, thinking of the rows and rows of lean-to bars cobbled together with bits of ply, music booming from tinny players threatening to shatter the temporary structures that appeared every Christmas, and pound them into the ochre dirt. "Okay, but you must have your cellphone in your pocket. Don't take a bag, and wear flatties!"

"Okay, thanks Mum."

"Kate, you live in London on your own where I have no idea what you are up to! I can hardly stop you here, but thank you for asking."

"Well it is a bit different here isn't it?" she asked, darting away from Miss Meg's joyous shake and tail wag at being released from her watery purgatory.

"Just remember not to drink anything that you don't see opened in front of you."

"I know Mum, I know."

"I know you know possum, it just makes me feel better knowing I've said it!"

"Will Dad be okay about it?"

"Yes of course. You will probably be the only two white girls there, so be ready for some staring."

"Yeah, I guess. There are a few of guys going, we'll be fine."

Both girls were delivered home in the early hours, driven from the *fiesta* by their desire to pee, but not in one of few long drops available.

They'd had fun, but what our daughter hadn't realised was that beer, not something she drank normally anyway, has greater amounts of formaldehyde in Africa than most other places. An ingredient that might preserve the ale but also induces a dreadful hangover. She suffered the next day.

Freedoms are restricted in other countries, either by law or logistics. In the United States where the legal age for alcohol consumption is 21, coming home for the holidays from Europe, university age young adults visiting their parents in suburban America find the restrictions, and lack of public transport, frustrating. Something also felt by American teens brought up in Europe, who have grown up with the relative freedom of the gradual easing into a life less controlled by a parent, insofar as getting from A to B. Public transport has slowly become part of their life until they travel confidently around their adopted city, as well of course as negotiating airports.

Take –Away Slice: I don't believe TCKs are rootless or homeless individuals with no sense of 'home'. "They just," as Norma McCaig who coined the phrase 'global nomad' put it, "spread their roots horizontally rather than vertically." Instead they turn out to be well-adjusted and adaptable young men and women with a sense of adventure, a sense of belonging wherever they happen to find themselves and a remarkable empathy for all peoples. They will also know their way around airports.

Fourth Slice:
Customs, Culture and Calypso

"What is it?" we asked, rushing out on deck from the nursery, a large room that always smelt of soggy nappies, cabbage and eggs, and where each morning we children were ignominiously deposited.

"The gully-gully man," said the uniformed nanny.

"Who is he?"

"He makes snakes dance. An' he does tricks," said an old Suez hand of about eight, as we peered through the railings at the man in a dress clambering up the side of the ship.

Mum and I were aboard the P&O steamship, the *S.S. Chitral*, sailing to join my father in Malaysia. We were nearing Bahrain, after gliding through the Suez Canal where I almost believed if I stretched my arms out really, really far I could touch the sand on both the banks.

"That's called a bum-boat," said another boy, pointing to the tender as it bumped alongside.

"You can't say that. That's rude," a little girl in a gingham dress protested.

We watched the man work two baskets with lids, like our laundry baskets in Aba, on to the deck. African faces meant home to me and I found the gully-gully man's sallow skin strangely intimidating. His face was stubbled and jowly, and his uneven teeth yellow, made more so by a thin black moustache. Or maybe it was his long, dirty toenails curling over the ends of dusty sandals, showing from under the hem of his not-quite-white *dish dash* as he clambered aboard after his baskets.

"What's he going to do?" I asked the know-it-all.

"Wait 'n' see," he told me.

Sitting cross-legged in a circle we watched as the gully-gully man settled himself behind the baskets. I liked his fez with a tassel he flipped from across his eyes each time he lifted the reed pipe to his mouth. But it was his obvious power that truly terrified me. The cobra writhed up and out as the music pierced the woven cane of the basket, and with eyes hooded, hovered, and then struck with head flattened and tongue darting at the rows of mesmerized children.

We screamed, but didn't move. Smaller snakes were brought out of the other basket for those interested in holding them. I wasn't, and I longed for the familiarity of Ali and Sam.

One of the most wonderful benefits of growing up a TCK, or raising children in different lands, is the opportunity to view, and sometimes be a part of, local festivals. The event, whatever it is, provides lessons in geography, history, social commentary, religion, politics and plain old human nature all rolled up into one colourful, more often than not noisy, display of local customs and traditions.

"Sweetie, there will be lots of men with hooks and spikes stuck into their skin," Dad warned me, as we made our way to Batu Caves on the outskirts of KL.

"Why?" I asked. Nudity was not a surprise, it did not shock me. But watching Thiapusam in Malaysia did.

"Because they are Hindus and it is a very special day for them. They show their devotion to Lord Murugan by putting skewers in themselves. But they mustn't show pain."

"Why doesn't it hurt?" I asked, from the back seat of our Humber, windows wound down to catch any breeze.

"They put themselves into a trance and that makes them feel less pain," he explained.

It didn't seem a very satisfactory explanation then, and it still doesn't. Some of the hooks dug into the men's backs had bags bulging with coconut milk, reminding me of bursting udders. I couldn't understand why there was no blood.

"What's that?" I asked, pointing to a wooden structure decorated with feathers and flowers, slung across a man's shoulders.

"It's called a *kavadi*," my ever-knowledgeable father said, as we watched the devotees reach the base of stairs and toss a cube of paraffin into the burning fires before staggering up 272 steps to the caves, dodging the monkeys all the way.

It was both repulsive and mesmerising to a seven-year old. I learnt not all monkeys were like Munnings, the one I had grown up with in Nigeria, when one pulled my plait hard enough to make me cry.

It still surprises me that children can be so accepting of strange, sometimes painful sights. Though one incident stayed with me many years because it was, I think, the first time I realised my father could not fix everything, and I was disappointed.

We were driving to the Cameron Highlands, about 200 kilometres north of KL in Pahang, for a week away from the humidity. Our car was the only one on a long straight stretch as we crossed the plains to the base of the highlands, there was jungle on one side and on the other a ditch, and then a wide verge before the regimented lines of a rubber plantation stood silent sentinel.

The windows were of course down, it being before the days of air-conditioning in cars. My parents were probably smoking and I was sitting in the middle of the back seat leaning forward to talk, seat belts not yet having been invented.

"What's that noise?" I asked, sticking my head out of the window straining to see around the only bend in the road.

"I don't know, sweetie," Mum said, and she tried to interest me in a travel lolly, something reserved for long boring car trips.

"There!" I said, pointing ahead. "Why's that man hitting that woman?" I shouted, terrified at the sight of a woman cowering on the grass, being held by her long black plait with one hand while the other hammered punches, but knowing my father would slow the car and deal with the situation.

"I don't know Apple," Mum said, having given up on the lolly bribe.

"Daddy you have to stop him," I said, surprised the car was not slowing.

"Apple," he said as we whizzed past, "They are Tamils, and different races have different ways of doing things."

"But you said a man must never hit a women. You have to stop him," I said in tears, as the wailing followed us along the road, once again straight.

"We can't interfere in other people's customs," he said, gripping the steering wheel tightly even though there were no corners coming up. I sobbed in the back seat until I was distracted by a bullock cart plodding along carrying a covey of brightly saried women to a wedding. But the violent image stayed with me.

Years later I thought of that incident when I attended an FIGT Houston Affiliate meeting.

"Here is the cultural iceberg," intoned the presenter, as she put a large laminated photo of an iceberg on an easel. "You see how much greater an area there is below the waterline," she continued, handing out stick-it notes with words such as religion, facial expression, favourite authors, gender, etiquette and so on, printed on them. "I want you to put the words where you think they fit on the iceberg."

After the usual glances attendees give to each other when presented with a task, people slowly rose and stuck their notes on the enlarged photo. It is an exercise used often in cultural adaptation lectures, but it is always interesting to see understanding dawn with the realisation so many cultural differences are well below the surface.

I have always loved the beat of drums, swaying bodies and stamping feet. Maybe that's why the Mount Hagen Show in Papua New Guinea fascinated me. Born out of the Australian Government's attempt to sponsor harmony between the feuding tribes, ever ready to throw spears across the valleys at each other, it had, since it's inception in 1964, grown to be a well-organised event by 1977. Still not known internationally, it drew local expats as well as many tribes.

John, three other VSOs and I had planned a weekend away from work to go to the show. We were young and thought nothing of driving ten hours up to the Highlands on Friday and back on Monday.

The showground was a melange of colour, sounds and clumps of men and women, all milling in their tribes. Men from

Tari, deeper in the Western Highlands, wore their distinctive headgear of hair and moss and decorated with red plumes from the Bird of Paradise. With beads and bone encircling their necks, above yellow painted faces with a red line down the nose, sometimes enhanced by a piece of wire poked through the septum, they were startling figures to bump into in the crowds.

The men from Chimbu were not so flamboyant, relying more on their reputation, stocky stature and gleaming dark skin to instil terror. Short, plain arse-grasses hung from their waists. The white feathers entwined through vines in their hair contrasted strangely with the bows, arrows and clubs they carried.

From Asaro in the Eastern Highlands came the Mudmen. They wore very little. Short skirts made from grass barely covering their modesty hung from twine around their hips, along with clay shapes professing to their prowess. But their full head masks were truly awesome. Made of mud and clay in grotesque shapes, huge in comparison to their head size, they wrought fear in the bravest of hearts. Legend had it their village had been defeated by another tribe, and they had been forced to dive into the Asaro River where they hid until dusk. Their enemy saw them emerge, covered in river mud, and thought they were spirits and so fled, never to return.

The day was spent surrounded by feathers, clay, drums and hot gyrating flesh. Groups of women ready to showcase their tribal dances, some modestly covered by the ugly *meri* smocks insisted on by the early missionaries, others bare breasted, swayed their grass-encased hips to the rhythms beating everywhere.

I envied their nakedness, cool and unencumbered by bras and tee-shirts, the freedom of spirit and lack of body consciousness refreshing to see after the more assertive nationals from the coastal regions.

"What the hell?" Richard, the man who had introduced me to John a few months earlier, and also a VSO, said as we viewed our accommodation at the end of the long, hot and noisy day.

"Oh no," I said, looking at the uneven and puddled concrete floor, the rows of rickety shelves and the single bulb swaying in the chill breeze that whispered through the cracks in the walls.

"I'll bet your dad didn't know it was this unfinished when he said we could use it," John said, coming up behind me. My father had offered us camping rights in a rice warehouse his company was building on the outskirts of Mount Hagen.

"I think not. What shall we do?" I asked the five faces looking at me accusingly.

"We could try the hotel or rest house."

"Not a hope, they've been booked for months and anyway we can't afford them," said Malcolm, our host in Mendi the night before, a couple of hours further into the highlands. "We could kip in the trucks."

"It'll be fine," John said. "We can put our sleeping bags on the shelves. At least we can stretch out."

It was a long night, spent intermittently dozing on wobbly shelves or playing cards balanced on a piece of timber across our knees, sipping on beer when hot cocoa would have been preferable.

Morning did not come soon enough. We decamped to the Mount Hagen Hotel where we took turns sneaking into the bathrooms for morning ablutions and relief, and then filched coffee from the urns left out for the paying guests.

One night of discomfort seemed little to pay for the spectacle we'd watched.

Living in Thailand eight years later brought all sorts of new festivities into our lives, and one of the gentlest and prettiest is the festival of *Loi Krathong*, held at the full moon of the twelfth lunar month in the Thai calendar, which falls sometime in mid-November. The waters are high from the end of the monsoon season so the crops cannot be harvested, what better way to pass the time than to give thanks for blessings received?

"Wat doze?" Kate asked, pointing to piles of polystyrene discs leaning awkwardly amongst the buckets of orchids at our usual flower vendor's stall.

"Dey for to make *loi krathong,* Cake," said the owner.

"Wat dat?" my inquisitive daughter asked.

"Come, I show. Madam you shop, come back later," I was instructed.

I nipped into *Villa* next door for some staples, and by the time I got back outside Kate and our florist had the materials needed for us to make our own *loi krathongs*.

Sometimes I am too reticent about getting involved in local customs, not wanting to intrude on a custom that is not mine to share. In the true Thai spirit of generosity and in the politest way possible I was told "Do not to be a fool, *kha*". (*Kha*, or *krap* being the male equivalent, is one of those particularly useful words that some languages have which don't really mean anything but make a sentence sound less abrupt.)

A young Thai girl's education is not considered complete until she has mastered the painstakingly fiddly task of creating the most beautiful floating raft imaginable, but I had no idea how I was going to manage.

The intricate rafts, some in shapes of a lotus in full bloom, a swan, Mount Meru from Buddhist mythology, or *chedis* are tightly woven from banana leaves. Decorated with any combination of blossoms, candles, coins, betel nuts and joss sticks, and occasionally tufts of hair or nail clippings of the human variety in a symbolic gesture of releasing one's character flaws, the *loi krathongs* are set adrift from the banks of the *klongs* and rivers, the seashore or any waterway, with candles flickering.

Like many ancient festivals around the world, this too has varied origins but essentially any ill fortune floats away on the rafts and the river goddess, Mae Phra Khongha, is appeased.

"Ah Madam, good," said Es, the woman who kept the house clean and kept me on track about Thai protocol, as we unloaded the car. "I wan say you buy dees tings. I learn you make *loi krathong*."

All the necessary paraphernalia for the lesson was laid out on the patio floor in strict order of need; polystyrene disc, banana leaves, orchids, coins and candles.

"You see, like dis," Es said, weaving shredded leaves around the disc. "My mummy use bled, velly hard, not like dis," she said stabbing the polystyrene. "Dis more easy."

It might have been easier for Es but not being a crafty kind of person, I found the whole exercise a trying endeavour that ended up lacerating my unskilled fingers and producing a less than perfect example of a lotus blossom. Kate soon tired of the enterprise and much preferred toddling around wearing flowers in her hair.

"It not so good Madam," Es said. "But first time eh," she encouraged me.

As the sun went down and the *soi* lights flickered on, casting soft shadows around the garden, we held our own little *loi krathong* ceremony at the pond.

Even Kate's excited chatter stilled as Es knelt beside the water and made a *wai* to her beautifully woven and decorated *loi krathong*. Her prayers said, she gently slid the raft into the pond and we watched, mesmerized, as it floated around pushed by the flow from the pump trying manfully to aerate the water.

Mine was next. It sank ignominiously to the depths, albeit shallow ones, startling the fish into a frenzy of activity. Kate, resisting all attempts at being held, knelt beside Es, ready to float her lovely *loi krathong*, courtesy of Es's handiwork.

"See Mummy," she said, pointing to the precious things she'd put in the raft, "My dolly in for to be lucky." She *wai*ed, as Es had taught her and since she had just learned her nighttime prayer 'gentle Jesus, meek and mild', she insisted we recite it together. It was one of those quiet moments when all the world seems to be in harmony.

"*Mai pen lai,* Mummy" Kate said as her *loi krathong* sploshed in, sending droplets of water over her nightie. And she was right, it didn't matter.

Misunderstandings do arise though, no matter how well versed we feel we are in cultural differences. I was dozing in a hospital room in Bangkok after the birth of our son Edward, watching the panel above my bed lift with the delayed breeze as it rippled across the ceiling tiles each time the door opened.

"*Sawahdeekha* Madam," greeted a diminutive nurse, as she bustled in with some purple vanda orchids delivered by a friend.

"*Sawahdeekha*," I replied. "*Kobkhunkha,*" I thanked as she handed me a glass of water.

"*Mai pen lai.* Aah Madam, so sollee for boy," she went on.

"What?" I said, jolted to a painful sitting position. "What's wrong? My baby?"

"Oh no, no, Madam, baby he fine," she said, seeing my tears flowing. "But boy born in tiger year vely stlong, vely difficult, better wait for labbit," she explained patting me on my shoulder.

I fell back on the pillows, not quite able to laugh at the misunderstanding just yet.

Moving very young children around the world is, apart from worrying about medical facilities, easier than when they start making real friends and also understanding where they are. We have always been an ardent board game and puzzler family, and we've managed to find games and puzzles that helped place the kids in their new environment. *Explore Europe* was a game that not only taught the geography of Europe but also about using public transport, buying tickets, making connections, transferring from ferry to train to plane and so on, and it was fun.

When we left Asia we had thought we were heading to England, but a few weeks into our supposed repatriation, not far from where John grew up, we were transferred to Scotland. It may only have been eight hours up the road, but culturally it was very different. We knew how to do the eight-some reel from hours spent at the St Andrew's Ball in Bangkok, but couldn't understand the milkman. Kate and Edward for the first time faced an ingrained antipathy to the English in their school playground, even at the ages of five and eight, and there were some uncomfortable moments. It opened my eyes to the ridiculousness of holding old hatreds that we, as parents, pass on to our children.

Moving to Europe from Asia also brought some of our own quirks to the fore. Grocery shopping was a family activity with the kids being sent on errands to find various products from the shelves.

"Okay guys, we need rice please," I said, checking the list at the entrance to ASDA on the Bridge of Dee in Aberdeen. They scuttled off and I did my usual race around to gather as much as I could before they found me again. My trolley was filling nicely when I realised they had been gone quite a while. I started searching the aisles knowing they would be together, that being one of the hard and fast rules of the game.

As panic was edging through reason I spotted them.

"What are you doing?" I asked, rather louder than I meant to, as I rushed along to where they were sitting in the aisle surrounded by bags of rice, with curious shoppers giving them a wide berth.

"Looking for weevils Mummy," Edward explained loudly, shaking another bag and poking the plastic in an attempt to dislodge any critters.

"Oh God, get up both of you," I laughed. "I don't think they let weevils into Scotland," I explained.

"How come?" Asked Kate.

"Well I guess they clean the rice better when they know it's coming to Europe," I said. "Come on, help me put these back on the shelf."

"So we won't have to let them float to the top of the water?" Kate continued.

"No, I don't think so," I said. "But we'll double check before we cook it shall we?"

Seven years later the United States was new to us all, apart from John who had been travelling there regularly since our time in Trinidad fourteen years earlier. A puzzle showing the states, their flowers and animals, was a great help to us all in those early days, and trying to stay one step ahead of the kids in American history was a challenge, but a great deal more fun than trying to do the same in Maths or any of the sciences.

One of my greatest concerns about relocating to America was the perceived notion that there was a gun in every house. I really did worry about it.

"If you are ever in a friend's house and a gun is brought out, you get to a phone and you call me immediately, then you get out of the house. Okay?" I drummed into the kids as we moved into suburbia.

I wasn't correct in my perception, but there are a lot around.

"Hello?" I answered, the phone beside the bed, noting it was two in the morning.

"Apple, it's me."

"What's up, Liz?" I asked. John was already throwing on clothes, knowing the teenager across the street, home alone for the first time as both parents were on business trips, would only call if worried.

"There's a strange noise coming from the garden."

"Okay, don't worry. John's on his way over now," I said, watching him cross the road as I spoke, holding back an indignant Meg from accompanying him. I heard their dog barking as John checked around the bushes outside and let himself into the back garden.

The phone rang again.

"Apple, I can see a man in the garden," Liz cried. "I've got Dad's gun out."

"Liz, it's John. Put the gun down now. He's walking to the front door, okay? Can you see his shape through the glass? Have you put the gun down? Put it down now," I said.

I saw her open the door, sobbing with fright. I was almost sobbing too. After checking under every bed, every room, every cupboard and the garage John tried to persuade Liz and her friend to come over to us for the rest of the night. They declined. The incident made me even more aware of how accidents with guns do happen.

Some customs are difficult to adjust to, not just guns, initiation rites or how we treat our fellow man, sometimes it's a series of events. "I don't think I can do that before the holidays" or "It'll be easier after the holidays" were phrases that confused me our first holiday season in the United States. We hadn't realised it essentially lasted from the end of October through to New Year's Day and I struggled to sustain eight weeks of 'goodwill to all men'.

"Oh that's sick," Edward exclaimed from the back of car.

"What is?" Kate asked, ready to be contrary.

"In that garden. Look. Those graves have got their kids names on them."

"Gross!" She agreed, busy studying the headstones with 'RIP Travis' or 'RIP Crystal' etched into the grey polystyrene.

I allowed myself to be coerced into buying spooky lights, which we tastefully draped over the hawthorn bushes in our front garden for the start of Halloween. Witches, hobgoblins, ghosts and ghouls abounded, along with recordings of scary music connected to motion sensors designed to make me levitate each time I set one off. A black cat with glitzy silver streaks and creepy green luminescent eyes that, Mona Lisa-like, followed me whenever I happened to walk past, took up residence under the pine tree.

"You and Kate could take turns standing out in the garden too," John observed on seeing the latest addition, a life-size witch with her ubiquitous broom, and recently having had to intervene in an argument. Having two pre-menstrual women in the house was obviously getting to him. For once my teenage daughter and I were in accord and his comment was treated with disdain from Kate, and a rueful smile from me.

The 'trick' though mainly 'treating' was over and the kids went through all shades of green from an over indulgence of all things sweet. The shops were magically bare of everything purple or black and in a final swish of a witch's wand they were full of rusts and oranges and goods autumnal.

Thanksgiving was on the doorstep. Jack o' lanterns, scarecrows, pumpkins, hay bales and corn took over from tombstones and hobgoblins. My hibiscus bushes conveniently came into bloom again, their ostentatious marmalade-coloured blossoms complementing the cheerfully dressed scarecrow – my only concession to Thanksgiving.

"I'm not cooking a Thanksgiving lunch," I informed the family, feeling not the slightest obligation to feed my family turkey and pecan pie. "You can wait for Christmas!"

"Awh Mum," moaned Edward.

"I feed you most of the three hundred and sixty-five days of the year," I said, my argument irrefutable. "I'm having a day off!"

Some new American friends very generously invited us to share in their Thanksgiving and we had a lovely introduction to the tradition. Our contributions were of a horticultural nature, of the eye pleasing and palate cleansing variety. I didn't quite yet understand the need to watch 'the game'.

"Oh my God, you are not going to believe this." I spluttered to John, as I returned from walking Miss Meg the next morning in a feeble attempt to shift half a pound of turkey and fixin's from my hips.

"What?" he said, enjoying a quiet cup of coffee and not very keen to get into a conversation.

"Santa's in the garden next door."

"You're kidding?"

"No I'm not!"

"Bloody hell," he said, sneaking a peek from behind the dining room curtains.

Later in the day I was accosted by one of the doyennes of our *cul de sac*. She patiently explained the need to present a united image for 'the best decorated street' in our subdivision. It would be our combined attempt to wrest the Christmas Cup, which I had always thought a punch of the alcoholic kind, from the tight-fisted grasp of the street two rows down, who had held it for a record-breaking three years.

"Um, have we got any plywood in the garage?" I timed my request to John carefully.

"No *we* don't, but I might have. Why?" he answered warily.

"Well, the street has decided to have a theme this year."

"Oh really? I wasn't aware the street had a voice." Often facetious in moments of suspicion, I ignored him and ploughed on with my carefully worked out justification.

"It's a gingerbread theme. I think it'd be good to join in." And then the clincher, "It's the kids' first Christmas here. It would be nice for them to feel a part of everything that's happening." A low blow I knew, but guaranteed to work.

"Has the street specified exactly what it wants?" John asked.

"Not exactly. Just gingerbready. I thought we could just make a façade for the house and then shapes for the people."

"People?" he queried, "And just who is we?"

"Well I'll help. And the kids can paint them all."

On cue, they exploded in.

"Hey, Dad, you should see the cool house Brett's making for their front yard. It's like the one in *Hansel and Gretel*. Can we make one too?" they said in unison.

"Has it been iced?" their father asked.

"Don't be silly," Kate said. She was learning 'haughty' very quickly. "If you do the shapes, we'll paint."

The matter was settled as far as I was concerned. I was fairly sure by day's end there would at least be a gingerbread house, if not the occupants. I was right. Providing John with tea and sustenance as he sawed and sanded the day away, I thought of the many projects he had taken on for, and with, the kids. Like the time he helped them make a sort of trishaw out of a cable drum they'd found on our back lane in Aberdeen. That cart fixed to the back of a bike provided entertainment, and a few scratched knees, for the entire summer holiday.

As dusk approached the vast majority of gardens in our little pocket of Texan utopia were twinkling with fairy lights, and icicles adorning every hanging branch and eave. Sleighs and reindeer were artistically arranged in one corner. Nativity scenes in another, and on our street, gingerbread houses.

Goodwill was felt by one and all when we were the proud recipients of the Christmas Cup.

The day arrived. Santa, luckily, had received one of our change-of-address cards and found us. Another turkey was consumed, this time cooked by me, but with not quite so many trimmings as the November one.

"Good grief," John said, as we set off for a walk on St Stephen's Day. "All the Christmas trees have been tossed out already."

"Let's not take our lights down 'til after New Year," Kate said, eyeing fathers busily untangling fairy lights that had garlanded the boughs since the day after Thanksgiving. "I don't mind taking the gingerbread stuff down now though."

'Boxing Day' seemed to be just that. The day when all the angels, the baubles and bells, the yearly offering from the kid's art class and the holly and the ivy were boxed up until the day after Thanksgiving the following year. It was also the day the shops were inundated with reboxed presents, rejects from the recipients for one reason or another.

"Well I'm not taking the tree down until Epiphany," I announced. "Is it the 5th or 6th?" I asked John, as I do every year.

"The 6th," he replied, "The same as last year."

Yo-Yo Ma, the famed cellist, was born to Chinese parents in France and moved to the United States when he was four. In his essay in National Public Radio's *All Things Considered*, he spoke of his struggle to fit into one of three cultures until realising he had the privilege of taking pieces from all three; the cultural depth of China, the artistic traditions of France and the commitment to opportunity of America.

I think that is how most global nomads live their lives. Taking a little bit from everywhere they've touched down. For me, being invited to share, and sometimes participate in, another culture's special moments has been one of the highlights of an expatriate life, which is probably why I am at a complete loss to answer an oft asked question, "Which is your favourite country?"

I don't have a favourite country or culture. Just like I don't have a favourite style of music or a favourite cuisine, there are elements I like from many, though drums do get my feet going and calypso, the precursor to reggae and ska, gets my hips gyrating though not quite as smoothly as when I was younger.

Long before I lived in Trinidad, I loved the rhythm and simplicity of the lyrics in calypso, I grew up listening to Dad's records of Harry Belafonte and that most unusual calypso duo, the Danish couple Nina and Frederick.

"But Daddy, why is he leaving his little girl in Kingston Town?" I would ask tearfully.

"He doesn't mean his daughter, sweetie," Dad would explain again and again, "He means his girlfriend."

"But why is he leaving her?"

"Because he has to go to work somewhere else."

"You won't will you, Daddy?"

"Of course not, sweetie-pie," he'd reply, and jump the needle over to *The Banana Boat Song*, and we'd sing "Day-o, day-o, day light come and me wan' go home", and all would be well again until the next time we played calypso.

Take-Away Slice: I think one of the hardest things to do as a guest in someone's country is accept that some things will repulse you, whether it is a food or a custom. The food is easy, swallow quickly or spit it out, though surreptitiously of course. The custom, particularly if it involves long-term pain and real suffering, is much harder. Female circumcision, acid throwing, stoning, mutilation and so on, are not easy things to watch or understand.

But don't we, as visitors, have to realise that we cannot, and should not, burst in with our ways? Change has to evolve gradually and will, I'm sure, be most effective if it comes from within. As expatriates we can use our knowledge, and possibly wider world vision, to act as educators and if possible, enablers, whilst accepting that we are short-term residents and will in all likelihood not have to deal with any fall out.

Fifth Slice: Service with a Smile

"*Mem,*" Ah Boon said, as he frog marched me to where Mum was sitting on the veranda overlooking the sloping lawns, wonderful for tray races, of our terraced garden in Singapore. "Apuh she kill my bird."

"What?" Mum said, lowering the paper and stubbing out her cigarette.

"Mummy, I didn't," I said, my cowboy hat shaking in consternation. "It's not real," I shouted at Ah Boon, waving my plastic pistol at him.

"*Mem,* she shoot bird. He dead."

"Apple, don't shout! Ah Boon," she placated, "It is a toy gun. It did not kill your turkey. I will replace it."

He slid back to the kitchen eyeing me with great disfavour. And then Mum took me to task.

"What happened?"

"Me and Kenneth were the goodies 'coz we've got cowboy hats. The others were the baddies. We found them feathers an' we chased them to the back and it was lying down."

"The turkey?" Mum clarified.

"Yeah."

"Yes," she corrected. "Then what?"

"We left it 'coz we was chasing the Indians. And then Ah Boon yelled and sended everyone home. And we didn't killed it."

"All right. I'll sort it out. But, and I mean this Apple, none of you are to play behind the servants' quarters. That is their home and off limits to you all."

"But what if the baddies run there?"

"You make sure they don't, otherwise you won't be allowed to play anywhere on that side of the house."

"Okay," I grumbled. "But we didn't killed it."

"You didn't 'kill' it Apple, not 'killed'. No I know you didn't, but it might have died from the shock of seeing a gang of Cowboys and Indians racing around."

"It was lied down already," I repeated.

A peripatetic lifestyle comes, in some locations, with a very obvious bonus, household help. Servants. Staff, if you want to sound very grand.

Until I lived in London, in a house subdivided into a warren of bed-sits with shared bathrooms, I had never had to clean a loo. Three of us shared the first floor facilities. Frau Schmidt, of advanced years, strange habits and elevated sensitivities and, across the hall, an elderly Englishman with lascivious tendencies and foul breath, and I dodged each on our dash every morning.

It was rather a shock. And still one of my least favoured domestic tasks. I am not a domestic goddess, or actually a goddess of any kind. I do what I have to in order to keep a reasonably clean home, but there are far, far too many other things in life greatly more rewarding. Because of that I have the greatest respect for anyone who does domestic work.

It sounds perhaps patronising and arrogant if we say those who worked for us over the years cared about us, but as a child that's certainly how I felt. I know for my part it was returned. But who really knows how people feel about us? My parents had a thorough regard for everyone who worked for us and we were inordinately lucky.

In Nigeria Ali and Sam looked after us. Ali's family lived on the Biafran border and even though there was room for them, he did not want them with us. Instead he sent funds back and visited them when he could. Sam was from Kano and not married. Ali and Sam were my stalwarts, and they were what I cried about most whenever we left the country to go on leave. I don't think I understood we would never be going back when we left for the last time, which was probably a good thing.

The only servant I can ever remember not liking was Ah Boon. Mum inherited him when we moved into our house in Singapore. He was an older Chinese *amah* who had very little patience for swarms of children playing in the garden and running through the house.

My relationship with Ah Boon never improved, but we moved back to KL shortly after the turkey incident so I don't think I was greatly injured by his lack of *esprit de corps.*

My ally in arms against him was Samsuri, Dad's driver. Samsuri was Malay, and even as a child I felt him to be a gentle soul. He collected me from school most days and regaled me with stories from his *kampong* and about his children. Ah Boon did not like Samsuri smoking on the back porch near where the washing was hung, which was a bit rich considering he used to smoke while he ironed. Samsuri and I were often banished to the garage.

We all had servants, and drivers and gardeners – how we treated them was very dependent on how our parents treated them. Even at a young age we knew who was 'old' expat and who was not, the relationship between servant and *tuan* or *mem* told many stories. I learnt my lesson early.

"Inside, now!" Mum said, hauling me into the sitting room, not long after we returned to KL from Singapore and just after Ah Moi came to work for us. "Just who do you think you are?"

"What?" I asked, rubbing my arm but knowing Mum had heard me cheeking Ah Moi. I had been snipping out a paper doll from the last page of a comic when she'd asked me to move so she could sweep. I had refused with the toss of my plait and a smart-aleck comment.

"You will go and apologise, and if I ever hear you speaking to Ah Moi like that again you won't be sitting for a week. You will also sweep up the mess you have made."

"Now?" I asked, for once having nothing to say, but at eight knowing the enormity of my rudeness.

"Yes, now! Ah Moi is not here to clean up after you, and certainly does not deserve being spoken to like that. I am ashamed of you."

I never forgot the lesson, or Ah Moi's graciousness at my red-faced apology. It was also a lesson instilled in our children very early in their little lives, so much so that if one of their friends cheeked their own *amah*, or worse in Kate and Edward's eyes, ours, the kids were appalled and were quick to tell me. It made me think rather less of the parents.

Ah Moi, Ah Yong and Ebi were a large part of my world for the next eight years. So too was Ah Moi's daughter, Mak Peck Yoke. We were the same age and moved freely between homes, both for play purposes and eating. Our homes were separated by a long covered path leading to the servants quarters, on which we spent most afternoons undertaking the rather revolting job of deticking the dogs.

"Ugh, fat one," Peck Yoke said, dropping a blood-filled grey tick from between Charlie's paws into the jar of salted water beside her. He was the least amenable to the procedure, objecting to being wedged between our legs as we examined under his arms, in his soft floppy ears and in between his paws.

The other three were more willing. It was really my only chore, along with cleaning the fish tank, though I knew Peck Yoke had many more. She had lots more homework than I did and was already trilingual in Cantonese, Malay and English. She married a Swede so is now fluent in that language too.

We cycled the *lorongs* around our house with complete freedom, our boundary being the main road, *Jalan Pekeleling.* It seemed a large area to roam made more so by the huge gardens of many of the houses. We had five acres, the bottom part being a mangosteen grove that was dank, dark and eerie and only entered when we were sent to pick fruit.

A huge concrete monsoon drain ran along the edge of *Lorong Kuda,* so called because it backed onto the racecourse, *kuda* meaning horse. We knew exactly which section held the most neon-striped guppies that could be caught and transferred to the tank in the hallway.

"Let's go under the bridge," I suggested one afternoon.

"We're not allowed," she said.

"Not on the road, but no one said we couldn't go under it." Peck Yoke was easily persuaded. We dumped the bikes, took off our flip-flops and armed with fishing nets and jars sloshed through the man-sized culvert and into the undergrowth that tangled overhead on the other side. Forbidden delights, and so much more fun than the cleared area on our side of the road.

"Hello chilren," came a voice from further along the drain. "I play wid you," continued the voice, growing nearer. We saw, as he emerged through the bamboo and vines, that it belonged to an Indian, as old as our fathers. He sat, skinny legs dangling over the edge of the drain and watched, throwing a comment every now and then. We ignored him.

"I show you to catch fish," he said eventually, and slid down into the drain and leaning over, put his arms around me and grasped my hands, holding the fishing net.

"Let's go home," Peck Yoke said, as I squirmed. Something did not feel right and with a twist and a shove I ran, following her splattering back to our side of the road and safety. We clambered up to the verge, threw ourselves onto our bikes and raced home.

We never talked about it and we never crossed under the boundary again, though I remember having to admit to carelessness because of the lost fishing nets. As children often do, we sensed something wrong but couldn't quite put our fingers on it so therefore blocked it out. It was only recently, when Peck Yoke and I reconnected on Facebook after a ten-year gap that she brought the incident up. I suppose it was only then I realised how lucky we were not to have been hurt.

When, as a young wife and mother, we moved to Bangkok it seemed perfectly natural to have a house girl. Es came into our lives very easily. She showed up at the gate along with the moving truck and offered her services. I liked her. Her references seemed good, but how many of us have written a glowing reference while leaving out something as well? She started the next day and stayed with us a year.

Pregnant and dozing one afternoon in front of Kate's favourite video, *The Jungle Book*, I came to and realised she had wandered away. Her screaming mingled with wailing levitated me off the sofa and out the door to find her running back to the house from Es's quarters.

"Mummy, Mummy," she sobbed, eyes wide and wet, "Dan hit Es."

I scooped her up, took her inside and calmed her down. We rewound *The Jungle Book* to her favourite part where Ballou sings *Bare Necessities*.

"Where you going?" she asked, as I gave her an ice lolly.

"To see Es. I'll be back in a couple of minutes. You stay here and watch Ballou. Okay?"

"'kay," she hiccupped.

I stormed out and for once did not knock on Es's door. Dan, a part-time actor and a part-time gardener for us, was standing over her. Her eye was already swollen shut.

"Get out," I shouted, shaking all over.

He moved toward me, and before I could move my bulk aside brushed past me shouting in Thai.

"Out, now," I said again, as he hesitated, "Or I call the police." His English was not good and my Thai did not have the words to lash at him, but he understood 'police'. Screaming at Es and me he left. I followed him to the gate, at a distance, and locked it.

Kate had heard me shouting and had come back out and was sitting on Es's lap.

"Don' cry Es, don' cry Es," she kept saying, stroking her swelling cheek.

With tears streaming I went and got ice and a flannel and helped Es wash her poor bruised face. She would not let me take her to the hospital even though I was worried her arm was broken.

"No, madam, I okay, I sorree."

"Oh Es, you don't have to be sorry," I said, as the three of us sat on her bed crying.

I was furious with myself. I had suspected she was being hit because of bruises she insisted she got from bumping into things, and I had, to my shame, never pursued it.

"He cannot come back here. Ever." I said. "I don't want you to be hurt, and I don't want Kate to see anything like that again."

"He my husban'," Es said.

"That does not make it okay for him to hurt you."

"Where I go?"

"You stay here with us. We can help you." All seemed to calm down and then she came in one Sunday evening.

"Madam, my husban' need me. I go now."

And she left that night. I wrote her a reference, a glowing one, which was deserved, but I also wrote that her husband should not be allowed on the premises.

After Es came Nit. She was a nice woman, older and would, I thought, be adept at handling an impish toddler when I was busy with a late pregnancy, and new baby.

"I do, I do," I heard through the whirr of air conditioning one afternoon as I took my enforced bed rest, followed by peals of laughter. Something about it sounded forbidden and I lumbered up and out onto the terrace overlooking the garden.

Nit was sitting on the edge of the pond with Kate floating naked in the water with *koi* darting around her splashing legs. Her hair streamed out behind her as she gleefully dunked her head under to watch the fish.

"Kate, out now!" I bellowed down.

Both Nit and Kate looked up, guilty at being caught. A couple of days later Kate was at the hospital with amoebic dysentery and Nit was out of a job. It was the only time I had to let someone go and it was horrid, but I could not have a two and a half year old dictating what she could and could not do.

Dao was next, but was with us just a short time as three weeks after Edward was born we were on the move again, this time to Singapore, where once we found housing, Julie, a Filipina, moved in. She was a pleasant competent young woman, but I did not have the same rapport with her as I have had with all the others.

Kay tells the story of Margie, her Filipina *amah* in Singapore who was trying to join her husband in a Middle Eastern country. After months of waiting for a visa and then finally being promised one, the day before her flight Margie went to the Embassy to get the stamp.

"You must come back at eight tonight," she was told by an immigration official.

In tears Margie related the story to Kay who, horrified at the implication of sex for a visa, 'phoned her husband, Kevin. He rang the number Margie had been told to call when she neared the Embassy at the designated hour, a direct line to the official.

"Hello, I am Margie's employer," he said in his gruff voice, "I wanted to confirm your appointment with her before I cancel my meeting with the Minister this evening, because I will naturally be driving her at that hour."

"Oh no, sir, there has been some mistake. If she comes to the Embassy now her passport will be stamped."

"Wonderful," said Kay's husband, "I'm so pleased I won't have to cancel my meeting," and hung up.

We were transferred back to Thailand two weeks before Edward's first birthday and that happy relocation brought Bo into our lives, where she stayed for three years. She has stayed in our hearts a lot longer.

Sundays were her days off and she rarely came home until late. We had been out and as we drove up I saw her door was open and reminded the children it was her day off and they were not to disturb her. I was a little surprised she did not call out when we came in but thought nothing more about it.

Going upstairs I heard a keening and ran on up to the third floor where I found Bo and a young girl huddled behind our bathroom door.

"Oh my God, Bo, what's the matter?" I said, dropping to my knees in front of them.

"Bad man at gate," she sobbed.

"Who is this?" I asked, patting the girl on her shoulder.

"My nee. He her daddy."

"Who?"

"Bad man at gate."

"There's no one at the gate Bo. We just came home. Come downstairs, let me make you tea." She loved Earl Grey.

"No, madam."

"Okay." I sat on the bathroom floor with them. "Tell me what happened."

"My sissa daughter, she name Kat, she run. She come here, fin' me."

"Ran away from who? Her father?"

"No, bad place."

"What place?"

"Bad place mens go."

"How did she get there?" I asked looking at the girl, very beautiful but only about twelve it seemed.

"Her daddy take her. Get *baht.*"

"Oh shit," I said, sickened to think of a father selling his daughter. I persuaded them to come downstairs and suggested they stay in the spare bedroom until we could get things sorted out.

"No madam, she stay me," Bo said.

"Bo, you stay with her in the room."

"No madam, she sleep me."

It was the start of a dodgy month. Fortunately John was at home because the police, lawyers, the British Embassy and hit men all came into our lives.

We were accused of stealing Kat. Her father would appear drunk and screaming at the gates demanding firstly money and then delivering threats. We took them seriously when other men appeared with messages of the same ilk.

Eventually it was agreed Kat would live with us, and her mother, appalled at her husband's perfidy, signed her over to us for the length of our stay in Thailand after we promised to employ her. Bo said she had to work if she was to live with us, and I left it up to them to sort the division of labour.

Kat became the children's playmate cum nanny and happily spent hours playing with bricks and toys and generally being a child herself, for the first time in many years I understood from Bo. At nearly 15, she did not want to go back to school but wanted to learn dressmaking, and she learnt English from us. It was better than a brothel.

So sometimes we can help.

Virasek was our driver during all the kerfuffle with Kat. He literally guarded the children when they were at the swings near the gate, anxious they were not subjected to the rantings from her father and his cronies. He was also the only one I allowed to occasionally collect Kate from school at lunchtime. She adored him and would skip happily by his side chattering away in her English Thai patois. There was a friendly rivalry between him and Bo for the children's affections, though he was the only driver Bo would allow over the threshold.

"Edwa', you walk here!" called Bo, clapping her hands and trying to get our chunky son off his bottom. He was nearly fifteen months old so it was time.

"Come, come, come me Edwa'," Virasek would urge. "You walk me!"

Edward chose, much to Bo's chagrin, to make his first stuttering steps to Virasek as Bo and I looked on, and Kate laughed for joy.

"He my hero!" Bo said, when Edward toddled back to her.

Bo came with us to Singapore when we were transferred back two years later, in many ways playing the role Ali had in my early life, by providing some continuity in our children's lives. She hated living there and missed Thailand terribly so when we were relocated to Scotland eight months later she returned home, despite being offered numerous jobs in Singapore.

Taking her to the airport goes down in our family history as being one of the worst times. The children sobbed, clinging to her legs. I sobbed trying to prise them away. She sobbed as she bent to rub cheeks with them one last time. She and I did not hug, even after all we had been through together. We *waied* each other, me ensuring I bowed at the same level, and she returned to the Land of Smiles and one of my most favourite of places.

There are the nay sayers who decry the ideal of having servants, perhaps thinking to serve is to be servile. Often they are newly arrived, first-time expatriates who have an ingrained sensibility, and the naïve and erroneous assumption that we are all the same. We are not. Some of us are far luckier than others. And people forget that if an *amah* can find employment with an expatriate she is far more likely to be well remunerated and cared for.

In many countries it is often a poor relation who takes on the mantle of home help in the guise of helping family, but in truth it is often low-paid, if at all, servitude. In others servants are little more than slaves, their passports taken for 'safe keeping', low wages are kept from them with the excuse their salary, meagre as it is, is being used to pay for their food and lodging. These servants, nearly always women trying to send funds back to their families, work seven days a week and are often locked in with no contact with others from their own country. It is a repugnant state of affairs and one that should be legislated against, everywhere.

My attitude has always been if I can provide employment for someone, and possibly help with education, then I am contributing to the country's often hardest working, least-helped people. It is of course not an entirely altruistic attitude. I hate housework. Salaries have always come out of our pocket, and we have always paid generously, provided bags of rice and any other commodity that was appropriate.

I expected no difference when we relocated to West Africa. We had been in Malabo about six months and quite by chance I learned that while we were paying Isabel, the other staff houses were being cleaned at the expense of the Company.

"Why," I screeched at my poor spouse, "Are we paying for Isabel and the others are not?"

"I assume because we are here on married status and they aren't."

"And you think that's okay?"

"I hadn't actually thought about it."

"Well, I think you should," I stormed. "Do any of them put up visiting people? Do any of them host receptions, dinner parties, brunches for customers?"

"No of course not."

"Exactly. So I put up with strangers staying in my home. I walk into town and trail around all the shops and the market looking for food I then prepare, serve and clean up after evening dos, and we are the ones who pay for the maid." I was incandescent with rage.

"Put like that it doesn't seem right," John said.

I could not believe a large, US, multi-national company would treat 'a trailing spouse' with so little regard and the attitude, 'well he has his wife there, she can clean and cook for him.'

It is the only time I have ever aired a company grievance to other wives. Over the Continental card table I did a quick survey.

"Do you mind me asking, but do you pay for your house help here?"

"No of course not," came back the reply again, and again, and again.

I brought the subject up once more, much to the discomfit of my spouse, the one I trail after. He promised to sort it out. He did.

I like to think I am reasonably patient with fellow expatriates. I do understand how difficult life can be in a new country, I really do. But little irritates me more than the berating and belittling of the people who help make our lives that little easier, more luxurious, at very little cost to us.

"My maid shrank my silk blouse this morning," a woman ranted over the Mah Jong table. "I am so angry at her."

"Did you show her how to wash it?" I asked.

"No. She didn't ask."

"She might never have seen a silk blouse before."

"Then she should have asked," grumbled the woman.

"You can always buy another blouse," I commented and moved tables.

It was a short while later, in the same country, another woman complained at her maid's lack of personal hygiene.

"It's the dry season. There is no water in the town standpipes," I explained. "Why don't you buy her some soap and deodorant, give her a towel and offer the use of one of your bathrooms?"

"In my house?"

"Yes. You've got four. And let her wash her family's clothes in the washing machine."

"I couldn't do that," she said.

"Why not?" I asked.

"Well, I just couldn't."

I left that table also.

Having live-in help, whilst a wonderful benefit if small children are around, can feel intrusive particularly if they live in the house itself, with no separate kitchen or entrance. It is up to us, the employer, to set boundaries that are fair to all. Days off and salary are naturally negotiated upfront, so too should be the number of hours worked each day and access to the kitchen suiting you both.

If I asked for babysitting at night I paid extra, or gave time off in lieu. One of the strictest rules in our house when the children were young, was that whoever was working for us was not to be disturbed on their day off.

One of my foibles is a dislike of facing dirty dishes in the morning so I invariably cleaned up after our dinner, not to mention it helped deter cockroaches. One of my greatest pleasures was not having to deal with breakfast each morning. We would all come downstairs together to find the table set and the start of the day relaxed.

I know I relied very heavily on Es and Bo in Thailand, and Julie in Singapore, the first time we were there. John was out of the country a great deal and it made my life infinitely easier to have help with the children. It allowed me freedom to work part-time, albeit as a volunteer, but it also gave me a chance to go to the theatre or a party knowing they were in good hands. It gave me time for me, which so many young mothers do not have.

There is however a flip side, and as in all things we have to find a balance. Stories of a child refusing to go to her mother, or choosing his *amah* over his mother after a fall, or the *amah* bathing and putting the child to bed every night, are often heard around the coffee table, almost a throwback to Victorian times. It hurts to see, and I'm sure it hurts to be on the receiving end. It is easy to be lulled, but the blowback is awful for all concerned particularly when the time comes for either you or your help to move on, or even on home leaves when the *amah* is not with you. The realisation dawns that you don't actually know how little Johnnie likes his eggs cooked and that's not good for either of you.

The other area where it's easy to fall down is the level of our children's participation in the house. Memories of my first day at NEGS came back to me as Kate grew from toddlerhood, and from the time the children could make a bed, they were expected to do so, despite having servants, though they did not have to change the sheets.

Dottie, a woman I have worked closely with at Families in Global Transition, tells the story of their time living in Mexico City.

"Hey Mom, where are my track clothes?" her daughter called.

"In the laundry," Dottie replied.

Five minutes later her daughter appeared at the door looking bewildered.

"Mom, where's the laundry?" she asked.

"That was when I knew we had to spend our next summer at Hilton Head learning the basics of housekeeping," Dottie laughed.

In Equatorial Guinea Stephen taught me. We had asked our landlord if we could employ Stephen as our guard, a misnomer as he was physically a frail man, but I defied anyone to get around his tongue. He also knew where every single pipe and wire was placed in the building which, having seen most of the connections being made, seemed a good fall back plan for us, there being no actual building plans. The landlord was delighted to get Stephen off his books and onto ours, and so were we.

Stephen. How to describe Stephen? The man who became my gatekeeper, my dog watcher, my co-gardener and my tutor on African studies, while never once crossing that sometimes nebulous boundary of employer and employee.

Stephen was Ghanaian but had been in Equatorial Guinea many years. He had great affection for the British, and as a native of one of the first independent countries in Africa, freed from the supposedly oppressive mantle of colonialism, he had nothing but regret that the British had left. He had returned to Ghana for occasional visits. On one trip he married, and on two subsequent visits he seeded two daughters. They were the reason he stayed in a country not his own, and assiduously sent money back for their education, his salary now greatly increased due to working for 'a big American company', to his village just outside Accra.

His proudest possession was a little radio on which he listened to the BBC World Service and every football match played by his beloved Everton. His spoken English was melodic, his vocabulary and turn-of-phrase quaintly old-fashioned.

He was, we later found out, the same age as John – forty-nine. There looked to be a twenty-year age difference with my husband being the winner. Stephen's legs were spindly but strong, scarred from years of working on the cocoa plantations slashing *lalang* grass, along with mosquito bites that had turned septic. His toes splayed over the edges of his worn-down flip-flops. His shaved head showed scars of a life not always safe. His lungs were not good, though he told me he had never smoked, but he had fought a long and weary battle with tuberculosis.

Every morning he would call up to us as we had breakfast on the terrace, "Good morning, massa, good morning, madam. I trust the night passed well."

On particularly lung-filled mornings I would call down, "Stephen are you okay? Your cough is bad this morning. Did you take the medicine I gave you?"

"Oh yes, madam. It is this Malabo air. It is very bad for the catarrh."

I could only agree and go back to my coffee. John would go downstairs ready to drive to the office, with Miss Meg close at his heels. She would, on reaching the outside world, stretch long and languorously with her rump in the air.

"Oh, massa look," Stephen said, "Megarn, she prostrate herself to you." His words, spoken nearly every morning, started my day with a smile for over two years.

That fine line, the one between employer and employee, can be especially difficult when you both live on the same compound. While our house was being built we argued the case with the landlord for the guardhouse, originally meant to be one very small cubbyhole, to be extended to encompass three small rooms and a bathroom. I think it took another small bag of cement to close the deal, but we did get Stephen a reasonable little house. He still lived and slept in one room though, with his possessions neatly hung on wires strung across the corners. He used one as storage and rented the third.

Stephen had a wonderful sense of humour and could also be a bit naughty. His chuckle would start deep in his belly and then explode out of his thin chest with a great wamph.

There was a ruckus at the gates one morning and, my curiosity piqued, I eavesdropped from the terrace. It took me a while to decipher what was happening but I was by then quite good at discerning the lilting words.

"Eh! Ol' Man? Goo' mornin' I wan tek yur barro?"

"No, he bizi."

Stephen, when speaking to me, spoke a pure English, but when conversing with fellow Africans he reverted to a patois understood by any West African, whether Ghanaian, Cameroonian, Nigerian, Gambian or Togan. The words swirled in a rich mixture of the Queen's English, native tongues, a little French, German and of course Spanish from our bit of the Continent.

"Ee no bizi. I see 'im stan dere."

"No, he bizi," Stephen said again, returning to his gas stove and the tea he was brewing.

"Ol' Man, I beg yu plis. Gib me won hoa!"

"Wat yu gib I?" Stephen responded.

"Ey, man, I nogat notin. I jes neet won hoa, tek bric dow' de line."

"Yu neet me barro, yu gimme wat?"

I felt this would be a long negotiation so poured more coffee, pulled up a chair but stayed out of sight. I already knew Stephen was a harsh critic of his fellow Africans, but I had not realized his antipathy could be so antagonistic. "These black men cannot be trusted" was one of his favourite warnings.

The wheelbarrow in question was not a deluxe model. The wheel held air for a maximum of three minutes, the barrow had rusted away on one side and the handles were guaranteed to produce instant blisters. I was not being mean by not replacing it. There were no wheelbarrows to be bought, or borrowed it seemed, on the island.

"Wat yu wan'?" asked our new neighbour.

"Yu go' w'men." I winced thinking I might have to intervene after all. "Yor w'man, she cok me."

"Won nigh'," the sweating man at the gate said.

"Won wek," Stephen countered.

"Yu gib de fuud."

I relaxed, realising it was not a negotiation over how many nights one of the women would be available for Stephen's entertainment, but rather a culinary deal.

"Okay, ba no de eggs."

"Okay Ol' Man, deel."

Stephen was delighted and later informed me he would have a cooked meal delivered every evening for a week. He was a tough negotiator.

As Miss Meg and I wandered down the track later in the cool of the afternoon, heading for the jungle over the stream at the bottom of the hill, I saw the wheelbarrow being upended, bricks and building debris spilling from its eroded sides. Painted in Stephen's firm hand on the rusted bottom were the words 'mama apple'.

When wheelbarrows did finally appear in the market I sent Stephen off to get one. He returned proudly pushing a pillar-box red barrow with smart black rubber handles, and a tyre that stayed inflated. Before a clod of earth could be tossed in, 'mama apple 2' was painted on its sparkling bottom. I felt payment for its usage would be feasts for at least a month.

We spent many hours, Stephen and I, making our mud compound a garden and often talked about politics; his knowledge of West African affairs was encyclopedic and his opinions right-wing. He believed the mostly benign rule of the British should have been emulated by the new rulers of independent Africa but recognised, and berated, the greed that overtook many of them. We talked literature. He told me stories from his village in Ghana.

"Madam Apple, I am most upset."

"Oh no, Stephen, what's the matter?" I asked, worried someone had offended him, or that I had.

"That magazine, *The Week*. It is a story I do not understand. You will please explain to me."

"What was it about?" I asked.

"Killing de people," he said. "The family, they take their modder or fadder or sista or brodder to Switzerland and kill dem." Stephen's normally articulate English would lapse when he was upset. "Madam, explain me please why a person would do dis t'ing?"

"Do you mean the piece about Dignitas?" I asked, remembering reading something about them a few weeks earlier, before passing the magazine along to Stephen.

"Yes, Madam. It is very bad place. God does not allow murder. How can dey murder dere family? It is not up to us to choose, it is up to God. He decides when he wants us to join him," he said, pointing to the sky, as if God was watching and listening with interest through the equatorial glare, to the labours of a black man and a white woman sharing the gardening chores in the sweaty heat.

"It's very difficult Stephen. Those people who go there, go because they want to die. Some people do not want to be a burden to their family. They would rather choose when they die, hopefully with dignity rather than waste away, maybe in pain, with no control over their life."

"But Madam, dat is what family and God is dere for, to ease pain. It is a son's duty to care for his parents," he said, with utter conviction.

What could I say in the face of such deep-felt beliefs that would not sound disrespectful to him or his God?

Stephen, being the oldest man on the street, was regarded with great respect and people would come to him for advice on all manner of things, normally starting their query with the words, "Ol' Man, wat yu say 'bout...?"

When we left, he and James, another employee, gave us three carvings. The ones of a man and a woman they gave John.

"You hab de balance of man and woman in your blod, massa," they told him.

To me they gave a carving of a turbaned woman fitting into the shape of Africa.

"You are our Mama Africa, Madam Apple," Stephen said.

I cried as I shook their hands, holding them in both of mine. I had learnt so much from two kind and wise African men.

Every time I board a plane now I am grateful I no longer travel with children. What has always been a stress inducer, in even the most organised mother, is made ever more so by new rules and regulations not actually guaranteed to protect us. But the ineptitude of some parents travelling with children, notwithstanding the hurdles put up by the authorities, is astounding.

It is not fair to ask a child to travel across the world (which when shown their new location in an atlas doesn't look far from their current location), without ensuring you have thought of pretty much every eventuality.

Even with the kids I used to love flying. And so did they. We used to try for night flights, putting on pyjamas in a plane is so much more fun than on *terra firma*, and there were always a couple of new, wrapped up small presents to open half way through the flight. It was exciting. Getting on a plane in one country, flying high above clouds giving such wonderful reign to the imagination, and plop, landing in another country with completely different smells, though you don't smell them now until you actually leave the terminal, was thrilling.

The first flight I can really remember was almost half a century ago and was Port Harcourt in Nigeria to London via Rome. I know this because I found my BOAC logbooks not long ago. I was about five and half.

I can remember walking across the apron, smelling the aviation fuel already whirring around the engines. My parents were 'dressed' to travel. My father in a suit and tie, Mum in a skirt and twin-set, always pearls, and a jacket for our arrival.

I'm sure Dad would've liked her to wear a hat, but she drew the line at that.

There were two classes even then though nobody had much room. But wherever you sat the meals were served on trays with white cloths, china, proper cutlery and silver salt and pepper shakers. It was, of course, silver service with a plentiful selection of wine, beer and liquor poured into the appropriate shaped crystal. I was offered orange or lemon squash. Everything was served by apparitions in navy blue uniforms with coiffed hair and manicured nails; modulated voices that could discuss a raft of topics, all with a pleasant smile and a willingness to help.

There was no in-flight entertainment one could plug into. Reading papers a week old was a treat for many of the men and when that palled, cards were sometimes played with the new acquaintance to your left or right.

I played noughts and crosses and draughts with my parents, as they sipped whisky and smoked into the night to pass the time. I was often the only child on board and would invariably get a trip to the cockpit to meet the captain and his crew, but the biggest thrill was helping the airhostesses offer sweets as we prepared to land.

"Would you like a sweetie, sir?" I'd ask very importantly.

"Well thank you, my dear."

I couldn't wait to grow up and be an airhostess.

Somewhere over the miles and the years flying became an arduous event to be managed and got through. Hostesses became stewards and stewardesses, then flight attendants and about the only advantage I can see now is that a fug of yellow smoke no longer hangs over the sardines lining the fuselage. There are of course exceptions both in airlines and staff, but on the whole flying is not a pleasant experience, and there is very little service with a smile.

Take-Away Slice: If we allow ourselves not to know it all, to be open and willing to listen, sometimes to things not said, or said between the lines, those people that help us in the house or garden, or drive us around, are a wonderful source of local information, from politics to which vendor is best to buy from in the market. If we watch them interact with each other we can learn the subtleties of their culture and that is worth a very great deal.

Sixth Slice: Education, a Conundrum

"Daddy, why do I have to do the maypole thing?" I asked one night, as he sat on the edge of my bed. We were back living in Somerset, a year after my last term there. He was between Africa and Asia, job wise.

"Because you're part of the school and everyone learns how to dance around the Maypole in the summer term in England. I did."

"Yes but you lived here. I'm from Africa."

"No sweetie-pie, you're not. You're English."

"Mummy's not. I don't want to be. I'm African."

"Sweetie we've left Africa, and now England is home. So you have to learn English things, like you learnt African things."

"What about Ali?"

"He's fine."

"I miss him. I want to go back."

"I know. But we can't."

"I want to be 'stralian like Mummy. Why do I have to be English?"

"Because I am, and you were born here."

"Well I don't like the Maypole." I imagine the conversation would've continued dancing around the pole if my father had not tucked me in and kissed me a firm goodnight.

Education surely is one of the most talked about issues in a globally mobile family, either *sotto voce* between parents trying to decide whether to accept an assignment in Ulan Bataar, or between the whole family once a decision has been made.

There was never any discussion about schooling with me. We were moving and I would naturally have to start at a new school. There were no choices.

I don't believe it ever occurred to me I was a different colour to some of my classmates in Nigeria, and it was only in a rural English school I realised there were no other colours in the classroom. I hated all the clothes I had to wear. I hated having to wear lace-up shoes. I hated having to change for sports in a freezing locker room and I hated sports too.

England was not home for long and my next school was in KL, and much more to my liking. I liked the colours back in the classroom. I liked everyone's 'special' days from Chinese New Year, with all the cymbals and fireworks, to Hari Raya Puasa, which celebrated the end of Ramadan, to Deepavili, the Hindu Festival of Lights leading Rama home from exile. I liked my school day ending at lunchtime. I liked the time I spent with my father in the car as he dropped me off on his way to work. Everything was so much more vivid and wild than in England, and I liked being warm again.

A year later we drove the logger-lorry laden road through miles and miles of rubber plantations to Singapore where I went to Raeburn Park School. It did not start successfully.

Samsuri, Dad's driver, came and collected me early and Mum and I arrived home at the same time, me from school and her from the Red Cross.

"What's up sweetie-pie," she asked, feeling my forehead.

"My head hurts," I said, tears trickling down my face, "And everywhere."

"Let's put the air-conditioning on in my bedroom and you can lie in the cool for a while and see if that helps," she said.

It didn't, and after ascertaining my hurting head and aching body were not ploys to avoid a new school, after many blood tests in the end of each finger and, it seemed, pints taken from both arms, it was agreed I was suffering from rheumatic fever. I was put on bed rest and only allowed to walk to the loo. My poor mother had to carry me everywhere else.

We did innumerable jigsaws with thousands of pieces. I read. And I listened to the tiny little transistor radio John and Julia, my uncle and aunt, gave me when they visited us on their way back to England from the Solomon Islands, where they lived. It was the most wonderful thing I had ever been given and on which I first heard the Beatles.

Months later it was decided to remove my tonsils and hey presto I was fixed and tried Raeburn Park again. This time it worked, for a year.

And then back to KL where I once again went to The Garden School.

By the time I was nearly ten it was decided educational stability might be appropriate. I would go NEGS. It did not seem strange. All my English friends and many of my Asian ones were heading to England to boarding school, there being no alternative considered viable then. I never questioned going to Australia.

Going from the British education system to the Australian one was not that difficult, although I did have to work through a couple of books before I left KL.

"What in God's name are social studies?" my father asked, flicking through the workbooks when they arrived. "This is geography and people. Commonsense."

Not the best attitude to show a daughter reluctant to do any extra work when I could be outside playing with Peck Yoke.

"She has to do them," Mum said.

"She will also have to continue her French," I remember Dad saying. "It's ridiculous they don't teach it there for another two years."

There were no tears when I left home the first time in January 1969. They came after my first holiday back to KL in August, once the bloom of new things had worn off. I cried on the plane, and the train, and my first couple of nights back in a dormitory shared with five others and then I got on with life. It was a pattern that repeated itself for a few years, and probably only stopped when I realized how very unattractive I looked with red-rimmed eyes and a swollen nose.

That first time though, Mum took me. The whole uniform-buying procedure was arduous for someone used to light cotton dresses, and I still didn't like wearing shoes.

"Why do I have to wear these?" I asked my mother who was trying to clip stockings to my new suspender belt. "Why can't I just wear socks?"

"Because it's the only way your stockings will stay up. And they are part of the uniform."

"They hurt. And they're scratchy," I complained. The layers of clothes, knickers, bloomers, vest, shirt, tie, tunic and the dreaded leg wear that had to be negotiated each morning were one of the worst things about my early days at NEGS. Saturdays were bliss. We were allowed to wear jodhpurs until teatime.

NEGS, became my stability. Great fun, perhaps too much fun, as academically I did not shine and my father's earlier hopes for a brilliant daughter faded with each report card. But I learnt a lot.

My first morning was one of the most instructive in the entire seven years. Being roused to the strident clang of the wake-up bell, and other people, was strange for an only child. Feigning sleep I watched, clutching Pambam my panda, as the others in my dormitory busied themselves with sheet tucking and shoe cleaning, two things I'd never had to do and had no idea how to tackle. When I finally found the courage to slide my legs over the side of the bed and get on with my first day, it took me so long to figure out the suspender belt and hospital corners that when another bell clanged to hustle us over to the dining hall for our first breakfast, I was last to leave the dorm.

The Dining Hall was cavernous, with windows twelve feet above the floor which could only be opened with the clever manipulation of a series of cords. The Staff sat at the High Table on the stage and were served by senior students. The Hall seated a hundred and fifty girls and the shuffle of three hundred feet on the wooden floors reverberated around the high walls. We stood behind the chairs at our designated table of twelve and waited for grace to be sung, in Latin. Then we sat, but only after the prefect who headed the table sat. It was she who ladled the food, it was she who reminded us of our manners, it was she who meted out punishment for intransigence.

"You two," the prefect pointed to the two of us nearest the serving bench between the dining tables, "Are the servers and clearers. You collect the platters of food from the counter over there, then when we've all finished eating you clear everyone's plates and pile them up there, cutlery on one plate. Then you take them out to the kitchens."

It was very different to the dining table I was used to, and I sat very quietly until I got the hang of serving and clearing and then setting the tables for the next shift, or the next meal. I could do that, thanks to Sam in Nigeria.

At the end of the meal, and after grace had again been sung, we would filter out between the prefects now lining the central aisle and charged with checking the shine on our shoes or the knot of our tie.

It was a lot to take in for a girl, pudgy and with a crisp Pommie accent, who had been brought up in Africa and Asia with servants.

But I settled. I felt sorry for girls who had only ever had governesses or had been taught by correspondence through School of the Air. I couldn't understand how you could grow up and only go to town once a month and not really have friends.

"Have you been to England?"

"'Course," I said.

"What about France?"

"Yeah, an' Africa." But I couldn't catch a sheep and I didn't know how to make a cup of tea.

I could though thankfully hold my own on a horse. I learnt to ride around the tin mines in KL, but once in Australia quickly adapted from a dressage saddle to the thigh-hugging stock saddle, and adopted the comfortable slouch of stock riding that could be upheld all day. I discovered the joy of riding bareback in a muddy dam on a hot afternoon after a morning of mustering cattle. I learnt about life on the land. I learnt not to be squeamish about eating a cow or a sheep I had petted days before. I learnt about dipping sheep for blowfly. I learnt about the wonders of lambing. I found out the damage an emu could do to a car meandering home at dawn after a party a hundred miles down the road. I learnt I loved the russet colours of outback Australia and the laconic attitude of the men and women on the land. I learnt the power of understatement, when 'just down the road' could mean six hundred miles. I also learnt to end all sentences with a question.

And more important than anything else, I made lifelong friends.

But no matter how welcome I was made to feel, I knew I was a little different. In the first few years it was not always easy. Things I had taken for granted growing up in an international environment were suddenly challenged. I had different sensibilities and attitudes particularly to 'coloured' people. There was no actual racism but rather an assumption of idleness and an easy use of terms I found offensive. It took me a long time to shut up and not get emotional, not so much with my pals who got used to my outbursts, but from older folk. I was, however, met with only kindness from families with whom I spent many halfterms and holidays, and where some of my fondest memories are embedded.

I don't think there is a teen alive who hasn't felt some small regret that the long summer holidays are over, despite looking forward to seeing friends again, and for some, even the thought of classes is exhilarating. I never fell into that heady category, but I know they exist. And those are the ones going back to school with friends they know and have grown up with from kindergarten.

Spare a thought for those displaced kids who, at the end of the last school year, knew they would be moving on, again. Following their parents and their shipment to a new location, again. Starting a new school, again.

In so many ways the life expatriates lead now is far more complex and complicated. With the mushrooming of international high schools around the world has come a whole new set of issues with regard to relocation and education. Whether to board, or not to board, is a huge question involving the whole family. But whatever the decision, bags are packed either for a new posting or for boarding school. My teen years were spent knowing I would be at NEGS no matter where else in the world we would live. It was my constant, and for that I am really grateful.

Home schooling, on location, boarding? It is an emotive issue with no hard and fast answer. Add to the mix the cultural divergences between countries, and within countries, particularly with regard to boarding schools and you have a crucible of opinions. Britain, Australia, Canada, some Asian and African countries and increasingly Russia, consider the boarding school option as potential, not punishment.

In America some states view boarding schools as something to be aspired to, while here in Texas it is seen more as a boot camp for young offenders, a behaviourial last resort. Slap 'em into shape academies.

But for many on the nomadic trail, boarding school can offer teens a chance to thrive in a stable environment through some of their most important educational years, without going through the dislocation of multiple moves in an already turbulent time of their lives. It gives a child the opportunity to experience continuity with peers, consistency in curriculum, and a sense of community, exempt from the upheavals of a mobile life, while still benefiting from the global experience with family during vacation time.

I do not mean to imply that children educated on location, either in a local or an international school, do not do well, many are hugely successful. A miniature united nations often exists in the international schools allowing a valuable lesson in cultural awareness and understanding.

International schools now have such a vast range of options with more and more leaning towards the International Baccalaureate that academically it is almost possible to seamlessly move school. For teens particularly, each move can be a huge hurdle socially and like everything about parenting it's hard to predict what their reactions will be. And sometimes the one you anticipate will transfer easily is the one who struggles, or vice versa.

In our global life our daughter stayed, successfully, with us on location in Houston. Our son, after two years at school in the same place, did not. After tearful discussions John and I felt we had to offer him the choice of boarding school. We sent off for prospectuses from thirty schools in England and planned to sit down together and talk about it with him. Like many plans, things didn't work out quite that way.

"Hey Mum," Edward said, staggering in from school, sweaty and laden down with a rucksack and saxophone.

"Hey yourself," I said. "Did you have a good day? Would you like something to eat?"

"No and yes please. I'm starved," he said.

"Have you got lots of homework?"

"Yeah. Lots. Band practice was crap this morning. I hate Mr Jones. He takes all the fun out of music. I think he wants to make us hate playing. And coach was in a foul mood. He shouted at everyone."

"Chook, what would you think about boarding school in England?" I asked, the words out before I'd even thought how to say it, before I'd even thought.

"You're going to send me away?" tears sprang to his eyes as he looked at me horrified.

"No my love, not if you don't want. It was just something Dad and I thought you might be interested in," I said, as I tried to hug him.

"You don't love me," he whispered, pushing me away. "Why isn't Kate going?" He shouted, as if he had morphed into his sister, our dramatic child. Never in my worst-case scenarios had I expected that reaction from my normally rational and laid back son.

"Oh Edward you know that's not true. You couldn't be more loved. It was just an idea."

He ran sobbing into our bedroom on the ground floor, slammed the door and locked it. Locked doors have never been allowed in our home. This time I tried to talk through it though Edward had thrown himself against it thinking I would try to unlock it. I 'phoned John who was fortunately in town and blurted out the enormity of my mistimed question.

"Give him time. He'll come out soon. Let him guide you," he said, always calm. "I'll be home early."

I went back to the kitchen, watching the door, as I peeled carrots. It eventually opened and Edward's dear, tear-stained face peered around the corner at me.

"I'm sorry, Mum," he said, nearly undoing my promise not to lose control.

"Edward, you are loved. Dearly. It was only an idea as things don't seem to be going right for you here," I said, hugging him tight. "Come and have something to eat and drink."

"Are those the schools?" he asked, pointing to the array of coloured prospectuses I had spread out on the coffee table.

"Yes."

"Will you look at them with me?"

I threw off my pinnie in a nanosecond and sat on the sofa with one of the children who held my heart. We sat close and compared brochures.

A little while later Kate whisked in, home for a quick bite before ballet rehearsals. She might have sometimes been disdainful of her younger brother but was still not too much of a teenager to see when something was very wrong.

"Why are you sending him away?" she cried, seeing the brochures.

"It's okay Kate," Edward said. "I don't have to go. But I might like to."

I was stunned. The three of us sat and talked about boarding school as if it were the most natural thing in the world. By the time John got home, early as promised, our son was positively enthusiastic. I was a mangled heap of emotions and the man who loved me, no matter what, gave me a much-needed hug.

Edward and John, along with my father, spent the following Spring Break touring schools. The final choice was Edward's, which fortunately coincided with the one we favoured. He went the following September.

Trite as it sounds, each child is different and each child warrants individual assessment. Not all children will benefit from the boarding experience, even if a sibling is at the same school, and a school which is right for one may not be the best fit for another.

When to go is a whole other question. But whatever age the child goes, whether seven, thirteen or sixteen, it is wrenching. To let your child go sooner than expected is a huge shift which has to be fully accepted by both parents, in order for the child to have a chance of assimilating happily and successfully into a boarding school.

I am the product of a boarding school education, John is not. And yet he was the more open to that option for our son. I loved boarding. Academically, I learnt a little. Educationally, I learnt a lot. And I had fun, great fun. So why didn't I want my children to go?

Because as a parent I did not want to miss out on what my parents missed, all those myriad steps our children go through to become young adults. I resented the thought I might not be a part of it, but that was the way then. Times had changed and we did see our son play rugby, cricket, basketball and act – certainly not as much as if he was at school where we lived, but we tried. Was it the best decision for him? Absolutely. Would it have been the right decision for our daughter? Absolutely not.

I think boarding school changes relationships, yours with your child, theirs with their siblings. Edward, though, disagrees and told me, "I don't think it changed, it just matured faster than if I had stayed at home." And you as the parent have to be prepared to let go sooner than expected. Your teen might make decisions or choices you would not have made for them, but they have to make mistakes, and you have to trust the ethics you instilled in their childhood come to the fore.

Leaving Edward at boarding school was high on the Worst Day of My Life list, far, far worse than me being left thirty years earlier.

"Why do I need hankies?" Edward asked, as I finished stitching the last nametags. "I never use them."

"Because your blazer was far too expensive to be used as one," I replied.

"That is gross, Mum."

"Well, how about because the list says you need them?" There are still hankies in John's drawer with his son's name on them, they were little used at school.

The morning after his thirteenth birthday all fun thoughts were wiped out at the breakfast table as the reality hit. The B-Day I had been dreading, the day Blundells became his new home. We ate quickly and went back upstairs to transfer goodies from seven plastic supermarket bags to the tuck box.

Our rooms at the B&B had a short connecting hall and we sat there, on the floor, carefully loading the tuck, squash, cocoa and chocolate on the bottom, sweeties, then crisps on top. We weren't talking. I looked over at Edward, soaking him in, remembering every expression, when our eyes caught. His were moist and that was all it took. We sobbed.

"I promise I won't cry at school," I told him. "But I will leave quickly, okay?"

"That'd be best, Mum," he said.

His uniform was hovering, ready, hung on the door. I dressed with care remembering how important it was for my parents to look 'just right' on the few occasions they came to NEGS.

"It's been two years since I tied a tie," Edward commented. "Since Aberdeen. Feels weird."

"Do you need help?" I asked.

"No Mum!" he replied, barely suppressing an eye roll.

After unloading tuck boxes and trunks in dormitories, new parents and children were invited to hear Headmaster Jonathon Leigh welcome us to the school. "Our aim is to turn out young men and women with integrity, and without arrogance," were the words that stuck in my mind as I sat there, miserable and proud at the same time. Back at the respective houses parents were siphoned away from children, to have tea with the housemaster and meet other parents. Seeing red-eyed mothers clutching tissues reinforced my promise to Edward. I would not cry.

"Oh you must be feeling awful," said one, "Living all the way over in America. I live twenty miles down the road and feel terrible. How will you cope?"

"Edward will be fine, and so will I," I said stiffly, and moved to talk to a couple who appeared more in control.

Our sons met us at the door and walked us to our cars.

"Remember what Mr Berrow said," I reminded Edward. "I won't call for three weeks, but I'm only in Edinburgh, with Marian, if you do need me, okay? And I'll be here for your first exeat."

"Okay, Mum. Will you go now?" he said, opening my car door for me.

"Yup," I said hugging him. "Always know you are loved, no matter what."

"I know Mum. Me too. 'Bye."

I got in the car, not looking at him as he shut my door. As I turned the corner the sobs hit and a mile down the road, in the nearest lay-by, I stopped.

Driving to Somerset through the back lanes on that pleasant early September evening I passed a pub, as one does in rural England. Pulling in, I went to the bar not feeling able to face my mother's matter-of-fact manner just yet.

"A large gin and tonic, and a ham sandwich please. Over in that corner if you don't mind," I said to the barman, who did not raise his head from polishing a glass.

"Food's served in the dining room from six."

"I want a large gin and tonic and a ham sandwich in that corner please," I repeated.

He glanced up, saw my red streaky face with tears ready to spill.

"Righ' away love. You okay?"

"Yes," I said.

I calmed down and thought of Mr Leigh's words. Words that came back to me every single time I said goodbye to my son, whether at an airport or at school. Arriving at my mother's house a couple of hours later, after just the one gin and tonic, I thought I was ready to be positive and cheerful.

"Sweetie," she said hugging me hard, "You must be feeling like hell. Come on, I've got the wine on ice."

"Oh Mum," I sobbed, "This is horrible. I didn't think you'd understand."

"How do you think I felt when I left you at NEGS, Apple?" she asked.

"I didn't know. You didn't cry."

"Would it have helped if I did?" she asked.

Leaving a child of any age at boarding school is hard. Being left at boarding school is hard. Homesickness is hell though it tends to be short-lived, but you've got to give a fair amount of time to let your child settle and adapt. A year allows a chance to experience all the activities on offer, as well as holidays in the parents' current location and a return to their 'other' home, school.

Another advantage of boarding school, apart from a stable education, was that it allowed me to make my mistakes out of my parents' sight. Drinking a flagon of cheap sherry, sitting on tractor tyres after one particular wool-shed party, remains one of the seriously low points in my life. Thankfully I can remember very little of the event, though the story goes that my cousin, Annie, and I were hosed down on the flatbed of the Ute and then put to bed. I do remember the fury of her parents the next day, particularly as we were quite unable to be back at school for the first day of term.

"We are so disappointed in you, Apple." Annie's mum, my mother's cousin, said. "We thought better of you. I'm not going to write to Ida, but I do expect you to tell her."

"I'm sorry," just doesn't do at times like that. Annie and I spent the remainder of the day trying to keep out of everyone's way. We decided to drive up to the dam for a swim. Through the haze of a hangover I do remember backing into the gatepost as we left. I don't believe we told Annie's parents about that.

Some move to a country where English is not a widely spoken language and go with the option that this could be the best chance for a child to absorb a language from a young age. It's a tough decision. Made more so when little Stevie comes home from school bereft at having left the school, back home, where he was understood and had friends, to finding himself in a school where maybe only one person speaks English.

It's easy to begin to question the wisdom when the child continues to come home in tears, or shows other desperate tendencies. Everyone agrees to give it a little longer and just as capitulation is on the cards, nerves are frayed to raw dangling threads, Stevie comes home and says, "Yanni asked me to his house to play tomorrow. Can I go?"

He wonders why his mother dissolves in a puddle, shrugs as he chooses *baklava* instead of wanting an Oreo, his plaintive request every afternoon for the previous three months. His mother reaches for the Retsina, not caring if it's red or white, as he turns the television on to a local station, understanding and laughing at the Greek cartoons, instead of putting a DVD from home in the slot. The expression 'it's all Greek to me' takes on a whole new meaning.

Homeschooling was never an option that crossed my mind, I'm not patient enough or frankly good enough at certain subjects to ably assist, and maths instantly springs to mind, but

I feel peers are such an important part of a teen's life that on the peripatetic wheel we live as expatriates, friends take on an even more important role. Nagging at the back of my mind were girls I went to NEGS with, who until they went to boarding school had very little contact with other children, which I think is a shame.

It is our friends, our peers, with whom we face the world when we first leave home as the emerging generation, and it is then that we, the parents, really start to bow out of our children's lives and let them live theirs.

The adjustment issues for those educated on location, whether in the home or at an international school, tend to occur when teens return to base for university. Often they find they have little in common with their new 'non global' peers and it can be hard assimilating into a more traditional, and sometimes insular, environment. It is easier now with the Internet providing instant communication and an insight into who is listening to what as far as music is concerned. Sports too have crossed the oceans with games traditionally played in one country often seen on televisions across the world. But assimilation can still be a problem, and is one shared by many adults repatriating.

Take Away Slice: Whatever decision is made there will be moments of angst, "Should we have done that instead?" but all we, as parents, can do is work with what we know about our children and research the options available. Whatever the decision, whether an international school, home schooling, boarding school or a local one, time has to be given for the child to adapt. And that means you, the one on the front line, have to stay steady, at least in front of them, until that magical moment when you realise they are happy. And then you will be too.

Seventh Slice: Volunteering is Work

"Can you write?"

"A little," I replied, wondering where the question was going.

"Can you type?"

"Yes," I said, more confident in that answer.

"Good. I want you to start a quarterly magazine covering the Far Eastern Region," Group Captain Leonard Cheshire said with a smile. "It's something we've been wanting to do for a while. This would seem the perfect opportunity."

"But I've never done anything like that before. A school magazine, and just writing for me."

"You'll be first rate. I know it," GC said. "Brother Kevin will help, won't you?" he asked the Marist brother, who was the Cheshire Homes Regional Secretary.

"Argh, to be sure I will," the grey-haired, bespectacled former high-school principal said.

Brother Kevin had been in Singapore for forty years. I had been there two months, not counting my childhood. I had gone to the Cheshire Home on Serangoon Garden Road to volunteer my services for reading or maybe playing board games with the residents, all physically disabled, not writing a magazine.

It was the start of five years, with two more relocations back up and down the length of Malaysia from Singapore to Bangkok, in one of the hardest volunteer jobs I have ever done. Our region covered eight countries, eleven languages and twenty-five homes. It was a magazine to be written by the residents, predominantly in English, and edited by me. It was before the days of computers when cut and paste meant scissors and glue and it was one of the most satisfying jobs I've ever had.

"You promised me the piece by today," I accused a man able only to type with a stick in his mouth.

"Ayee Apuh, you so hard on me lah."

"No I'm not. You've had three months. How far along are you?"

"Almos' leady."

"Would it help if I typed and you dictated?" I asked. His negative response told me he probably hadn't started. "Okay. Do you still want to write it?"

"I do it."

"By Friday?"

"Okay lah!" he said, and switched his attention back to Edward busy clambering up on his wheelchair.

Working with the residents in Singapore was in some ways more rewarding for me as I got to know them better than those in the two homes in Thailand, my Thai never being very proficient. But even before the days of email I had wonderful correspondence with many of those strong men and women fighting their disabilities with immense fortitude. Letters and articles from India, the Philippines, Indonesia, Malaysia, Hong Kong and Japan were all included.

On the Group Captain's second visit to Singapore while I was there, a meeting was held in our Chairman's home. Justice

Lai Kew Chai was a high court judge who in the court room I'm sure was fierce but with regard our common interests, the Cheshire Homes, was a staunch supporter and utterly delightful.

It had been arranged that after the meeting spouses would attend a dinner. As Oriental mores dictated then, the men were seated at one table and the women, hosted by the Justice's charming wife, at another. I could only glare as John sat in animated conversation with GC, a man I truly believed good, and who was also very interesting.

An RAF fighter pilot awarded the Victoria Cross, GC had also been an observer in the B-29 bomber, Bockscar, when it shed its load, the second atomic bomb, Fat Man, over Nagasaki. GC was deeply affected by the devastation, and I think probably spent the rest of his life trying to atone for the horrors inflicted.

"Um, Apple? I've been wondering, how would you feel about taking on the occasional special project? Fund raiser sort of things?" GC asked after dinner, men and women once again mingling.

"I've never done anything like that," I said.

"Well you'd never written and edited a magazine before," he pointed out, his thin shoulders and head thrusting forward, pale eyes watching me. "So how about it?"

"Okay."

I think it has been a combination of John's constant support, no matter the current passion, and GC's utter belief I could do anything I put my mind to, that has given me the self-belief to do things I had never considered.

"What were you two talking about at dinner?" I asked, in the taxi going home later, Singapore alive on the streets around us.

"Cricket," John answered.

"Cricket!" I shrieked. "You were sitting next to probably one of the greatest humanitarians in the world and you talked cricket?"

"Yup. He loves it. Said it was pleasant to talk about something other than work."

"Oh," I said.

Cheshire Homes not only brought me into contact with people from all over Asia and their respective cultures, even though I didn't get to travel to all the countries we covered, it also allowed my children an important insight into living with disabilities. One they didn't realise they were learning. It nearly came a cropper once.

"Where's Edward?" I asked Kate one afternoon, as we left Brother Kevin's office strewn with glued and corrected pages of the upcoming edition of *Cheshire News*.

"He went with Annie," she said, skipping along beside me greeting everyone we passed in the corridors and on the stairs.

As we reached the ground floor I heard a squeal of delight. Edward was sitting on the lap of an electric wheel-chaired man, immobile but for his right hand and head. They were careening along the walkway, a drainage ditch between the path and the hibiscus hedge, my three-year old son in charge of the controls.

"Edward!" I screeched. "Stop!" Running, Kate and I caught up with them as they neared the edge. "What the hell were you thinking?" I shouted at Lee Hoi, grabbing Edward off his lap.

"Oh Apple, we were having fun," Lee Hoi laughed. "Edward was safe."

"Oh my God, I wasn't worried about him. He bounces. I was worried about you ending up in the ditch!"

Both Kate and Edward were totally oblivious to the disability around them, rather like they were oblivious to different ethnicities in their little lives. That to me always made up for the odd tangle we found ourselves in with various relocations. When we opened a home in Kunming, China, the first in a communist country, it really was a red-letter day but one I sadly missed due to our final Asian relocation.

At NEGS I had not excelled academically. There had been far too many distractions, drama, dancing, singing and general fun. But when I couldn't work due to language issues in Holland, I realised I needed something to keep my mind occupied.

It was the start of a quest to find something I could do that would transfer wherever I went, and which I enjoyed. So I enrolled in a distance learning Montessori teacher training course, with the practical test taken in London. I knew very early on I would never teach, not being of a patient disposition, but I enjoyed the learning and it was fascinating to see Kate and Edward's progress through a Montessori lens.

Money – isn't it a funny and sensitive topic, especially amongst the trailing spouse brigade? It is not something I've ever really worried about, which sounds horribly arrogant. I think a lot of that was my upbringing; I never saw Mum earn, though she did go back to nursing when I was a baby and we lived in Nigeria. Once we moved to Asia working was not an option due to visa restrictions, but I saw her finding volunteer work as a fulfilling way to contribute, not only to the host country but also through the different contacts she made, which in turn helped my father.

Money was in short supply when we first married and, unable to work in Holland, I found it difficult to ask for funds not directly related to the household, which came out of a joint bank account, for a present for John for example, or a frippery for me. Without my knowing, he set up a direct debit to my UK bank account and started putting in a little each month so when we went to England I had money to spend. It was his recognition that I was valued, even though I wasn't actually bringing home any bacon. It was such a kindness, and so quietly done, I have never forgotten; in a large way it has helped me accept my own value as an accompanying spouse.

In all our moves as a couple I have never been put under pressure to go and earn. I think some of that had to do with John being away so much and we felt it was important for me to be around for the children, pretty much on demand. And of course I have been inordinately lucky that financially, even in the early days, I have not had to work. But neither have I ever felt I needed to earn in order to validate my existence.

I have, though, always kept busy with volunteer work, either in women's groups, the Cheshire Homes, school organisations or whatever took my fancy.

But in Thailand, although I found my volunteer work with Cheshire Homes rewarding I was beginning to think we might end up in Britain and I might have to work to help with the coffers. I have always been interested in buildings and interiors so started an interior design course, again by correspondence, from a college in England. It took me four years to finish, the part I enjoyed most being the history and essay writing.

It was timely as by the end of it we were living in Aberdeen, and while what I earnt did not greatly effect our bottom line it did make me leave the house on cold, har-ridden days when I might otherwise have buried myself in a duvet with a book. I worked with an interior designer, Mikhail Pietranek, whose showroom was perfectly placed between home and the kid's school, before branching out on my own.

I was an adequate designer with a good eye for colour and spatial design but I am not an artist and found it difficult getting my ideas across visually. Neither was I a good businesswoman. But it worked in well with the children's timetable and I met a lot of people whose paths I would probably not have crossed otherwise.

I much preferred the commercial projects to residential, finding them more challenging and with less involvement in people's personal affairs, likes and dislikes. I had to galvanise myself though, to go out for meetings in the dreekit weather of Scottish winter evenings, invariably the time residential meetings were called.

"Apple, do you not think this would work well in here?" a client asked, showing me a photo of dramatic swagged drapes clipped from *House and Garden* magazine.

"I think, Mrs McGregor, we have to look carefully at the proportions of the different rooms. That room," I said, pointing to the photograph, "Is more a salon and has very high ceilings. This room has a much lower ceiling and much smaller windows. I think perhaps we would swamp the area with fabric, which would make it feel even smaller, particularly if you decide to keep all this furniture in here."

"Ach, that's just wha' Jimmie said," Mrs McGregor admitted. My opinion of her taciturn husband inched up a little. "But aah want swags somewhere," she added.

"Perhaps we could really go to town in your bedroom," I suggested.

"Aye, we could at that," she agreed. "What have you to say to that, Jimmie?"

"Aye, lass, whatever," he responded, knocking his pipe against the fireplace.

A couple of local architects would use my services every now and then which is how I got involved with, first, a Chinese restaurant in Edinburgh which I never actually saw, and then a Japanese restaurant in Aberdeen which I saw far too much off.

Owned and run by canny Chinese brothers who wanted to be the first Japanese restaurant in town it was a bit of battle not mixing the two styles, and getting them to agree to ditch all things Chinese. We compromised on a couple of minor points.

"Mrs Apple, I no wan' change all plates. Too expensive. No one know dese not Japanese."

"A Japanese customer would Mr Hong," I said, sorting through dinner bowls with Chinese characters on them. Look," I pointed at the catering catalogue I'd ordered, "Here are some plain bowls that would work with whatever you do. You could get them in deep red, which would represent the rising sun on the Japanese flag and they'd look dramatic on your black dinner plates."

"Aah, okay. I like. You get."

John and I were offered limitless dining rights when they finally opened, unfortunately Japanese cuisine is probably my least favourite.

Over a few years I gathered a fantastic group of tradesmen whose broad Doric accents I finally learnt to understand, but who were happy to decipher my drawings, and whose ingenuity and skill managed to make me look good. John was also a great help, his civil engineering background coming in handy with my more fanciful ideas.

"Love, what exactly are you going to tie that wall to?" John asked one evening, peering over my shoulder at a drawing for a bathroom in a lovely old Victorian house.

"To that outside wall."

"You do know you'd have to get planning to permission to do that, and a certified builder."

"No I wouldn't if I'm not changing the shape of the outside wall."

"Yes you would, because you will have to build into the wall."

"Oh bugger, how can I get around that?"

"Sky hooks," he suggested helpfully.

I went back to the drawing board and modified my grandiose ideas.

I enjoyed the work, but I was thinking more and more about writing and signed up for another course. One I never finished as another move was on the cards.

"You know you won't be able to work in the States?" John said, as we discussed the pros and cons of a relocation to Houston.

"I know. That's okay. I can always find something to do and the kids will need some TLC to get settled," I replied.

I had not banked on living in the suburbs, which for all the right reasons we chose to do. Good schools, safe environment, close to John's office and the airport, a necessity as he was still travelling a great deal. But a wilderness for me. I was not a good suburban mom and found the general air of complacency difficult to swallow. I was more used to the hurly burly of life in less ordered places, not the sanitised version offered in suburbia.

My fortieth birthday opened doors I had not expected and got me back to a less antiseptic outlook. My present consisted of a year full of extras. First scuba diving lessons, then the diving gear, then the diving holiday in Cozumel and then, serendipitously, a job. I was by now legal to work, three years after our arrival in America, our papers finally having been accepted at the Green Card office. I filled in one day a week at a local dive store, with the hours inching up weekly. I never made much money, but we all had top of the range equipment. And then the doors shut for good and our satellite shop was absorbed back into the mother store in another part of town. But like most things it all worked out for the best. Edward and I were on our way home after soccer practice one evening and swung into another dive store, this one in Humble, about half and hour's drive from home.

"Hey Apple, whatcha doin' here?" Colin, an instructor I knew from the old place said, hugging me, "Do ya know Rebecca?"

"Hi yourself, and no I don't," I said, shaking Rebecca's hand.

"Apple used to work in the Kingwood shop," Colin explained.

"Right," she said offhandedly, and Edward and I continued our look around her place. As we arrived home the phone was ringing.

"Apple? It's Rebecca, from WWDiving. Would you be interested in working here?"

"What as?"

"We want to start a newsletter, Colin says you write," she said.

I worked part-time for two years, writing, selling, preparing destination presentations for the dive leaders to give customers before trips and generally having fun. It got me out of the 'burbs and mixing with people with slightly wider interests. Scuba diving is a great leveller. Your dive buddy might be a CEO one day, or a plumber the next, but we all look pretty awful underwater wearing a mask and regulator.

"You know you won't be able to work?" John said, a repeat of five years earlier.

"I know," I said again. "But something always seems to turn up. Let's go."

In preparation for life in Malabo, Equatorial Guinea, I spent a month studying harder than I had ever studied before. I went to a language college in Oxford, deposited myself with Jane, an old St Godric's friend and Kate's godmother, and relearnt first the rudiments of English grammar and then how to teach it as a foreign language. It was an intense month, but I managed to pass the practical and final exam, not without huge input from my hostess who helped me make props deep into the night.

"How did our clock do?" Jane asked one evening, unwinding her scarf and tossing it on the newel post as she came home from work.

"It was great," I answered. "The hairpin did the job with the hands. I even managed to work 'from dusk 'til dawn' into the conversation."

"Great! What have we got to make tonight?"

"I just need you to cut these travel brochures up. I'm looking for anything to do with cities."

"Fun. Let me get a cup of tea and I'll get started."

I have been so lucky with friends!

It was through a new friend life in EG took an upswing, not that I hadn't been busy trying to get our home built.

"Where are you?" John called, as he slammed the truck door, bent to pat Miss Meg and leapt up the stairs trying not to fall over her as she joined him on his dash.

"In the kitchen," I yelled back. "What are you doing home?"

"You've got an interview in half an hour."

"What for? I didn't know I was looking for a job."

"Well you are now. Dave Lindsay put your name forward as Commercial Attaché for the British Embassy in Yaoundé."

"Yaoundé? Am I missing something?"

"No, no. You'd report to the Ambassador there but work here."

"Darling, I don't like to state the obvious, but I have never done anything remotely like that before."

"I told him that but really it's a connecting people sort of job. And you do that all the time. Just talk to them. Might be fun."

"Who am I talking to?"

"Mark Lyall Grant. He's who I had breakfast with. Head of the Africa desk at the FCO. Dave was there too."

"Oh God. Okay. Can you print off my resumé while I get changed? Oh shit, I have no idea where my proper shoes are."

"What's it under?" John called from the computer.

"Resumé I should think," I said. "Feel free to tweak before you print."

"Where's the interview?" I shouted from the shower, thankful the power wasn't off and we had water pressure.

"The airport. That's why it's so sudden. They're leaving in a couple of hours."

"I hope it's air conditioned," I muttered to my spouse under my breath, "I'm going to sweat like a barbequed pig otherwise," thinking of the lined dress I could wear which would look vaguely professional.

We were still at the boxes stage of moving into our finally finished house. Fortunately my one pair of shoes, found in the second box opened, were not covered in mould but squeezing feet into them, once again used to the freedom of going bare, was not pleasant.

The interview was conducted in the VIP lounge of the Malabo International Airport. A breeze-block building with a tin roof and sporadic air-conditioning. The bar was surrounded by a bevy of colourful women, braided and beaded hair swinging in time to their chatter, obviously well connected and all waiting for a flight to Madrid, whiling away the time with their favourite tipple, Bayley's Irish Cream on ice. The deep armchairs in ubiquitous velour were filled with men in suits, all African, talking loudly into cell phones. It was dark and a little musty. The windows were shrouded in heavy damask-like curtains drooping where the hooks had given way, or moths had eaten fabric. The carpeted floor was sticky from spilt drinks.

John and Valerie, the Commercial Attaché from Douala in Cameroon, stood a discrete distance away as I was interviewed. Half an hour later I had the job subject to security clearances. A couple of months later Honorary Consul was added to my role and they sort of rolled into one.

The whole process reminded me of my first job in PNG, right place at the right time sort of thing. The biggest difference was in PNG I was paid and in EG I wasn't. The annual stipend was negligible, but it was fun and a job that needed doing. I wondered at the irony of Guinea being part of the name of both countries, it meaning 'black man'.

My new boss, the British Ambassador based in Cameroon, also covered Chad, Gabon and the Central African Republic as well as EG. He relied on a squad of Hon Cons to keep him informed of goings on in each of the countries. On his next visit to the country he decided to introduce me to the President, the official seal on his 'woman in EG'.

"What time do the government offices close?" the Ambassador asked, as we drank yet another cup of tea on the terrace waiting for the command call from the President's office, a good twenty-four hours after his arrival on the island.

"Officially at four, but really whenever a minister feels like it," I replied. The wait was making me nervous. I had never met a president before, and I was worried about my dodgy Spanish and long-forgotten French.

"Well it's almost four now. It's not going to happen today," he said removing his shoes and tie, undoing his cufflinks and rolling up his sleeves.

His cell phone rang and with a resigned nod he redressed, I retrieved my tight shoes from under the sofa and we scurried down to the Presidential Palace.

After being hustled through the police cordon at the end of the Plaza de Presidencia and through a side door by the grand staircase, we were deposited in an anteroom. I had plenty of time to examine my surroundings over the next few hours as I shivered in the frigid air conditioning ricocheting around the room stuffed full of chintz covered sofas, and a low coffee table with no coffee. At one stage I was so cold I opened the door to the late afternoon torpor only to be pushed back in by the man standing guard outside. Not sure we wouldn't be recorded, our conversation was desultory and quiet.

Finally, one of the Lebanese bodyguards summoned us, they being considered more trustworthy and less likely to turn on their employer. Odd really, as it was Lebanese mercenaries who executed the former president, uncle of the present incumbent.

"You give me," he said, seizing my handbag as I walked along the corridor, two paces behind the Ambassador. The contents would have sorely disappointed him, a mobile phone, lipstick, a Chinese fan and a silver toothpick I had every confidence could be used as a weapon should it be necessary.

The doors to the presidential chamber were flung open and lights burst in our face. The TV station, owned by the

President, was there to record the first official meeting with the new British Ambassador. The room, lavishly decorated, gave no indication we were in Africa, rather like the anteroom we had spent so much time in.

"*Su excellencio,*" I said, as we shook hands. I bowed my head slightly, having made up my mind I would not curtsey as I was introduced as *La Senora Consul Honoraria.*

The meeting, an amicable affair largely ignoring me, gave me ample time to study the country's leader. Purported to be about sixty-three, and to have fought prostate cancer, though naturally not in his own country, he was a dapper man. He smiled a lot and spoke very, very quietly. He closed his eyes often and I couldn't be sure whether it helped him think or if he was catching a few zzz's, as the Minister for Foreign Affairs took over the speaking. Sometimes in English for my benefit.

President Obiang Nguema Mbasoga and his cohorts had an exemplary record of agreeing to suggestions made, whether by the World Bank, an oil company or a foreign diplomat, and then doing exactly as he pleased. His record for human rights abuses was not stellar, though not as bad as his predecessor. It was an interesting experience repeated four or five times during my time in EG. Not all the meetings were as benign.

As we left the premises half an hour after the meeting actually started, and about two hours after our arrival at the palace, we were again accosted by TV lights and a local journalist asking the Ambassador for his impression of his President.

I stepped out of the lens' focus and listened to the Ambassador's diplomatic response.

On our return to the house our cold tea was discarded and the wine opened. John returned from work to find his wife and her new boss happily ensconced on the terrace enjoyed sundowners and olives and now casually dressed in shorts and tee-shirts.

"Madam Apple?" Stephen, our earnest guard, asked not long after I took on the role of Hon Con.

"Yes Stephen, what's up?"

"You work for British Government?"

"Yes, I suppose I do."

"Is good. We fly flag?"

"No. It's better for the master if we don't. Because his company is American."

"Okay. But still better to fly flag. Massa Jim does," he remarked, looking across the weeds separating our two houses on the dirt lane to the US Chargé d'Affaires home and office.

Stephen took great pride in both John's and my jobs and took it upon himself to become a fiercesome gatekeeper.

"Hi Stephen," I called, stamping mud off my feet as I came through the small side gate. "Hello Miss Meg," I bent to scratch behind her ears.

"Oh Madam, man come see you."

"Who was it?"

"Black man. I tell him go away."

"Which black man?" I asked, amused that in a town full of black men I was expected to know this particular one.

"Bad man, very black, from town."

"Stephen you mustn't do that," I said. "Maybe he needed help."

"No. He want visa. I tell him go Yaoundé."

Stephen was quite right. I could not issue visas, only applications, but his customer care attitude could have done with a bit of gentling.

In between my official duties I taught English at a school in

N'bili *barrio*, a warren of lean-to huts along dusty paths with narrow drains. Dusty that is, until rain fell when they turned into a churning quagmire of all things unpleasant.

"There is no moaney," the Spanish nun warned.

"That's okay," I replied.

"Ju can teech two class?"

"Sure," I said. "But not more than twelve in a class. Okay?"

"Si, si," she replied.

On the given day a couple of weeks later I walked in, laden down with papers I had photocopied for two classes. I was a little nervous, both at finding the school amongst the maze, and about walking through the *barrio* and past the ramshackle bars with youths loafing around them.

"Buenas dias senora," the smiling nun said, taking my hand and drawing me to the classroom.

I should know better. Never trust a smiling nun who agrees with everything you say. My first class held twenty-eight men and women ranging in age from 16 to 50 with vastly different levels of English. The nun shrugged at my gasp. The next class, which ran immediately after, was slightly easier with only twenty-two who were considered advanced English speakers. It was challenging, but once the students got used to me leaping on a table to demonstrate a preposition, or tossing a beanbag at them to answer a question, it was fun.

"*Senora,* ju titch diffren'," said one young man.

"I know Juan, but you remember my lessons don't you?"

Africans have a wonderful ear for language and many speak many tongues, from their own tribal language to French, English, German, and in EG, Spanish. But translating the spoken word to paper was altogether another challenge.

I was amazed as I made my way out between the shacks

after my first afternoon, past infants being bathed in buckets with water taken from the trickle in the ditch, to be greeted by many with *hola maestra, buenas tardes professora,* or *hey manzana* by some of the cheekier boys, thinking themselves very clever translating 'Apple'. Word travelled fast in *barrio*.

The only other time I was a little anxious about walking there was after an attempted coup. John had suggested I miss class, but I didn't want to let anyone down, even though the market was still closed and the streets were tense with police and the military snatching people with impunity, but on the whole not Europeans.

I nearly burst into tears as I approached the entrance, through a rubbish heap and around the broken wire fence. There were three of 'my boys' waiting to escort me in.

"Good arpernoon Teacher," they unisoned, grinning. "We wark wid you today."

How could I ever feel threatened after such kindness?

It reminded me that sometimes in our foreign travels we are the ones who put up roadblocks by our own insecurities. By our standards and fears of groups of people. I have felt far more intimidated by a clutch of yobos on a London street wearing hoodies, than I ever have in an African or Asian nation, or even in PNG.

Even comments like, "*Hola blanca,* you lub me huh?" received while walking through the market were made in jest and could be easily deflected. My answer would often be along the lines of, "Hey black man, no I don't. Do you have tomatoes for me today?" Laughter would erupt and we would go about our business.

Walking through the market one day with Edward, after he had been working in the company yard all through the summer holidays of his penultimate year at Blundells, was an experience never forgotten.

"Hey Edvard, you buy me drink?"

"*Hola* my friend, you wan nailz dis arpernoon? You buy huh?"

"*Buenas tardes senor*, yu no see me long time. Where you be?"

He too was completely at ease, and laughed and joked his way through the alleyways, though we always avoided the meat line. Skinned monkeys, their glazed, unseeing eyes staring at me from the poles they hung on, still turned my stomach and brought me to tears. I wasn't fond of the rats either, big and hairy, lying dead on the counters ready for someone's cooking pot.

Markets are always a good indicator of the civilian population's mood. True to form the Malabo market would close in a heartbeat the moment whispers of unrest flitted through the streets. It was incredible how quickly hundreds of people could melt into the background at the first sign of trouble. Many of the stallholders were Ghanaian, Nigerian and Cameronian and they were invariably the ones picked up in swoops by the security forces, accused of fomenting dissent.

Part of my role as Honorary Consul was to register as many British citizens as I could persuade to go through the painless process. Most were employed in the oilfield and felt secure in their company's promise to care for them. They were right, but it is still a good policy to register with the representative from one's passport country.

Talking freely about local politics and personalities in and around Malabo was best done in the privacy of one's home. John became used to arriving home in the evening and seeing another strange man, a visiting businessman or journalist, on our terrace drinking his beer, as we chatted about the country.

"Have you ever been to EG before?" I asked.

"No, but all these African countries are similar. I've spent the better part of twenty-five years in and around West Africa," said one old Africa hand.

"I think you will find this one isn't," I said, astounded at the arrogance. There might be similarities but each country, each tribe, has distinct differences. "For a start it's Spanish speaking."

And so the conversation would continue. Often at the end of their trip they would return to our terrace and debrief me. Occasionally someone would have the grace to say, "You were right, it is different here."

"Hello, Apple Gidley," I answered the phone one Sunday afternoon, turning the sound down on the cricket test match.

"*Hola Señora Jidlee*, I am friend of friend son. He trouble. He tell me call ju."

"Okay, who is it? And what is your name?"

"My name Angelica. It Mark," the woman replied. "Polis have 'im."

"Where? What did he do?"

"De gaol. He drink an' hit polisman. *Si*, an' he 'ave ganja."

"Oh for God's sake," I said, forgetting the Consular manual stated quite clearly, Do Not Judge, and turning the cricket off asked, "Is he okay?"

"*Si Señora, lo se.*"

"When did they arrest him?"

"Night time. I fine 'im *ahora*."

"Are you still at the police station?

"*Si*," Angelica replied.

"Tell him I'll be there in a hour. Tell him not to speak to anyone. Okay?"

"*Si*, I shou' him tru bars. *Gracias Señora.*"

"*De nada,*" I said, knowing my Sunday was over.

Mark was in the country under the auspices of his father and though in his twenties and working for a different company, the government thinking could easily be to deport them both. Something I knew his father would be very upset about, having spent the previous twelve months trying to get a contract signed for a British construction company.

I had been to the police station and holding cells a few times already, but this was my first attempt at a gaol break. John was in Gabon and I was scared. It took half an hour to walk down and by the time I got there the water I was carrying for Mark was warm and the loo roll soggy, neither commodity being available to those on the wrong side of the bars.

"*Hola, buenas tardes Señor,*" I said to the uniformed man, idly flicking flies behind a chipped desk in the stuffy anteroom. The fan rotated once every minute. The seats lining the walls were filled with men and women all waiting for something.

I had noticed Africans often seem to be waiting. Sitting perfectly still. Sometimes for no discernible event, like a bus or a shop to open, just waiting. They don't get irritated. They just wait. I have never been able to emulate the skill.

"*Buenas tardes Señora,*" he grunted, as I explained who I was and handed over my card with the wonderful crest of Her Majesty's Government embossed on the top. He looked at it both ways, up and down, and grunted again as Angelica hustled into the room, offering to interpret for me. We joined the waiting ranks until about an hour later we were waved into the office. The blast of cool air was bliss.

The officer behind the pockmarked desk remained seated, but at least smiled as he indicated we should sit. In front of him were an open envelope, ganja spilling out, a wooden axe handle and a pad filled with scrawled writing.

The door opened again and Mark was pushed in, hands still cuffed. His eyes were bloodshot and bleary. His face bruised and his shirt and trousers bloodied. His demeanour chastened.

"Are you okay? Have you been hit since you've been here?" I asked, trying not to look shocked. Fifteen hours in a police lock up, an open courtyard with a narrow, covered walkway around it, with no water or food and a pail for lavatorial needs, does not lend itself to sartorial elegance. "Don't let on you know me," I added in a rush, in case the policeman spoke a little English.

"No, I'm okay. Got a headache though."

"Please uncuff him," I asked the jailer through Angelica. "Drink this," I said to Mark, handing him the tepid water, "You're probably dehydrated."

For the next few hours the conversation, sometimes in my poor Spanish and sometimes in English and translated by Angelica, went back and forth. There was no denying the issue. If a Guineano man had been drunk and disorderly in London, laid into a policeman with an axe handle and then been found to have a pocketful of marijuana he would certainly have been arrested.

The officer was at least pleasant, not the more usual bully-type, and he finally agreed to release Mark under my cognisance as long as we returned in the morning to meet with the Chief of Police, a very different character. We were shown out and as the officer shook hands with Angelica and I, he and I smilingly agreed Mark was a foolish young man and we were both glad he was not our son.

Outside I forgot the consular manual.

"What the fuck were you playing at?"

"I dunno. Drank too much," Mark mumbled.

"Drinking too much in London is one thing, but here quite another," I said. "And then you whack a cop and then they find ganja. You are unbelievable."

"I'm sorry Apple."

"Yeah, I know. It's okay. I'm sorry I spoke like that. Did anyone hit you?" I asked again, thinking *I am not the person for this job*.

"Only the cop I hit. But they poked me with a baton and threw me against the wall in here. I hurt my shoulder."

"Do you want to see a medic?" I asked.

"No, I just want to sleep."

"Okay, but listen to me Mark. You have got to behave here. Quite apart from not wanting to end up in gaol, you've got to think of your dad. He's worked so hard to get that contract signed. Don't blow it for him."

"Yeah, I know." He shuffled his feet like a four-year-old caught peeing on the roses.

"Okay, go home get some sleep. First though, phone your dad and tell him you might have to pay a fine to stay out of gaol and you'll need to have funds available. When's he due back?"

"Dunno."

"Okay, I'll meet you here tomorrow morning. Nine sharp. Be shaved, dressed properly – no shorts – and with your shoes cleaned."

"Alright. Thanks Apple. I'm sorry," he muttered.

"That's okay. We'll get it sorted tomorrow. No drinking tonight though."

We went our separate ways. Angelica and Mark to the hotel he was living in and me back up the hill. I realised as I started walking that my hands were shaking. Sitting on my terrace later with a glass of wine I thought of what I'd said to Mark..

Many of these kids we traipse around the world do live with an added burden. The fear of disappointing our parents is, I think, part of the normal growing up process but when the threat of a visa being rescinded, with the added possibility of a parent losing a job for a teenager's misdemeanour hangs over them, the onus is greater.

The next morning we met at the gates and spent six hours in a grander room being castigated by Carlos, the Chief of Police. Painstakingly the stenographer typed Mark's confession and promise on a manual Olivetti typewriter, both being translated on the fly by Angelica.

Mark promised to behave on the understanding that if he didn't, he would be heavily fined and deported immediately. We eventually left, exhausted, but without a fine being levied, the Chief having agreed that in the interests of both our country's mutual respect for each other it would be a diplomatic gesture, on this sole occasion.

My first gaol break had been successful, but more importantly I had a friendly man on the inside. Not the Chief, but the helpful man from the previous day.

It was not a full-time job but a twenty-four hour one, and I learnt to dread calls at odd times. Any incident involving cameras was bad news and no matter how much I suggested people were circumspect with their snapping, some were still arrested. The trick was to get to the police station before they were processed into the holding cell – the open-air courtyard behind bars containing both men and women. The paperwork was less onerous and did not always need to involve the Chief of Police, a villainous and corrupt man.

The March 2004 attempted *coup* involving Simon Mann and Nick du Toit raised tensions and had repercussions for many months. The plan, we later learned, was to instigate a *coups d'etat* deposing Obiang and install the exiled opposition leader, Severo Moto, who was purported to be *en route* from Spain. .

Contrary to various reports and books written about the incident, the expatriate community was not on lock-down at the start of it. Many of us were on an oil company's compound at a farewell party, some of us performing in a skit celebrating a couple's departure. A busload from the Punta Europa camp were delayed a short while which meant the skit had to be performed a second time, not quite as successfully due to the increased number of drinks consumed by the cast.

Word of unrest filtered through and sobered the party when phones starting beeping telling of arrests on the streets of company employees, predominantly African rather than European. It was decided to end the celebrations and get to our respective homes before things escalated, though we didn't know what the 'things' were at that stage.

The morning brought rumblings of a *coup* and that the market was closed, and there was a heavy military and police presence. Rumours of arrests continued.

Another started circulating about the arrest in Harare, Zimbabwe, of Simon Mann, an Englishman, caught attempting to load weapons onto a plane bound for Malabo and filled with mercenaries from South Africa, many of whom had worked for Mann on other nefarious contracts.

An email appeared on my screen from the Foreign Office in London, asking me to forward an attached press release to the relevant media, denying any involvement from Britain. I replied I would try, but explained the President owned all the media. As anticipated, I was not successful.

Other African nationals took the brunt of the fall out. Our Cameroonian neighbours being some of them. It was a large house enclosed by a high wall and was home to a number of 'ladies of the night'. They did not ply their wares on the premises but lived there with their children and various others.

"John, come here," I called the next morning, as I watched the scene unfold from behind the curtain of our bedroom window, having heard screaming from the compound.

A truck laden with pistol-wielding policemen stormed in, corralling all those at home in the yard. Faces were pistol-whipped, arms twisted and women thrown around. One hysterical woman, her baby on her hip, was slapped and pushed to the wall. Most were loaded onto the truck and driven away. Money exchanged hands and some were left behind. It was noisy, violent and frightening, and there was nothing we could do.

"Good morning Apple," the crisp voice of the Ambassador clipped across the line from Cameroon.

"Good morning sir, you're back. Did you have a good trip?" I asked, knowing he had been in London for meetings.

"They started out alright and then this upset in EG rather changed the focus. I have been summoned by President Obiang. He is sending his plane for me tomorrow morning, due to arrive in Malabo at nine I'm told. Not a good sign."

"Okay, I'll meet you and we can talk here."

"No, I'm afraid not. I have been told an official car will meet the plane and then we will swing by and collect you. Can you be ready anytime after nine."

"Yes of course, can you remember how to get to us?"

"The gentleman making the arrangements knows exactly where you live. We might be in for a little roasting. Right, until tomorrow."

I put down the phone and wondered at my naiveté in assuming I was not watched and that John and I had managed to keep our different jobs separate in the minds of the government.

Feet squeezed once more into confining shoes, I waited next morning on the terrace, a part of me rather hoping the government car would get stuck in the mudbath outside our gates after the night's torrential downfall. I couldn't even have a coffee as I didn't want to be searching for a loo at the Palace.

The escort arrived just before eleven. Stephen looked suspiciously at the car's darkened windows but allowed me out the gate.

"I tell massa what time you leave," he comforted me.

"Where are we going?" I asked the men in the front seat, as we turned right towards N'bili where I taught, instead of into town towards the Palace. The Ambassador glanced my way.

"Panapa," we were told.

"Porqué?" I asked why.

"Panapa," the slim young man in a black suit repeated.

The gates to the Panapa Conference Centre were swung open as we approached, and shut immediately we were through. We wove our way along roads sided by American-style houses, mostly empty, being reserved for visiting dignatories or other special guests. Pulling up outside a bungalow with high walls, we were met by an armed man, also in a suit, who ushered us through the front door, heavy with locks, with a wave of his AK47.

"Sit. You wait 'ere," the man from the car said as he left, locking the front door behind him."

I stood and went to the window in time to see him give a cigarette to our guard, climb into the car and be driven away.

"What now?" I asked the Ambassador, uncomfortable at being locked in.

"We wait," he said.

"Has this ever happened to you before?"

"No, I can't say it has. But we'll be okay."

"I know, I just don't like it."

"They didn't take our phones," he commented.

We waited. And then we waited some more. The décor was similar to the anteroom at the Palace, though velour replaced chintz and the bright sunny day was allowed no entry through the heavy curtains. Four and half hours later, after a cup of instant coffee with condensed milk begged from the maid in the kitchen, we were collected by the same young man. He again gave a cigarette to the rifle-wielding guard.

As we pulled away from the kerb another car pulled in behind us. As we left the Panapa compound we fell in behind a waiting car at the entrance and in convoy were driven to the Palace. This time my bag, still containing the silver cocktail stick, was taken away before we were put in the anteroom.

Another hour passed before finally being herded to meet the President. There were no cameras this time. Just the Foreign Minister, and the Minister of Labour, a man with an unsavoury reputation. I had met the latter only once, when trying to release an Englishman after he'd been detained, stripped at the army barracks and finally taken to the police station, all for taking photos near a government installation. He had actually been taking photos of Mount Pico and children playing soccer in a clearing next to sword-edged *lalang* grass.

The meeting with the President, still conducted in a whisper, was not as convivial as previous ones. We were shown maps found on one of the *coup* suspects purporting to prove suspicious activities planned for, in and around Malabo. The Ambassador was repeatedly asked about the British connection, men in London alleged to be the financiers of the operation. The Minister of Labour hinted at repercussions for British firms already operating in the country and lack of contract signatures for those hoping to start.

Voices were never raised, but the good cop, bad cop routine was in evidence. Every time something vaguely threatening was said, the President sat back and closed his eyes. The half hour session felt much longer, and I was delighted to get out of the building and back to our terrace where we could at last talk freely.

John was already home, waiting with the whisky and the wine, having been phoned by a couple of people who had seen us in the back of the car during our whizzed convoy from Panapa to the Palace.

Those in the country accused of the *coup* attempt, South Africans, Guineanos and Azerbaijanis, were eventually brought to trial, which in turn brought a great many journalists in, visas being issued to circumvent accusations of foul play by the international community, Human Rights Watch and Amnesty International. There were still rumblings of British involvement, both through Simon Mann and his backers, Eli Calil and Mark Thatcher amongst others, but they were not on trial in EG at the time.

"Have you got your press passes?" I asked one journalist from a British broadsheet and his photographer, who joined me for coffee on the terrace.

"Yup, got them earlier this morning."

"All of them? Still and videography?"

"Don't need them when we have a press pass?"

"Yes you do," I argued. "And you will need a separate pass if you leave Malabo. You get that from the Protocol Office as well."

My cell phone rang as I played a winning hand at cards later that afternoon.

"Er, Apple? Hi. It's Frank. Er, from this morning."

"Oh, hi."

"We've got a bit of a situation here," he said.

"Where is here?" I asked with dread.

"Luba," he replied. "We've been arrested. And so has our interpreter."

"Frank, please tell me you went to Protocol?" My heart sank further knowing trying to get them released from the police in the town further down the island, where a deepwater harbour was being readied for the oil industry, was not going to be easy.

"Er, no. It was sort of spur of the moment."

"Okay," I said, the Consular manual floating in front of my eyes. "What happened? Are you using your own phone?"

"Yes, they've taken all the cameras but left my cell. They look pissed off."

"Okay, be quick then, they might still take it."

It transpired that on a whim they'd decided to dig around for a story on the illegal, but unenforced, bushmeat trade and knew, because I'd told them, about seeing skinned monkeys and pangolin for sale on the side of the road to Luba. All was well until they reached the township, and had taken a photo of a woman skinning a goat and then roasting it over a fire beside the canal. In itself an innocent action, but she had taken umbrage and when they continued shooting from a distance had called her cousin, the cop.

"What should we do?" Frank asked.

"I have to make a couple of calls here. Don't say or sign anything. Phone me back in fifteen minutes, or when you can," I said.

"Shit," I said to my card partners. "Sorry, got to go."

I didn't have any contacts in Luba, and the Chief of Police in Malabo did not particularly like me after various meetings which had not proved financially satisfactory to him, so I decided to call the Minister of Justice, with whom I had a slight rapport. He also spoke excellent English and had just become engaged to a British broadcast journalist.

"Your Excellency," I said, grateful he had even taken my call, and outlined the situation. "Do you think, sir, you could arrange to have the journalists sent back to Malabo where it will be easier for us all to sort out this misunderstanding?" I finished.

He promised to call back in fifteen minutes. I regret to say I doubted him. But ten minutes later he called to say they would be driven back and I was to meet them at the Police Station. "I will attempt to stop by later, but I have an important meeting this evening," he added.

As I thanked the minister profusely I hoped his meeting wasn't with the President, but grateful I didn't have to go to Luba. It was way out of my comfort zone as far as gaol breaking was concerned.

"Hello, Frank?" I said as my phone rang.

"Yes. What's happening? People are getting unhappy here. There's been some shouting."

"Stay calm and polite. You're going to be driven back here. Don't use your phone for anything else and call me when you pass the Panapa Conference Centre on the way into Malabo.

It's on the left hand side and has a huge statue in front of it. I'll meet you at the station."

John dropped me off at the police station at about ten thirty, unhappy about leaving me there alone at night.

"I'll be fine. I'll call if it gets ugly," I promised his worried face.

The little anteroom was full and my request to see the journalists was denied. I was told to sit on the bench. I asked again, this time loudly, hoping they would hear me from behind the door. It was a silly mistake as it only inflamed the situation and the man at the desk who before had merely been surly, became angry.

Through the slur of the drunken Spanish of the policemen and guards I began to understand what the problem was. Who was going to pay for the time spent escorting the prisoners from Luba to Malabo? Who was going to pay for their supper? How were they going to get back to Luba that night? I couldn't quite understand why two unarmed journalists required three cars to escort them, but I didn't have the words to ask. It was an angry room and I was the only woman in it and decided submission was the best tack to take. I sat, slouched, on the bench looking at the floor. Slowly everyone quietened.

A dishevelled civilian was shoved in front of me by two policemen, he introduced himself as Cristophe, the newsmen's interpreter, though in his real world he was the receptionist at the hotel at which they were staying.

"*Señora* you wan' I help?"

"Yes please," I answered, my Spanish still not good enough to decipher fast angry shouting. "Have they released you?"

"I ting so. Dey wan' me in room wid inglismen."

With Cris's help I asked the least angry-looking man to please let me give the journalists some water. As it appeared we were getting somewhere, another uniformed man charged in screaming, yanked Cris to his feet and arrested him again.

I tried to explain he was my official interpreter, which stretched the truth a little, and I needed him, which certainly didn't. It made no difference. Cris, now very frightened rather than just uneasy, was stripped of his belt which was used to tie his hands behind his back and he was frog-marched out, crying and shouting. It was horrible.

Businessmen, lawyers, journalists came into the country and, needing drivers and translators, would offer what appeared to the poorly paid Equato-Guinean, huge amounts of cash for their help. If trouble arose the visitor would leave on the next flight out and the poor sod they'd employed for a day or a week was left, often to face consequences not of their making. It might not be an immediate arrest, but their profile would be raised in the eyes of the authorities, and they and their family would often be detained on some pretext. And now I had joined that group of people by putting a man, trying to earn a little extra, in danger.

The door to the inner chamber was suddenly wrenched open by a soldier wanting to ask the guard something, and much to his annoyance I pushed in too, using the bottles of water as my excuse. The man guarding them, behind yet another scratched desk in the little cubby-hole of a room which was becoming familiar to me, allowed me to stay.

"Hello, Apple Gidley," I said seconds later, as my cell phone rang. The irritation on the gaoler's face did not bode well.

"Hi, Apple," said the worried man from the international desk of the newspaper, safe in his office in London. "We were just wondering if there was any news?"

"I'm with them now. I'll call as soon as we're out. Please don't call me again – it's not helping," I said and hung up, apologising to the guard.

The lines had been hot all afternoon between the Foreign Office, the newspaper, the Embassy in Yaoundé and me. I made a show of turning my phone off, hoping to ease the tension. Speaking was not allowed, but at least I was with them and very grateful for the working air-conditioner. I concentrated on the peeling paint and tried to think of words I would need and then the door opened.

"*Buenas tardes, Señora Consul,*" said the Minister, who I hardly recognised in his casual jeans, shirt and sandals, very different to the expensive suits and spit 'n' polish shoes of his normal attire. "It is good to see you again. You know *Señor* Carlos I understand."

"Good evening, Your Excellency," I said having leapt to my feet, shaking his outstretched hand. "Thank you so much for helping in this difficult situation." I shook the Chief of Police's hand but did not speak. He was an awkward man to gauge and I wasn't sure where he was in the game just yet. I soon learned.

"*Señora Consul,* you not call me eh?" he asked. "We are friends, yes? I have helped before." He was very angry. Angry the journalists had gone to Luba without informing Protocol. Angry they'd taken photos. Angry they'd been arrested. Angry I had gone way over his head to the Minister. Plain angry.

"I am very sorry, sir," I lied. "I did not know you had jurisdiction in Luba," I lied again.

"I control everywhere," he told me with an oily smile.

I knew that. He was on the dark side of shady and was known to have a violent temper and a fondness for attaching car batteries to nipples, and other sensitive areas.

He nodded and I introduced the journalist and photographer to both men, and spoke for them, apologising profusely for the 'misunderstandings' that had taken place. I added it was most important we resolve the matter promptly, so no one else was involved.

"Gentlemen, I hope this small inconvenience will not make you think badly of my country," said the Minister, quiet until then.

"No, not at all Your Excellency," the journalists chorused, having taken my lead in his title.

"I have recently become engaged to a British woman. A journalist also. Did you know that?' he asked them.

"Yes Your Excellency, Mrs Gidley told us."

"You are free to go. Please remember to inform Protocol of your movements. For your own protection, you understand." The Minister smiled as he shook hands again and ushered them past the still glowering *Señor* Carlos.

"Er, Your Excellency, what about my cameras?" asked the photo-journalist.

"You may take them. Please get a permit for them. Mrs Gidley?" he continued, putting a hand on my shoulder and smiling, "I would be most grateful if you could help with visas so my children may attend my wedding in London next month."

"I will certainly mention it to the Ambassador, Your Excellency," I said. "Oh, Sir? The interpreter working for these gentlemen, and who helped me, has been also detained. I would be so pleased if he could be released. He was only trying to assist foreigners to his country."

"He, too, can now go," the Minister said, waving a hand at Carlos.

The Consular manual states only British nationals may be assisted, but in this case there was a moral obligation. I was told later, in the politest possible terms, not to interfere again between foreign nationals.

With more handshakes the Minister and Carlos left the room with us close behind. The Minister went out to his Mercedes and Carlos to the holding yard. As I was hustling my charges, now clutching cameras, and Cris to the gates while phoning John to come and get us, a God-awful noise erupted behind the bars. We turned. Two of the prison warders, shirtless with arms outstretched against the rails, were being lashed with Cris's belt, buckle meeting flesh. Their screams were terrible. Instinctively the camera lens was pointed. Instinctively I pushed the men out the gates and along the road. We would not have been so fortunate getting out of the building a second time for taking photos where photos should not be taken.

"*Señora* Apple," Cris said. "Tank ju."

"Cris, it was our fault you were arrested."

"*Señora*, I wan' my belt," he said, turning back to the ugly building.

"These kind men will buy you a new belt, Cris," I promised, grabbing his arm and looking at the journalists. They nodded.

John drove up and with huge relief I climbed in the vehicle. After delivering the three men back to their hotel, we went home and had a drink that wasn't coffee. I realised I was shaking again.

Finding ourselves back in Houston six months later I was again lucky and fell into the role of helping oil executives and their wives, mainly American, prepare for a transfer to West Africa. It was in a way a continuation of my position in EG, talking to people, though I left some of the less pleasant aspects of the country out of my presentations. This was a job I was paid for.

My attitude towards a career probably started during my conversations with Dad over the dinner table in PNG. I was serious about wanting to explore social work as an option but was too young and easily swayed to follow it, in retrospect I obviously didn't have a passion for it. I think I would probably have been too emotional, certainly in my younger days.

I have though been inordinately lucky. Jobs, whether voluntary or paid, have just happened. I also think I had an advantage in that I did not have a career path planned. I had no visions of where I saw myself in five, ten or even twenty years. I wasn't even prepared to commit two years to Canberra when offered a position with the Australian diplomatic service after PNG. I was only sure I did not want a sedentary life. I certainly did not envisage marrying young, though I knew I wanted children at some stage.

Not having gone to university played a part in my not having a hard and fast plan for keeping myself afloat. I think it far harder if that career plan, studied and worked so hard for, is tilted or turned upside down by the person you inadvertently fall in love with, and who is offered a chance to travel and live an expatriate life, whether for one posting or multiple. It takes a lot of courage to change your own goals, to submit if you like, to your partner's career, even if it is well reimbursed. I admire tremendously the men and women who do leave behind burgeoning careers and follow their spouses around the world, and who have recreated themselves again, and sometimes again.

I am, I think, too lazy to be an entrepreneur. I toyed with the idea of shipping containers stuffed to the gunnels back to England from Thailand. Laurence, John's old friend and former boss in the landscaping business and who is an entrepreneur, was keen for us to go into exporting/importing Thai artefacts and I liked the idea of sourcing them, but the thought of dealing constantly with customs and officialdom in all its forms did not appeal.

I am a hard worker for causes I believe in, and little irritates me more, and quite a lot of things do irritate me, than people who sign up to volunteer and then enjoy the benefits with none of the graft. I am well aware volunteering is by it's very nature a tenuous venture, and things do crop up that can effect one's commitment, in which case bow out instead of letting the work fall to others, too often the same commited people who do most of the work anyway.

I am currently on the Advisory Board of the University Museum at Texas Southern University in Houston. A position I was asked to fill after serving on their Volunteer Circle for three years. It is a constant battle to get the recognition and funding from the State and private enterprises the Museum deserves, through the exhibitions presented and the educational and cultural opportunity given to students who may never before have been in an art gallery or museum. Funding for the arts is sadly overlooked in many places, but I firmly believe a balanced approach to education is far more productive than a sole focus on one aspect, whether it be sport, the sciences or indeed the arts.

To those who have subjugated their own dreams and are discontent, not having found a worthwhile way to fill their time, whether through volunteering, sport, or some other occupation, I would say it was a decision they made. Until they can accept it fully and embrace the change in their life, they will continue to be unhappy. And more importantly will almost certainly colour their children's attitude to a global life. That to me seems a terrible waste of an amazing opportunity.

Sometimes my radar is too attuned to other cultures to the detriment of my friends. I was reminded of this one afternoon when I was happily rootling around with the herbs on my Houston terrace. Re-potting in an attempt to defeat the five raccoons who descended nightly to dance amongst the mint, cilantro and parsley before sipping from the water well John had rather cleverly made, and then supping on the basil. My thinking was if the basil were tucked between the various mints, which they did not appear to like, the masked bandits might leave me enough basil for my pesto.

As my mind was pleasantly wandering to other gardens planted around the world and wondering what they now looked like, I was reminded of an unforgivable thought, or rather lack of.

Three friends of mine, one English and two American, and I meet occasionally for a quiet drink in an out-of-the-way coffee shop that happens to serve a delicious grapefruity sauvignon blanc at four in the afternoon. We meet about once every six weeks so can hardly be called seasoned partiers, but during the course of the last couple of years have got to know one another well, I thought.

"I've just had my first class on xeriscape gardening," commented Sandy, as we poured the wine.

"How was it? I thought you'd finished your garden," Kathleen said.

"I have, but I wanted to know more."

"I did a gardening course," Nicola mentioned.

"I didn't know that," I said. "When?"

"I finished just before we came here. Eighteen months, through the Royal Horticultural Society, and a year's internship with Andrew Wilson."

"Who's he?" Sandy asked.

"A well-known society gardener in England," Nicola answered. "I'd picked up business cards from the printers in the afternoon, and James came home that evening and said he'd been offered a position in Houston."

My dereliction, the one I had been ruminating on as I attempted to thwart the racoons, was that I had never enquired about her life before Texas apart from the usual, "Where were you last?" type of query expatriates tend to make, particularly on learning the spouse is employed by an oil company.

It is a common oversight, but one I thought I would never be party to. Too many times I have been judged a 'trailing spouse' with the same ambitions as Milne's bear, the one with very little brain and who is bothered by long words, concerned only about the pot of honey. But I did fall into that trap and I was ashamed.

Nicola, like many expatriate spouses, had upped sticks, packed up home, said goodbye to her children, who had decided to stay in Britain at boarding school, and relocated across an ocean to support her husband's career.

She had arrived, kick started the new-*arrivée* mode many pack in their carry-on bag along with a spare pair of knickers and a toothbrush, and thrown herself into life without her children in her new surroundings. She did not mention the fledgling career she had been carving out for herself in Surrey. She did not mention the profound disappointment that all her learning about landscaping, plant selection and design had to be put on hold, an English garden being different to the more arid-style of gardening required for the humid heat of Houston, with the threat of the occasional frost and snowfall.

And I hadn't even asked what her life was about before Houston. I had assumed because she seemed pleased to be here, because she threw herself into making a new home in Houston that her story was an open book.

Nicola might not want to put all her energies into her perfect garden to see only the first fruits of her labour before being relocated to another part of the world. I can understand that, never having seen any of my gardens come into full flower, even if here I do have mint and basil, raccoons notwithstanding, but I'm determined to never again forget to dig deeper.

Alan Paul, author of *Big in China*, made a comment at the 2011 Families in Global Transition conference encapsulating the lives of many accompanying spouses. "Expatriation was a way to reinvent myself," he said. It is so true of both men and women who have followed a spouse or lover to a foreign country.

Thinking about Alan's comment later, as I slathered on anti-wrinkle cream under the unforgiving glare of a hotel bathroom light, I thought of me.

My own reinventions bounced back from the mirror, wrinkles and all, and I realised that is what had unwittingly happened. I lack the imagination to be one of life's entrepreneurs but have still managed to do a variety of things. I do know I have often been grateful to my typing and organisational skills. The overriding factor in all cases was a willingness to have a go, though I drew the line at pole dancing.

There have, of course, been glitches along the way, but I think I would have gone through those self-doubts if I had been born and raised in one place. They were not a product of an itinerant life, but a by-product of motherhood, even though I recognised I was lucky enough to spend time solely raising my children. It was a brief time in my life when I was John's wife and their mother without, in my mind, my own identity.

Reflecting again I realised I never lost my identity, only the confidence to believe in myself.

Take-Away Slice: Volunteering is work, sometimes harder than a paid position because it is the cause keeping you there and not the salary. It is really important that we, the accompanying spouse, recognise the value of the different elements of our overseas experience, whether volunteering or starting up a business in a foreign land, maybe completely different to anything we've previously done, something I think we tend to forget. The many strands woven into making an overseas assignment successful, and the emotional logistics of keeping all the family on track and thriving, are immeasurable and great pride should be taken in the success. Of both our family and ourselves.

Eighth Slice: Staying Connected

"Look what I bought," I gloated, not long after we married and on a quick trip to John's parents in Gloucestershire.

"What is it?" he asked, peering out from under Murphy, our old VW Variant he was trying to repair enough to get us back to Holland the next day.

"A visitor's book! It's leather."

"Why do we need a visitor's book?" he asked.

"To remember," I told him.

Thirty years later it is fun to read through the comments written by friends over the years. The truly wonderful thing is many of them are still dear friends and continue to visit us wherever we happen to be living. Staying in touch is hard sometimes. And I think harder for men who on the whole do not have the same inclination, or maybe discipline, about keeping friendships going, about needing to share experiences and our lives.

The visitor's book is also a wonderful *aide-memoire* to queries like, "Who stayed with us in Trinidad?" and, "When did Laurence visit us in Thailand?" Some of the comments tell stories of their lives; a new bride, a baby, a relocation, others could lead one to think we offered not a sanctuary of calm, but a den of iniquity, but they keep coming back.

I blame the American Women's Club in Bangkok for my other record-keeping addiction, which in a way goes hand in hand with my visitor's book. Wandering around their annual craft market one year I pounced upon a 'party book', which fortuitously matched my blue and white china.

I have faithfully recorded every barbie, lunch or dinner party, farewell do, birthday celebration or just plain brunch. The names and menus are detailed, the wine also, though in EG I got tired of writing *rioja*, the only wine available. It has ended many arguments over who knows who, and when so-and-so met so-and-so. It is fun to go back, and strangely comforting to see the same names appearing as we bump into each other in different locations around the world. I am on my second book and fully anticipate filling it in until my funeral, when I would like my daughter to do the honours.

It is almost impossible to remember what it was like waiting for, longing for, flimsy blue aerogrammes to arrive from home, from a lover, from a friend. The arrival of telegrams however rarely spelt good news and communicating via *Poste Restante* in dusty post offices around the world filled with pitfalls. But strange as it seems now, long distance romances did prosper, families did stay together, and the world continued to revolve on its axis.

"Julie North!" The prefect, in charge of dispensing mail at NEGS from a small platform against the wall of the dining hall, tossed the crisp white envelope sharp and sure in the general direction of the answering voice. "Mary Alker!" Again the letter would follow its parabolic arc. "Everest!" "Chook!"

Those with names less common were dealt with familiarly. The letters darted precisely to the upraised hands, there being an element of pride in the throwing technique of the prefect. "Apple!" Mine, sent from Mum or Dad would eventually reach me, crumpled and stained from the many hands which caught and tossed the featherweight epistle as it fluttered from student to student on its final flight path. I didn't care, it was after all news from home, in those days Malaysia.

Communications have come a long way. But in some ways the speed of information, knowing everything our children are doing at any given time has, rather than increasing our, or their, freedom, actually hampered it.

There was an element of liberation knowing whatever the misdemeanour, the knowledge would not reach my parents for at least three weeks by which time, more often than not, the infraction had been forgotten or detention given and received.

In businesses with tentacles spread around the world, the role of the country manager was in many respects autonomous. As long as guidelines laid down in some far off head office across numerous time zones were generally followed, and profits made, the day-to-day running of the company was very much left to those on the ground. The men from London would arrive periodically every few years for two months to 'look over' the business and shake hands with local dignitaries. More often than not they would bring their wives, much to the regret of the country manager's spouse who would have to kowtow to their every whimsy.

Often those on the ground are in a far better position to make a decision than those in their air-conditioned towers in London, Houston, Madrid or wherever. Time is wasted on the back and forth of opinion, and frustration is felt on both sides of the oceans.

The ease of communication has also brought new stressors for both children and parents, particularly those families who have chosen the boarding school route. What sounded like an irredeemable issue over the phone when Stephie sobbed she had fallen out with her roommate Rosalyn, may well be over by the time an irritated house matron finds them both, now happily making cocoa together in the common room. Instant access to and from houseparents to homeparents, often without the child's awareness, can bring unneeded and unwanted interference in an issue often best resolved by the protagonists.

There are, of course, occasions when instant intervention is paramount, but on the whole children learn compassion, and compromise, from day to day encounters, good and bad. I think those lessons give them greater decision-making powers within appropriate parameters that can only stand them in good stead as adults.

But this is where it gets tricky now, with the overload of information spewing through the ether. We cannot make decisions without information. And knowing the information is freely available with the slightest touch of a finger gives us far greater rights, which in turn allows us greater freedom of choice. Where though does freedom occur if we are constantly being monitored, or indeed doing the monitoring?

On the global front freedom of choice, of sharing information, is at greatest risk in countries where the fear of sedition is also greatest. The term 'threaten public security' is often all that is needed to stifle freedom of speech and assembly.

So here is my dichotomy. On the one hand I thrive on the ease of the Internet, and admire the way in which social media is most definitely a catalyst for change in countries not as open as others. On the other, I fear for the over use and abuse of both.

How do we reach that happy medium of use and not abuse? How do we monitor children and teens so they are safe, but still able to explore and satisfy their curiosity?

Social media. What did we do before its advent? Certainly for expatriates and travellers it is a boon, and for many in countries staggering under dictatorships it has literally been a lifesaver, but it can also be an avenue for abuse. Occasionally in a manipulative and unpleasant way when used by someone determined to do evil, and sometimes by the user him or herself when it is used as a hide, somewhere to retreat to and not face the reality of the moment, maybe a new country or a new school.

'Friending' one's children on Facebook has caused an outcry from many teenagers and young people not wanting their parents as 'friends'. "It is the only way I can find out who my daughter is hanging out with," wrote one mother in a local paper. "I like to keep tabs on my son," wrote another. "My kids just don't understand the consequences of irresponsible postings," complained a father from New Jersey.

I know the concerns are all legitimate, but using social media as a spy cam on the lives of our children just doesn't seem right. We didn't grow up with today's technology and so have to forge our own path as parents through the morass of social media. It's not easy. Parents can see the rashness of posting photos from drunken orgies, or writing a post at the perceived unjustness of a teacher's action, of venting in general, all of which can be seen by prospective universities and employers, and in some instances governments of countries we may be resident in.

Perhaps the basic terminology is what we should focus on. Our children are not our friends; they are our children. And while, as they age, our relationship with them changes and friendship takes on a more prominent role, the bottom line stays the same, child and parent, until the sad day when there is a complete role reversal.

I am unashamedly old fashioned in one way at least, I truly believe allowing one's children the space to make mistakes, to fall down, is part of the growing up process. Of course we don't want our children to hurt themselves, or others, but some of those day-to-day knocks are the fastest lessons learnt. And in some ways that is even more important for expatriate children, whose world, while wide in many aspects, is not always wide in daily freedoms.

Picking up people around the world to share your life with is one of the greatest pleasures in life, and sometimes you know straight away they will continue to stay in it. I met Kevin while searching for clues under a rather nice teak dining table in Singapore. We were on opposing teams in a treasure hunt on New Year's Eve 1986; quietly, under that table, we formed an alliance, one that has not been broken in twenty-five years and through four countries. Kay, who I have mentioned before and who knows all my foibles and still calls me her friend, is his wife. Her kind commonsense along with her sense of the ridiculous, similar political views and book likes, have been an important part of my life. Their three children, the same age as ours, are my surrogate children whose highs and lows we have celebrated and bemoaned together.

Nick and Grainne came into our lives in Bangkok. For the following ten years I spent many hours retraining my children after each meeting, I gave up when they reached their teens.

"What are you both doing?" I asked my children one sultry afternoon in Pataya, Thailand. Most of the world was snoozing away the heat of the day after a morning on the beach.

"We're being cats," Kate chortled, as she and her brother continued to lap milk from bowls set in the sand outside the back door of the bungalow we were staying in.

"Grainne showed us," Edward laughed, licking his sticky and by then sandy hand, and cleaning behind his ear.

"Did she now?"

"She said they're her favourite animal," Kate purred.

I smiled across at Grainne, working on her tan on a lounger nearby and keeping an eye on her pets, my children, and marvelled a woman so petite and innocent could create such drama.

Nick and Grainne have been the perfect foil to John and I as parents. Reminding us of the silly side of life, sometimes forgotten in the morass of manners we try to instil in our kids. Now adults, both Kate and Edward count them as two of their closest friends, as do we. Weeks spent together on a canal boat, or a yacht, testament indeed to an enduring friendship.

Back in the dark ages before the Internet and Skype, we had what I called our Rogue's Gallery. Photos of people important to our lives were all framed and hung on one wall in every new location. The grandparents, all five of them, were obviously well represented. Uncles too. Special friends Nick and Grainne have had wall space for years, and also special friends the kids had left behind with each move. When they were very little we would go along the wall in the evening and say goodnight to them, as well as remembering them in their bedtime prayers. The 'God bless list' grew very long sometimes, a bedtime delaying tactic used by both children to good results over the years.

It was a small price to pay to keep all those special people in the children's thoughts and conversations when we might not see some of them for a couple of years.

Friends become so much more important in the teen years. Hand-in-hand with puberty is the assumption your family will be there no matter what, but friends, well they have to be nurtured on a daily basis. Each relocation rips a little piece of their social strata away, which can lead to real issues of abandonment for some children, with of course the add-on effect their behaviour has on the entire family.

Now with email and Skype it is infinitely easier to stay connected, but in a way it is sad the effort that went into writing has gone. Nothing quite beats holding a letter that has been held by someone loved on the other side of the world.

"Why don't you ask some of the girls around for supper and a movie?" I asked Kate.

"Everyone's busy," she dismissed the suggestion with a toss of her hair.

It is easy to say we should know our children's friends, but anyone who has suffered through the agonies of the teen years, both as a teen and a parent, understands those friendships are sometimes jealously guarded. That is part of teens trying to forge their own path before they leave the safety net of 'home' and head out into the world of college or work.

Of course this rational explanation was not obvious to me in those angst-filled years. But as with most things, a little distance can bring perspective and I think we have to trust our children to have, somewhere deep down, taken in those lessons we have tried to instil. The ones about think before you leap, or in this case before you post a diatribe or inappropriate photo on Facebook.

We all know, as parents of teens, we are on a hiding to nothing and whatever is said, or not said, is wrong in our teen's eyes. For once, though, I'm on the side of the kids. I think we have to shut our eyes, grit our teeth, and give them space, even if it is cyberspace, to have their friendships, their parties, their misadventures without us hovering over their shoulders.

How do we know mischief is not pinging along the airwaves? I guess we have to use our parental radars, those eyes in the back of our heads, and trust the open door policy works, and if and when an issue arises we are there to help sort it out, if it is wanted or indeed needed.

But no matter what the temptation, the one thing guaranteed to clang all communication down with our teens, is to reprimand our children on their social media pages. Their public humiliation serves no purpose and closes the nebulous window of trust we have painstakingly built.

I guess we have to try and remember social media for the TCK, the Third Culture Kid you are raising in Mongolia or Malaysia, could be a lifeline when next you uproot them. Keeping them in touch with their old buddies whilst making quiet inroads into a new social scene through the relative anonymity of 'friending' on Facebook.

Staying in touch takes effort. Sometimes we have to decline an invitation to a celebration on the other side of the world for practical or financial reasons, and sometimes it is just so much easier to say no. But other times it is truly wonderful to say, "What the hell?" and hop on a plane.

We were living in Malabo where Internet access was intermittent so when the cursor blinked and I saw an email from Adrian, a dear friend from earlier days, I opened it immediately.

"Getting married on September 27th, christening the next day. Can you come? Would you like to be godmother?"

Practicalities said, "No, too far," and "Too complicated".

"Yes and yes," I emailed back. "I'll be there evening of 25th, find me somewhere cheap and cheerful to stay."

To share two such important events in a friend's life was very precious, and Africa to Newfoundland, Canada for a long weekend seemed a reasonable distance to travel.

EG is not a country that encourages casual visitors. Americans can enter with impunity, thanks to an early deal the first major oil and gas company in the country struck with the Government, when oil was first found to be a viable commodity. Any other nationality must jump through hoops, and then jump again. There is also the issue of becoming a human pincushion in order to adequately protect oneself from every imaginable lurgy.

"Let's have a house party," I suggested one Sunday morning, as we sat sipping coffee on our terrace, ten months before John's fiftieth birthday. It was pleasantly quiet, the intrusive noise of generators for once not rumbling in the background.

"What? Here? Why?"

"No, in Spain, for your birthday."

"Who would come?"

"The family for a start," I said. "Lots of people," I went on.

"You can't ask people to spend a lot of money to go somewhere for a party," he objected.

"'Course you can," I argued. "And not just one night, a week. Anyone can say no."

"I'd feel awkward asking."

"Oh for God's sake, I wouldn't. It would be fun. We'll rent a big house for a week, people can stay with us, first come first served. And we could choose a day in the middle for the actual party."

"Hmmm," he said, and went back to the rugby score in a week-old paper from England, brought in by some returning rotator.

I took his response as positive and starting looking into it.

In October, a month before his birthday, so it fitted in with Edward's half term, we spent a week in the hills behind Malaga in Spain with forty-five family and friends from around the world. Some of course could not come, but those who did helped us celebrate in memorable style. Mention the words 'treasure hunt' to many of our friends and family and they will shake their heads and say, "Bloody Gidleys and their games!"

The effort everyone made was truly tremendous and underpinned the importance of staying in touch, no matter how hard it sometimes seems. That week also had the added poignancy of being the last time the family spent together with my parents-in-law.

Flying to England from Houston for a party in Dorset was another extravagant gesture, and I appreciate I am very lucky to able to do it. I also thank John for all his travelling back and forth across the globe, for the work and for the jetlag he gloops his way through, so I can steal his air miles.

The summer party on Waterloo Day was perfect and celebrated a ninetieth birthday. Jack and his wife Helen, have known me longer than I have known me. He was the first man I declared my love for, and he still has it. It was a case of fly and be damned, because those precious people might not be there the next time I want to land on their square.

It was serendipitous that his son, who hasn't loved me but is an old playing-in-the-monsoon-drains-of-Kuala-Lumpur pal, turned 50 in the same year and co-chaired the celebrations. Kate, her partner Wayne, and Edward all made the trek down the M3, giving proof that neither years nor miles need sever friendships.

I fell into bed at one in the morning having danced and sung with octogenarians, nonagenarians and even Jeff from the KL ditch days, hoping I would never forget such a happy day.

I admit to being sentimental and have kept every letter John has ever sent, so too the children's. Maybe the frequent times apart have worked for us, or maybe we like each other's company. I know a parent's separation affects you no matter your age, but whatever the reason we have been lucky with our marriage.

Staying connected can also mean staying in step with your partner, the one you have followed around the world. Expatriate life can put strains on a marriage, not only if one or either of you travel a lot, your spouse for work, you to your home base to stay connected with children and family there, but also from the very nature of your lives while on location, whether a cosmopolitan existence in the Emirates or a more rugged life in a third world country.

Cocktail parties, balls, receptions, days at the races can all join to create a false sense of togetherness. You arrive and leave together, therefore you must be together. You present a united front, but occasionally that is all it is, a front. Your lives have become so disconnected by the frivolity and frippery little time is actually spent talking.

You ask yourself when was the last time we discussed politics? When did we talk about something other than the children or logistical issues of who will be where, when?

Leaves are often spent stretching yourselves thin between families, before your spouse heads back to your temporary home on the edge of the Andaman Sea, or the rim of Lake Geneva and you stay 'home' for a little longer to miss Ramadan or to catch your son playing cello in the school concert, or maybe you vacation with another family from Lizzie's school, or your tennis club.

"We thought we'd go to New Zealand in June," your best friend, the one you met a year ago just after your arrival, says. "Why don't we all go together? Jim thought the kids can all keep each other occupied and we can split costs. What do you think?"

"Hey, that's a great idea," Janine says. "Let me talk to Liam, but I know he'll love it, particularly if it means he's got someone to go skiing off *piste* with. He knows I won't."

And so even your vacation is spent sharing time and energy that sometimes needs to be spent on your marriage.

Back at home, wherever home happens to be at the time, you unpack and each heads back to busy lives, converging over the breakfast bar to arrange the evening's entertainment.

"What time are we due at the Embassy?" Celia asks.

"I'll go straight from work. Not much point coming back here for half an hour. I've got a clean shirt in my briefcase," Roger replies. "I'll send the car to pick you up at 6:30, okay?"

"Fine, I'll see you there then," Celia says, bussing his cheek before heading out into the morning cool for her tennis lesson.

They join briefly at the steps of the Embassy and follow the reception line, nodding and smiling at others they recognise. After shaking hands with their hosts they separate and in a waltz of avoidance meet again four hours later in the car, driven by their driver.

"I'm bushed," Roger says taking his tie off and heading up the stairs, "I'm going to bed."

"I'll just check on the kids," Celia says.

By the time she gets back to their bedroom, gentle snores are reverberating from the bed dimly lit by the glow from the bathroom light.

On the rare night spent at home together, the computer or the television blinks enticingly, and even if they ignore the *brtt, brtt* of a Blackberry demanding attention, it breaks any chance of real and quiet conversation. And so each day repeats itself, until the connections are quietly and irrevocably broken.

Hardship postings create their own issues. The accompanying spouse may choose to spend longer than the proffered two weeks 'home' every three months.

"There's not much point going back with you Philip. It'll be Ramadan, and hot as hell, and then you'll be away for a couple of weeks. I'll be back at the end of the October."

"That's two months away."

"I know, but it'll go by quickly."

"For you maybe," he says peevishly. "What am I going to do?"

"Oh don't be silly, you'll be at work most of the time, and you fall asleep when you get home anyway. You won't notice I'm not here."

But he does notice, and resentment builds and eyes stray. Equally, hers do too sometimes. And before too long both have taken a step too far. And just sometimes both get so wound up in separate interests the axes don't cross anymore.

"Will you be in tonight, Tom?"

"Yes, but not till about 8. Got a meeting to discuss the extension to the Museum. What about you?"

"I'll be even later I'm afraid. Margie is having a farewell do for Samantha."

"Samantha?"

"Yes, the woman who helps at the orphanage with me. She's going to the Sudan. You did meet her, at the Brown's Christmas party."

"Don't remember. Well, have fun."

"Thanks, you too." And they *muah* each other's cheeks and head out the door.

Of course that doesn't just happen to expatriate couples, but often the intensity of social life interrupts the intimacy of real life, until the lines are blurred. Sometimes it is not even noticed until a relocation looms.

There are, though, many, many, many marriages that have become stronger with overseas postings, the trials as well as the triumphs bringing couples, and families, closer than they ever imagined.

Last summer, I found myself sitting one Sunday afternoon in the Half Moon pub in Sherborne, an ancient town in Dorset, England having had lunch with Jack and Helen, friends of my parents and the couple I have known all my life.

Melancholia seeped in, due in some part I'm sure to the wine consumed with my roast beef and Yorkshire pudding. I am not a good lunchtime imbiber. I was thinking about my earlier walk up the hill to my cousin's new abode, a charming old cottage on the edge of a large and ancient estate. Without a dog in tow I need a purpose to walk, I knew Adam was away so it had seemed the ideal time to drop a thank you note for a lovely evening the previous Friday through his letterbox. The walk, over a stile and up a steep bridle path through a grove of curving chestnuts, was solitary and rather lovely. The sun filtered through the canopy, drying patches of the path strewn with fallen leaves, slippery to the unwary. As I neared the crest of the hill, the trees gave way to fields newly ploughed and ready for autumn planting, offering a pastiche of Englishness seen normally only on postcards sold in the Cotswolds, or other spots popular with tourists.

I felt extraordinarily lucky to have had the chance to savour the benefits of an English summer afternoon, and it wasn't even raining. I was in the pub because I had a few hours to kill before my next commitment, a word connoting obligation, and nothing that weekend was obligatory.

Deepest Dorset draws me every time I go to England. My family, those keepers of memories made before I could keep my own, are all resident around the area, and since both my parents are now dead there was an added pathos. As my relations age I have realised the importance of continuity, not so much of lineage, but of remembrance. This has been brought particularly to the fore due to one aunt's decline into the miasma of Alzheimer's.

My thoughts led me to the closeness of my family, though never physically. As I grew I lived in Africa and Asia, some cousins grew up in Australia, some in the Caribbean, some in England, some in South America, and yet we are all close. As our parents have aged and died, our generation has stepped forward and renewed the familial bonds, compounded by our history of shared experiences snatched over brief interludes spent together in different corners of the world.

Maybe because of the extraordinary nature of our meetings as children, infrequent as they were in far flung parts, we have strong connections. As we age we draw closer still. We believe in family but do not see each other for years at a time, and yet we are all aware of where each of us is in the world, still scattered and testaments to a global upbringing.

I finished my wine and moved to tea before I spent another evening reminiscing with Julia, my much-loved aunt, recognising distance need not be detrimental, a nomadic life can lead to strong family ties albeit spread globally.

Take-Away Slice: One of the joys of a global life is the opportunity to meet interesting people, some of whom share our lives for evermore. With others we may form intense relationships for brief periods, a shared posting perhaps with wonderful memories but slowly drift apart without a continued injection of meetings. That's okay. It doesn't lessen the depth of the friendship when it was there, it doesn't diminish the fondness of those shared stories, the smile that a long-ago incident provokes.

Sometimes friendships are of, and remain, locked in a certain place, like old lovers. And that is something we should let our children know as we move them around the world, and as they grow up. Never regret a friendship, or a lover; it was special at the time.

Ninth Slice: Death at a Distance

"Hi," John said over the 'phone.

"Hi, what's up?"

"I've just spoken to Julia."

"What's happened?" I asked sitting down, knowing a call from my aunt would not be a good thing.

"They think Ida's had a stroke."

"Oh God, is she okay?" I asked, visualising my mother paralysed.

"Yes. But being very difficult and refusing to go to hospital."

"Bloody hell, what is it with her? She is so damn stubborn. I'd better go."

"Yes, I think so," John said. "Call Swiss and see if they can get you on tomorrow's flight. Let me know and I'll phone Julia back." Such were the difficulties of international communication at the time in Equatorial Guinea.

It was a week before Christmas and as I flew to England on Swiss, Kate flew to EG on Iberian Air. Edward was due a couple of days later.

"What are you doing here?" my mother asked, as she saw me walk through her conservatory door thirty-six hours later.

"Checking up on you, Mum," I said, as I kissed her.

"Who told you?"

"Doesn't matter. I have my spies. And I needed to see you were okay for myself."

"Of course I am, you shouldn't have come."

My mother's resilience and strength might have got her through some very difficult situations in her life, but those same traits made caring for her in her old age extraordinarily difficult.

She was all right, very slightly paralysed in her left hand, but it had knocked the physical stuffing out of her and for the first time she struggled with the stairs and bathing.

She was adamant I fly home for Christmas. I spent four frenetic days getting home help organised, a Stannah chair lift installed and meals delivered, a tall order that would never have been done without the understanding and competence of the various services involved. Mum also had wonderful neighbours in the village she had called home for the previous fifteen years. I could not have left her without their support.

I flew home on the 23rd December with a bagful of parsnips and a pot of whipping cream, two commodities unavailable in the local Malabo shops.

"Hi Mum," Kate said, as they all met me at the airport. "You are not going to believe what Granny has done!"

"Oh no, what?"

"Fired everyone!" she laughed.

"You are kidding me?"

"Nope," Edward said. "She's tough."

"Stubborn!" John murmured. "Bridget said not to worry, they'd keep an eye on her. She's going to them for Christmas anyway."

"I know, but honestly. What am I going to do? I don't know what I'do without Bridget and the other neighbours?"

"I know, we're very lucky. Well, there's no point worrying now. Let's enjoy Christmas and then we'll decide."

Always my favourite time of the year, Christmas was wonderful. Kate left in time to celebrate New Year's Eve in London, Edward had elected to stay a few extra days and would be flying back on the 2nd January. The day everything went pear shaped. John woke to a severe case of kidney stones and had to be medivaced to Douala in Cameroon. I went with him. Alida, a friend who worked for a local airline, kindly got Edward to his flight later that evening, and he got himself back to school in time to start his last year at Blundells.

The hospital in Douala was run efficiently and kindly but did not have the right doctor, he having been involved in a car crash while in France. John and I boarded a plane four days later, under the care of a nurse who had flown out from France in order to administer drugs on the flight to England. It was a long flight and I felt desperately sorry for John, and horribly ineffectual.

Once in hospital in London and a course of treatment decided upon, we could relax a little. My first action was to get on a bus and go to John Lewis on Oxford Street, a department store I knew would be able to kit me out in basic warm clothing. Not thinking I would be heading to cooler climes, I had packed only for Africa as we had hurried off our island. I was still wearing a cotton skirt and tee-shirt, bare legs and sandals. The flight attendants on Air France had taken pity on me and allowed me to keep one of the blankets to guard against the chill of an English January.

"Hey! Kate, Edward, hang on," I called along the street, as I saw their easy gaits ahead of me, heading to the hospital.

"Hi Mum, we were going to wait for you inside," Kate said hugging me hard, warmth in the chill wind barrelling down Maryleborne. "We didn't want to barge in on Dad. Is he okay?"

"Yes, he's fine now he's properly medicated, but he'll probably need surgery. Edward what are you doing here? Aren't you meant to be at Blundells?"

"I had to see Dad," he said with a shrug. I understood. John had been in terrible pain as we left Malabo and no child wants to see a parent like that.

"That's okay. You did tell the school though didn't you?"

"Yeah, I left a note."

"You left a note? Did you explain what was happening?"

"I told them I was getting the train to London and I'd be back in a couple of days."

"Oh God, Edward, I'd better phone now. They'll be tearing their hair out not knowing where you are, and why," I said, hugging my son and seeing Kate over his shoulder, ready to do battle on his behalf if necessary.

I spoke to the master of the sixth form house and explained the situation. To his credit he took the disappearance of one of his charges very well, and promised not to punish my son.

"I told the headmaster I knew it would have to be for a good reason," he said, "I do know Edward, Mrs Gidley. Send him back when he's seen his father."

It was difficult for them both to see John unwell, the first time ever, but at least it was in London and not Malabo, where the supplies of morphine would have run out very quickly.

Whoever came up with the notion that 'our forties are the best years' was obviously related to the same idiot who said 'our school years are the best...and so on'. Our forties and fifties are some of the saddest years because our stalwarts, our early history-keepers, our cheerleaders no matter what, our parents, come to the end of their lives and we become orphans. And that hurts whatever age you are.

As John recuperated from surgery in London, I dashed to Somerset to see my mother who was still unwell, but not admitting to it. A trip to the doctor did nothing to resolve the issue, as she would not allow me to go in with her. The next day I called him out to the house and as Mum lay upstairs, I explained the situation. After examining her he diagnosed compacted constipation, apparently a common occurrence after a stroke when the patient's mobility has suddenly decreased.

What followed were two days and nights of awfulness for my mother; one minute utterly dependent on me, the next reviling me for seeing her in such an undignified state. The evening of the second night, in between washing sheets again, I received a phone call.

"Apple, it's Julia. Sue died an hour ago," my aunt said with no preamble.

"Oh God, no, is Dad okay?" I asked, not bearing to think how he would cope with the loss of the love of his life, and his partner for the previous fifteen years.

"He's at Yeovil hospital. She died in the ambulance, the paramedics couldn't save her. Can you go?"

"Yes of course. But I have to get someone to sit with Mum. She can't be left. Will you call Dad please and let him know I'll be there as soon as possible?"

I told Mum what had happened, and for once vitriol about my father did not accompany her words. Again Bridget, one of her wonderful neighbours stepped in, and I raced to Yeovil to collect my poor father.

"Dad," I asked, once I'd got him home and sitting with a strong whisky, "Would you like me to stay tonight?"

"No, I don't think so," he said, "And anyway what about your mother?"

"I can ask Bridget to stay with her tonight, and I'll go back first thing in the morning. I think she's over the worst now."

"Thank you sweetie-pie, but actually I'd rather be alone," he said. "Just sit and talk to me for a while."

We sat, and talked, and cried about Sue who had made his life so happy. I stayed as he called her daughters in Australia and then went back to my mother.

The next few weeks went by in blur of moving landscapes as I travelled between the rolling hills of Somerset and Dorset, trying to help both parents. I did manage a quick trip to London to say goodbye to John before he headed back to Malabo, feeling very guilty he had to go home alone after a rough few weeks. He had stayed in London with my half-sister Val, a whole other story, while recuperating.

Life was in a way made easier when my mother was admitted to hospital, the same one I had collected my father from a week earlier, after failing to improve. At least I did not have to worry about leaving her alone at home when I was with my father, helping with funeral arrangements and getting his house ready for Sue's daughters arrival.

It was a difficult and sad time, and after six weeks I had to return home to Malabo, leaving a grieving father and an intransigent mother, determined not to leave her home again.

John in my absence had taken over as interim Honorary Consul and had organised a reception for all the British citizens on the island to meet the Ambassador. I had time to go home and say hello to Miss Meg, have a shower and head down to the restaurant chosen for the event. The Ambassador, who was staying with us, was already there seeing to last minute glitches, a job I should have been doing.

A few weeks later my wonderful obstinate mother fell again, and again refused to go to hospital.

"She's taken all the skin off her forehead," Bridget explained over the phone, "Fortunately the doctor was home, you remember he lives in the village, and came and sorted her out. I'll stay tonight."

I did not realise the explanation really was true. She had taken all the skin off, and it refused to heal. A week later she was finally taken into hospital, at ninety, objecting and kicking and screaming all the way.

"I can get a flight on Friday," I told Julia. There were no daily flights to London at the time.

"Really I don't think you need to come back at the moment. She's safe in hospital. Wait and see what happens over the next few days," she advised.

"Okay, Apple, you are going to have to come now," Julia said, a few weeks later after Mum was transferred to a cottage hospital nearer her village, and where it was easier for her friends to visit.

"The social workers have assessed her and say she can't live alone any more."

"What happened when they said that?"

"She screamed at them. Caused a tremendous scene in the ward."

"I can imagine. Okay, I'll be there in a couple of days."

Just after Mum's ninetieth birthday party, when she had only just stopped driving, and six months before her stroke, for which we held a wonderful lunch party including John, Kate and Edward, as well as thirty of her closest friends, I had spent a couple of days, unbeknownst to her, looking at residential homes in the area. It had been a thoroughly depressing time but had narrowed the options to one, the only one I could vaguely imagine her living in.

Before I saw her in hospital, after my latest arrival from Malabo, I went to the home and explained the situation to the owner. Fortunately for me, but horribly sad for another family, a room had become available, one on the ground floor and with a patio.

"We'll repaint in a couple of days and then your mother can move in anytime after that," Mrs McBride said. "Can I suggest you furnish it with her favourite pieces from home, even if some things don't usually belong in a bedroom?"

I signed on the dotted line and went to see Mum in the cottage hospital.

"Why are you here?" she asked. The greeting was becoming familiar.

"To see you, Mum. What the hell have you been doing to yourself?" I asked, looking at her poor forehead, still swollen and purplish.

"You should see the other one," Mum laughed, touching her head gently.

"Oh Mum," I said, sitting down and dreading the next few minutes. "What are we going to do?"

"Well, I've told them here I'm going home soon. What time is it?"

"Nearly six."

"Good they'll be coming with my whisky. They give me a glass with my pills. I told them I'd probably die if I took them with water."

"Ida always gets her tipple at six," called out a patient across the ward, "I don't like whisky," she added, "but I could do with a gin."

I thought I could do with a slug too.

"Mum, I've got some bad news," I started, after chatting for a while. "The social workers and doctors have assessed you, and the hospital won't release you to go home if you live alone. We're going to have to come up with a plan."

"Bloody rubbish. Of course I'm going home," she said.

"Only if you agree to have someone live in with you."

"Don't be silly, Apple, I'm not doing that. They'd drive me nuts."

My concern was actually finding someone to live with her even if she had agreed, and then trusting Mum not to fire them the minute I was on the plane.

"I'm sorry Mum, but that's the story. Either that or we move you into sheltered accommodation."

"You mean a home full of dribbling old men and women. No, I'm not going."

"I've looked at Hurd's Hill. You know, the home outside Langport, where your friend used to live. They have a nice suite with its own patio and bathroom that we could get." I couldn't look at her. I felt as if I'd betrayed her, and I had in a way.

"How dare you? Get out!" she exploded.

I sat for moment, but she continued shouting. The other patients on the ward were getting distressed, so I left to sympathetic nods from the women we'd chatted to a few moments earlier.

"She's tough," said the ward sister, the one I'd been talking to daily over the 'phone. "I find it hard to believe she's over ninety."

"I know, but this is going to be difficult."

"Have you found somewhere?"

"Yes, Hurd's Hill in Langport."

"Oh they're lovely there. Pricey though," she said.

"I know, we'll have to sell her house, but I can't tell her that yet."

"No, one thing at a time. You have to be patient. Come back tomorrow morning after breakfast, anytime. There are no set visiting hours. She'll calm down and fall asleep as soon as she's had supper. Don't worry love, it'll work out."

I went and cried in my hire car.

It took a couple of days and then like a switch Mum relented.

"Okay I'll go, but only because I want to leave this bloody place. Though they are very kind."

Money can become a huge issue if a retirement home is the best course of action. Private care homes are expensive and the family home might have to be sold to cover the costs. A wrenching decision for anyone to make, particularly if it's been in the family for many years. I hadn't grown up in the house, but memories were still bound up in the bricks and mortar.

Thoughts of finding the children, perched in little cane chairs they had somehow managed to get up into the apple tree on the edge of the patio, flashed through my mind as I drove back to Charters, Mum's home, and poured myself a drink.

In between hospital visits I started the horrid process of emptying my mother's house. Making decisions about her furniture, her possessions, her life. Fortunately she had agreed a few years previously to allow both Julia, my aunt, and I power of attorney should it be required. With the doctor's letter it was invoked.

The day she moved, her room at Hurd's Hill looked lovely, with her own bed, bedding and favourite chairs. Her curtains. Her favourite paintings and ornaments. I had spent a couple of nights making collages from all her photographs scattered around her house and generally trying to make it look welcoming.

"When we come later, may I bring Mum in the main entrance?" I asked Mrs McBride.

"Yes of course."

Mum was so relieved to be leaving the hospital, she was quite gay.

"We're going out for lunch first," I said, strapping her into the car.

"Oh good, where are we going?"

"To the trout place."

"Perfect, and then home. I can't wait."

I dreaded the afternoon ahead.

"Let's have a glass of wine with lunch," I suggested, needing all the Dutch courage I could muster.

"Mum," I said, once we were back in the car after lunch, "Remember I told you I had to move some of your things to Hurd's Hill? Well, Charters is a real mess, so much better you don't see it like it is," I stumbled on thinking of the boxes and empty rooms.

"Nonsense. I want to go home. I'm not going to Hurd's Hill. I've decided."

"Oh Mum, it's too late now. You're booked in. We have to go there," I said. The social workers had warned me not to take Mum back to her house before going to the residential home.

"She's been institutionalized for the last six weeks. If you take her home for a few days and then try and move her it will be far, far harder for her."

And so I drove her to the front entrance of her new home, feeling traitorous. We rang the bell and waited.

"Good afternoon Apple, and you must be Mrs Girling. Welcome." I could have kissed the carer for her gracious reception.

"Not bad is it, Mum?" I asked, pointing to the towering entrance hall, the chandeliers and huge flower displays.

"I suppose not."

"Come off it, you've never lived in a place this grand," I joked, wanting to cry.

"I want to see my room."

"Come on then, it's a lovely day. We could have our tea outside if you like, on your patio."

Mum settled, and before I flew back to Equatorial Guinea ten days later she said, "It's not too bad here."

There were a few upsets that made me feel as if I were dealing with a recalcitrant teenager breaking bounds at boarding school. Edward never gave us so much to worry about.

"Apple, I'm sorry, but please can you talk to your mother?" Mrs McBride said.

"What's happened now?" I asked, over the crackly line from Malabo.

"She ordered a taxi last week and went to the supermarket and came home with gin, whisky and beer."

"Well I promised her she could come and go. I'm sure it's for her guests," I suggested.

"Yes, of course and her friends are marvellous, they visit often either for tea or an evening drink, but she is drinking more and then she becomes very difficult. She fell again two nights ago and broke a bottle. Fortunately she didn't cut herself."

"Can you monitor the whisky? Give her a glass before dinner and then with her dinner and then that's it."

"Yes, we can do that. We keep quite a lot for other residents in the locked cabinet in the office."

"Okay then, I'll sort it out."

And so my next call to my mother was about the perils of booze and falling.

Mum lived at Hurd's Hill for just under two years before she died, peacefully, on Christmas Eve 2005. I wasn't with her but spoke to her just after she slipped into a coma that afternoon.

I am convinced she died then so I would never forget the day. Another Christmas was spent with John and my children, now grown and home in Houston from London, with fluctuating emotions.

I flew to England on the 27th December, the day after Nick and Grainne flew to Houston to stay with us for the New Year.

Mum's cremation was a family affair. Just Kate, Julia and I; John and Edward still being in Houston with our guests. From the crematorium we went to her village for a memorial service packing the church to the rafters, and then to the pub for a wonderful send off.

"How could you give your mother's eulogy?" I was asked.

"Because I didn't trust anyone else to do it as well."

As the wine flowed so too did the stories, aided by the photo collage Kate and I had put together the evening before.

"I didn't know Ida had done all those things," said person after person. People who thought they knew her well. "What an extraordinary woman!"

"Yes," I replied. "She was."

Her death, while sad, was made slightly less stressful because Charters had already been emptied and sold. Her possessions, apart from those in her room at Hurd's Hill, disposed of.

Kate went back to work in London, my wonderful friends Jane and Marian, who came to Ida's funeral from Oxford and Edinburgh respectively, went back to their lives and I cleaned out her room and arranged for the shipment of her favourite things back to my home in Houston.

On a cold misty morning, a few hours before I was due to fly home, I scattered her ashes around the village she loved, and that had loved her. I phoned John, waking him, crying hysterically as I screwed the lid back on some of her remaining ashes, which I had decided to take to Australia.

I don't think I have ever felt quite so sad or alone.

It is a miserable fact that often, as the sandwich generation of expatriates, our visits to base camp are mired in the practicalities of university-age children and aging parents. At the 2011 Families in Global Transition conference, friend and psychotherapist, Laura Stephens and I presented a session called *Death from a Distance*, which dealt not only with the grieving process, but also some thoughts on how to manage the last years of our parents' and other loved ones, from overseas. One of the suggestions we made, and this sounds obvious, but is something we often don't always do, was to spend time with them. Quality time.

In our expatriate lives the visits to our parent country can sometimes be fraught with time constraints, fitting people into squares like chessmen, trying to keep everybody happy and often failing.

The hardest thing for me, when the children were young, was dealing with the mundane issue of laundry. It always seemed rather rude appearing on someone's doorstep with an armful of dirty knickers, tee-shirts, jeans and socks saying, "Hello, lovely to see you, can I use the washing machine?" Mum understood and would offer but then insist on doing it herself because I couldn't possibly be trusted with her washing machine. I'd feel guilty she was doing laundry and not enjoying her grandchildren, which led to me lying, "No, no Mum it's okay – I did it on the last stop". I have sometimes been my own worst enemy. The plane ride back to wherever we lived at the time was almost a relief, "Whew we did it, I'm exhausted!" sort of feeling and then that pang and the voice saying *you didn't really spend time, real time, with anyone.*

In our haste to fit in all those chessmen it is sometimes hard to slow down enough to enjoy our parent's company even if their speech is a bit slower, a bit more convoluted than we remember, their hearing a little less acute.

And the really difficult thing about those times is we have to take the opportunity to talk about things no one likes to discuss; power of attorneys, wills, elder care, death, funerals and so on.

A Harvard surgeon, Atul Gawande, published an interesting article about 'letting go'. He wrote, "There was compelling evidence that suggested patients and the elderly faired better when sensitive topics had been addressed…and that patients reported a better quality of life in their final days, physicians showed a better appreciation of their patient's wishes and families showed less guilt and depression after the inevitable death."

It is not a discussion anyone wants to have, but it helps if we can keep at the back of our minds the belief we are ultimately helping make our parents', or any loved ones', dying less stressful. In a separate study, from a group out of the Massachusetts General Hospital, it was found that those patients who'd had palliative care discussions showed less depression and also 'happier' final days.

As we pluck up the courage to broach these subjects, it's worth remembering that unless power of attorney has already been invoked, your parent's specific permission has to be given before you can speak to their doctor. I know it helped me when I had to speak to Mum's doctors from long distance that I had already formed a relationship with them. You, and they, have a face to a name.

I had tried to talk to Mum over the years about alternative living arrangements as a 'just in case' but she was determined to leave her house 'in a box', and yet she was most specific about some things.

"Promise me, Apple you'll put the cats down if I die. They are too old to be moved to a new home."

"I promise, Mum, don't worry." It was then she told me, over thirty years after the event, she had put all our animals down when we left Malaysia.

"I cried all day," she said, "But it was the right thing to do. You promise me, about Fluff and Nutkins?"

"Yes Mum, I promise." As it turned out I didn't have to, they died before Mum went to Hurd's Hill.

"And another thing," she added, "I don't want that man at my funeral."

"I know Mum, he won't be," I assured her, knowing she was referring to my father. "You'll probably outlast him anyway," I joked.

If all your parents' wishes are clearly stated in a will it can ease the way through family decisions that can turn testy. A living will, or in the US an Advanced Medical Directive, can take the burden off children or siblings. When I brought up the subject of life support Mum just said, "Switch the bloody thing off."

At our presentation Laura was the voice of authority. My only qualification for speaking was experience, sadly five deaths in six years. Each one was difficult and each presented different issues, but what none of them presented was an issue with siblings, and for that I am extraordinarily grateful.

It was easier in a way for me. I was my mother's only child and so my decisions were mine alone, though obviously with input from John and doctors.

The death of a loved one across an ocean, a continent and probably a few time zones, and the ambivalent feelings of siblings all add to the intensity of emotions coursing through your jetlagged body.

"You left!" "You weren't here!" "You have no idea how hard it is!"

Even though I was an only child to my parents, I have a much-loved half sister, Val, who was my father's daughter from his first marriage. Sue, my father's paramour, had two daughters, who I had known for twenty-five years and John is one of three boys. Between us all we pretty much covered the gamut of family make-ups, but fortunately there has never been any unpleasantness to do with a parent's care, or possessions.

The choice of alternative living arrangements or a home is a whole other minefield. A sibling might be able to look after them but if not, the geographical decision is difficult. You are the one overseas, they cannot live with you. Do you move your parents to the other side of the country to be near family, for their convenience, or do you find somewhere near their own friends?

What is a horrendous time of grieving, and busyness, is made worse by resentment focused on the one who had the temerity to move abroad, whether of their own volition or at the will of work. At a time when all are hurting in their own individual ways, sibling resentments and our own guilt are not helpful emotions.

A parent dying is a messy business and is rarely simple, whether living next door or living on the other side of the world. All those surviving feel an element of guilt. For the person on the ground it is often regret at a cross word, or an impatient gesture brought on by the frustration of day-to-day responsibility. For the one abroad it is guilt at not having been able to do more, to be around more, to share that sad burden. Sometimes too, the one abroad feels wrong decisions are being made at home but swallows the words because of guilt at being away, and again resentment brews. Like I said, it's messy.

Expatriate life so often sounds glamorous as places like Dubai, Delhi or Djibouti pepper our conversation, and for those few short weeks we might be back at home base it is natural to talk about the good times abroad. Particularly to our parents who may well worry if they knew some of the issues faced in foreign countries. Life as an expat is not always roses, as any expat will tell you.

And when we fly home for a stroke, a fall, a final goodbye or a funeral the last thing we need to hear is, "How would you know?" "You weren't here". It is hard to suggest an alternative arrangement, or treatment, to one maybe made by the sibling at home. It is hard to wrest away control of visiting hours from a sibling intent on being in charge, or to suggest those nearest in geography take second place in the visiting roster to those juggling work hours and distance, whether for you, or your children trying to see a grandparent in hospital.

If those hard discussions are held before the inevitable

decline of our loved ones, openly and with all concerned, the trauma can be lessened a little. If we, the one flying in for a visit, can take the onus for starting the conversation maybe it will lessen the burden on the sibling at home. I know it's difficult to appear on a parent's doorstep after being away a year and launch into discussions of 'what ifs?' and 'have you dones?' But if we do, it will help in the long term.

With less opportunity for recriminations, maybe we can lessen the words that can't be taken back and instead work with a positive vocabulary of, "How can I help from over here?" and, "I'm so glad you're back".

My parents-in-law died within two years of each other. My father-in-law first, just six weeks before my mother: it was a truly awful time for John, who had no time to grieve properly for his loss before he was mopping me up after mine. Neither could he hop on a plane whenever he felt he should go back, though thankfully he was able to make a number of trips. His parents both died in their own home; while wonderful for them, it was difficult for their sons. There is never an easy solution, or one with which everyone is perfectly comfortable. There is nothing easy about death.

"I'm sorry to tell you Mrs Gidley, your father has lung cancer. It's inoperable," said the doctor, when I 'phoned from Houston for the test results. I had tried to prepare myself before dialling, Dad had smoked heavily since he was seventeen.

"How long do you think he has?" I asked, "Should I come immediately."

"He's comfortable now he's on medication. Maybe three months, but you should get here sooner rather than later."

"Oh Dad, what a bugger." I called him a little later in his hospital bed, after I'd wiped the tears away.

"Well sweetie-pie, it had to happen," replied my father. "Will you come over?"

"Of course, Daddy, as soon as the volcanic ash clears and they let planes fly across the Atlantic again. Hopefully just a few more days, and I'll be there."

He seemed almost cheerful, as if knowing the inevitable really wasn't much to worry about. He had never allowed me to talk about the future, but he had given me, the last time I'd seen him four months earlier, all the passwords to his computer files.

"How are you today, Dad?" I asked, as I had done the previous three days.

"Not too bad. The nurses are very kind. When are you coming?"

"As soon as I can fly, I promise."

"These bloody Icelanders, first their banks and now their volcanoes," he said.

"Yeah, I know, Dad."

Four days after a diagnosis of lung cancer, he died. One day before I could get back.

Emptying his house, going through his papers, finding his poems to various loves was another achy time. Again with the support of John, sadly from a distance, and my children, family and friends like Jack and Helen, and Nick and Grainne, we held a wonderful send off for the man who had infuriated us all sometimes with his pronouncements. It was a peculiarly difficult time for Val, my sister, who had only got to know Dad the last twenty years of his life. But at least we could all laugh and love him for his peccadilloes at his funeral.

"What are we are going to do with Grandpa's ties?" Kate asked, removing hanger after hanger of ties all hung by colour code.

"Keep them," I said. "Edward might want some of them. Toss any that are really worn or grubby, but none that have regimental or club emblems."

"What are you going to do with the rest of them? There are hundreds."

"I'm going to sew them together and make a Christmas tree skirt out of them."

"Oh my God, Mum, that is weird."

"No stranger than having Granny hanging behind the bar," I said, thinking of the pencil sketch done during the War of my mother that looks down on me when I have a drink in the evening.

As TCKs, particularly aging ones, it is something we have to remember as our children, TCKs themselves, find their place in the world, wherever it might be. They have grown up seeing us deal with the difficulties of our parents aging, and dying, from a distance. We are their role models, and I don't think we have the right to expect them to handle our old age any differently. I know my sense of guilt was lessened by knowing I had done as much as I could for my parents within the parameters of my life abroad. Fortunately for me, I was able to fly back and forth when necessary, which was not something they had been able to do for their parents.

Many so-called civilized countries have, in many ways, many lessons to learn from the rest of the world. The respect given to parents and seniors is imbued from an early age, as is the respect for education and the belief it can change a life. It is seen in the different parenting styles, and it is seen in the manner in which eldercare is undertaken in different parts of the world. And finally it is seen in the manner we bury our loved ones. I think sometimes we are far too sombre, a jazz band marching through the streets sounds much more fun, or drums beating out the rhythm of our life.

Take-Away Slice: Whether it's a death or to a lesser extent a relocation, and it would be fanciful and wrong to suggest the two feelings are of a similar magnitude, the ways of dealing with both are similar. It's happened, be sad and cry, say goodbye in the way that works best for you and then get on with the living the life you have chosen.

Grief plays havoc with your emotions – you feel angry, you feel despair and guilt, and sometimes you feel a certain detachment. Roland Barthes, a French semiotician and philosopher, wrote on the death of his mother, "Each of us has his own rhythm of suffering". I think that's true, you must be kind to yourself and I think it is easier if you too have prepared.

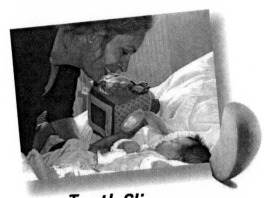

Tenth Slice:
Empty Nests and New Chicks

"Will you be okay?"

It should have been mother asking daughter, but it was the other way around. Kate was about to embark on her dream of becoming a professional dancer in London. We were in her hostel in Hampstead, her classes started the next day, and I was due to fly out.

"Yes of course, sweetheart," I said, through a mist of tears as I gave her a final hug, one that would have to keep me warm until the Christmas holidays, four months later. I flew back to Houston wondering why both my children were in England and I was in America.

Edward had essentially flown the proverbial nest three years earlier when he had gone to boarding school. At thirteen, even though it was the right decision for him, from a parental and emotional perspective he left far too early, and it was hard to adapt to not having a noisy, hungry boy in the house. Our weekends were no longer taken up with soccer tournaments, and

John missed the easy camaraderie he had with both Edward's friends and their fathers. It took me weeks to stop cooking too much for supper. Hearing the bounce of a basketball in the cul-de-sac outside our house would make me smile wryly, thinking of the times I'd wished I could deaden the noise of a ball hitting the kitchen wall when it missed the hoop. The lawn could once again be mown now the magnificent cricket matches, held most afternoons with Pakistani and Indian children, with a smattering of Americans interested in the willow, no longer tore up the grass. I missed it all.

"How could you send him away so young?" asked an American acquaintance, already prone to emotional outbursts six months before her eighteen-year-old was due to go to college forty miles up the road.

"Because he wanted to go, and it was the right decision for him."

"But what will you do?"

"What do you mean?"

"How will you fill your days?" she asked tearfully.

"Very easily," I said, moving away down the supermarket aisle before the sight of something Edward favoured reduced me to tears in front of the parent, known for her helicoptering style.

Edward, having left home at thirteen, did not lessen my angst when he and two mates spent a gap year, after school, wandering their way through Asia, Australia, New Zealand and South America.

"I don't expect daily reports," I told him, as we waved him off from Houston to join Patch and Mo in London for the start of their adventure, "But I would like an occasional 'we're okay Mum' text or email, okay?"

"I will," he promised.

"And I sure as hell don't want to know before you do anything stupid, like bungy jumping or gummying down a fast river, okay?" I went on, as I thought of the day I almost lost John before I'd even met him. "You can tell me after!"

When Kate left at eighteen, while I missed her it was a more natural loosening of the ties. She had been leading a relatively independent life, though living at home; her after school hours consumed by dance, both being taught and teaching as well as performing. She was itching to start her new life, and excited to be in London at the college of her choice.

As I sat on the Tube to Heathrow I remembered words said to me years earlier by an expat in Bangkok, sad at waving her early teenage children off to school at the airport.

"Someone once told me that as soon as your children are born you start losing them. And it's our job to ease their way. I just didn't anticipate it being this soon, or this hard," she said.

While both ours have been adored, more on some days than others, they have never been the sun, the moon and the stars to the exclusion of all else. My relationship with John has stayed strong, with the inevitable bumps of a long marriage and a few cross words, and my interests have remained varied. Certainly since the children grew out of the very needy stage of infancy.

My days were filled with work, and play, and I struggled to understand the mother who would insist on driving to a child's university every weekend to watch soccer, or football, or dance, whatever. By eighteen our children are ready to leave. University is the ideal stepping-stone; rules still govern them to some extent and expectations of good grades keep them focused, but they have an element of freedom from parental hovering.

"Please come Apple. You've done this, you know about having babies abroad."

"Of course I'll come," I said to my heavily pregnant young Australian friend. "Though I have to tell you, it makes me feel very old!" Baby showers are not my normal milieu, but I do occasionally make an exception. Maybe I was more open to the invitation because Kate had just announced she was expecting a baby the coming July. We were thrilled with the news, though I was a little sad the family dynamics were going change again so soon, particularly as the previous summer with Kate and Wayne, her partner, and Edward had been such fun, spent sailing the Adriatic with John at the helm.

Listening to the chatter over the coffee and wrapping paper about impending and early motherhood reminded me of those long ago days. Having a baby far away from home, from family and friends going through the same life-changing events, and in a country not one's own can be daunting. And now my daughter was doing the same thing, though she was technically home and I was the one away. Either way I wasn't going to be around for much of her pregnancy.

It's not the technical side of having a baby abroad that is the problem in most cases, it's the 'mum' quotient that makes it difficult. Sometimes when we are all grown up, we just need to be a child again.

Kate was born in the Netherlands and even in the dark ages of 1983, that country was progressive in its pre and antenatal care and I couldn't have wished for a better experience. Edward, three years later, was born in Thailand and again the care was wonderful. It had never occurred to me that my mother be present for either birth, but particularly with the first born, a little maternal nurturing can ease the way.

It doesn't mean a lack of confidence in yourself, your spouse, or your doctor, it means you can hand off for a nanosecond and revel in being cared for yourself. Having someone to moan to about fat feet, an aching back, or those little doubts which become huge in the middle of the night when sleep won't come because of a kicking belly. That's when you want your mum. And when you have a couple of oceans and continents between you, it can be hard.

Fathers-to-be are, on the whole, patient and put up with the inevitable emotional meltdowns whether Mum is around or not, but sometimes you want total unadulterated understanding and sympathy, not empathy. Girlfriends give empathy. Mums give sympathy, a hug and a cup of tea and then, if your mum is like my mum, a stern dose of now-buck-up-and-get-on-with-it. The only person in the world who can do that and not be relegated eternally to the crossed-off the Christmas card list.

It's an indefinable feeling even for those of us who haven't lived on the same continent as our mums for many years. It's visceral. And pregnancy and those first few days of motherhood are when it wells up along with the tears of tiredness, never far away.

The young women at the baby shower were mostly Australian, maybe that's why I felt pensive. They were a pragmatic and happy group, comfortable being pregnant and producing in Houston, but for a couple I sensed a void, an uncertainty.

"I'm not worried about having the baby, it's what comes after that which scares me, the whole parenting thing," one said, a little teary.

"That's natural," I replied. "There isn't a parent alive, or dead for that matter, who hasn't made mistakes. Ask my children. We all learn as we go along, no matter where our mums live."

And then those thoughts became more personal as my daughter's pregnancy progressed, across an ocean from her mum.

"Mum, I'd really like you to be here," Kate said, after showing me her bump over Skype.

"Oh Kate, I'd love to. Thank you. But not in the delivery room. That is a very special time for you and Wayne, the start of your own family. I'll be waiting outside."

Again thanking John for his air miles, I flew to London four days before the baby's due date. Twitching and anxious three nights later, I listened to the only other person in the brightly lit family room, a swarthy young man with a telephone clutched to his ear.

"'Allo? 'Allo?" he said, the last words I understood as the staccato Arabic sentences bounced around the quiet and chilly space. My thoughts were momentarily distracted from worrying about Kate as I focused on the language being spoken, and I wondered where in the Middle East he was from. My eyes kept drifting to the watch John had given me, pretty with a dark grey face on a gunmetal strap with diamantés instead of numbers, but almost impossible to read especially when tired and tense. Both of which I was then.

Another glance at my wrist showed me it was 11.24 when my companion's conversation ended with a snap as he closed his phone and smiled a little, shrugging in apology. I smiled back.

"You 'ave bin 'ere long time?" he asked.

"On and off since early afternoon," I responded, thinking of my rush back to the house to feed and exercise Kate's dog.

"Yes. It take time."

"It certainly does," I agreed.

We lapsed back into the silence, now and then disturbed by a juddering sigh from the vending machine ready to spew out a variety of chocolate bars and crisps ranging from plain to paprika and cheese. Another machine, though that one silent, offered Coke, Sprite and virulent coloured orange. No water. Next to it, with the insertion of coins, none of which I had, I could have had coffee with or without powdered milk, tea or hot chocolate. Various toys encouraging dexterity fought for space amongst the mess of videos scattered over a low plastic table, the off-white and scribbled on top cheered by pillar-box red legs.

As the hands crept to 11:38, my mind wandered over the last few days. Most of the first was spent in a fog of jetlag.

The next I spent with friends, first at Café des Amis du Vin, which was apt, and later at the Miró exhibition at the Tate Modern. A day that paid testament to friendships around the globe, picked up randomly in different countries, but always strong.

"How do you feel about becoming a grandmother?" Jo asked.

"Honestly? I'm thrilled for Kate and Wayne, but I feel kind of neutral. I was enjoying the kids being grown-ups," I replied, a little guilty.

Saturday saw me heading to the Forest of Dean to see my brother-in-law. Sitting on hard flip up seats in the open air watching *Richard III* performed by the Rococo Players, which whilst very good, reminded my of why I prefer Texas in summer. Wearing a borrowed fleece and Puffa jacket did nothing to alleviate the seeping chill of an English summer evening laden with a threatening drizzle. Finally, warming up later in bed my phone rang.

"I think I'm in labour, Mum," Kate said. We agreed I would head back along the A41 to London in the morning.

Back at the hospital I checked my watch again. At 11:59 I called John, waiting in Houston.

"What news?" he asked, before the phone was anywhere near his ear.

"None yet," I replied. "I'm getting nervous. I've been in the waiting room over an hour."

"Go and bang on the door," he suggested.

I scoffed though that is exactly what I wanted to do.

I had left the labour room full of good intentions, not wanting to intrude on Kate and Wayne's precious moment, the birth of their baby. Sometimes, down the years, when the going gets fraught, I think a reminder of what was shared at the very beginning is a good way to return to what is important.

At 00:14 my good intentions were ready to fly out the window. The urge to bang on the door and hurry my daughter along was building, and worry was mushrooming. If I could have laughed at myself pacing the halls outside the labour ward, a cell phone in either hand, I would have.

My companion-in-waiting joined me as I read the notices on the board, for the third time. The words appeared new.

"It take long, long time I tink," he said again.

I smiled tightly.

At 00:29 Ava arrived. I was instantly besotted. Neutrality blown away. A new phase in my life, global grandparenting.

At eleven weeks old my granddaughter became a trans-Atlantic traveller. She came to Houston while her parents celebrated a friend's wedding in Las Vegas. It was the greatest gift my daughter could have given us, a chance, as new global grandparents, to get to know our granddaughter, night-time feeds and all.

After a difficult few years in which five of our family have died, Ava is a reminder life, no matter where we live, is a continuum wonderful and precious. Along with the realisation that somehow along the way I have become one of the older generation.

I remembered Mum telling me Dad had been ambivalent about a grandchild, but when John 'phoned them in PNG to announce Kate's safe arrival, he had immediately called a number a friends, one of them my old boss Chris, and they'd drunk champagne for the rest of the day.

"Here, Dad, you feed her," I said, handing his granddaughter to him. He was in Brussels on a quick trip in his role as advisor to the PNG Government, and I had flown down from Emmen to see him with Kate, by then about three months old. It was the third weekend in November. This I know because the 1983 Beaujolais Nouveau had just been released.

"Er, no I don't think that's a very good idea," Dad said smiling at Kate's gurgling grin.

"Why not?"

"Well, I've never fed a baby."

"You never fed me? "

"No, I don't think so. I don't really remember. Your mother was there, and I think Adelaide as well. You probably don't remember her, she was your nanny."

"Well guess what, Dad? You're about to feed to your granddaughter."

I now understand Dad's ambivalence because it somehow surprised me that our child, who we traipsed from Europe to Asia to America with a short sojourn to the West Indies added to the mix, has had the temerity to grow up and have a child of her own, in England. The place she currently calls home, though in true TCK fashion anticipates leaving soon to return to the Caribbean with her partner and my grandchild, neither place being where I am.

Like my neutrality, Dad's ambivalence disappeared the moment he heard of her birth and he became a besotted grandparent the moment he set eyes on Kate. John, unlike my father, was a very hands-on parent and, when Ava arrived, swung into Grandpa mode with aplomb.

I never knew Mum's parents but had a loving, though long distant relationship with my father's. And yet I feel so lucky. Our children had caring relationships with grandparents, brought about by the efforts of all concerned, with letters and visits both to wherever we happened to be living, and with visits to them. An enterprise certainly made less complicated when my parents retired from their own globe trotting days.

For my parents-in-law an international nomadic lifestyle was not what they were used to, yet within Britain they had moved with the job, and so understood we too had to move with the job, albeit across oceans instead of counties. Their acceptance of an oceans-apart relationship with our children was eased by their willingness to step outside their boundaries and come to where we were. It enabled them to better understand our lives and their grandchildren's upbringing.

"Hello, sweetpea," I said on Skype, waggling my fingers in an attempt to get Ava to focus on me.

"Look, Ava," her mother said, directing her daughter's eyes to the screen, "It's Gigi."

We continued in this vein until it became obvious my rapidly growing granddaughter was really much more interested in the family dog than a strange blurry woman, whose voice she might vaguely recognise.

"Why Gigi?" Kay asked, first to know any new family happening and having been shown the latest photos.

"Because I can't very well be Granny Apple, can I?" I answered.

"'Spose not," she said, spluttering into her coffee. "How'd you come to that?"

"Well it should be obvious, but clearly isn't. Gorgeous Granny?" I said. "Or more prosaically Grumpy Granny, Granny Gidley, or how about Global Granny?"

It is without doubt easier now to build a loving relationship with children over the ether, Kate is adamant Ava knows her scattered family, some in Trinidad, some in America, and some in England. We will all be a part of her growing up.

Hopping on a plane holds no fears for my daughter, or granddaughter it seems, wherever they or we might live. We anticipate regular trips across whichever ocean separates us, but there is still no replacement for the neck-nuzzling delight of a little baby, or the joy of sharing new discoveries so prevalent in a child's life.

As a TCK mother of a TCK child and a soon-to-be TCK grandchild I might miss a lot of firsts. Global grandparenting is a new element in our lives, one I relish and look forward to, but it still seems strange the global life cycle has now turned a full rotation, and I will have to get used to saying goodbye to my grandchild, as well as my children.

Take-Away Slice: Saying goodbye never stops hurting and a dull ache settles into my heart every time I do, whether it is John or the kids. It drags me down for a couple of days and then my life takes over again until the next departure. I am the same with friends. Family and friends know I will leave quickly and not look back, a repetition of my mother leaving me at NEGS and me leaving Edward at Blundells, and then Kate and now Ava in London.

Eleventh Slice: Home is where...

"Let's go home," Kate cooed to Ava after a morning spent trawling the Houston malls.

"Agoo," her daughter agreed, flailing her arms and kicking her legs against the Baby Bjorn carrier holding her close to her mother, my daughter.

'Home' is a word we say all the time, whether returning from a shopping trip to our real home, or a temporary home, or whether we are returning to a hotel room after a day exploring Angkor Wat.

So why do we put so much store in that question 'where is home?' Why does it cause so much angst for TCKs? For long-time expatriates who say, "I don't know where home is anymore." Does it matter? Why do we have to have a static home?

I don't think we do.

Home is with me wherever I go, because home is my memories and being with John, and if the children, their partners and now Ava, happen to be around as well, then my home is full. It is not a single building or a single country, but many of them.

Which, when I consider some of the places we've called home, is fortunate. I have lived in some wonderful places, which for a short space of time I called home. But like all things, the ones not quite so comfortable or quite so attractive are the ones I remember, in some ways, with the fondest memories.

I consider temporary housing, the term used by HR departments and country managers, to span a month, six weeks at the most and so I was okay with John's warning that the temporary accommodation would be a little spartan in Equatorial Guinea. We were heading back to the continent I started out on and I was happy.

The drumbeat of Africa pulses lazily, but always within me. Not with the naiveté of tented safaris, big game and beautiful black babies, but with an understanding garnered from living in other developing countries. Childhood memories may have been hazy, but the urge to return has always been strong. Intangible. It took some getting to.

Turning off the main road from the Malabo Airport, I was pleasantly surprised to enter a large planted compound where tiny, irridescent blue and green humming birds darted amongst brilliant red and tangerine hibiscus blooms. To the right was a small copse of casuarinas and avocado trees giving shade and fruit, both being enjoyed by a gathering of lethargic young men.

"That's the First Lady's residence through there," John pointed to a gap in the chicken-wire fence being overrun with mauve Morning Glory.

"I'll have to keep Miss Meg on the leash," I said, as her ears perked up at the peacocks strutting around the gardenias.

"They only seem to come out in the evening and early

morning. She'll be fine," I was assured. "They make a strange noise though, almost sounds as if they're barking sometimes."

Around the bend on the brow of the slight hill, two buildings, each with three separate verandas, came into view. Their tin roofs were succumbing to the combined forces of searing African sun and thunderous monsoon rains, the black paint peeling off in shards. The walls were crumbling from the same onslaught.

"I did tell you we'd be sharing a roof with two others," John said, as the Toyota truck clanked to a stop and Francisco, the company greeter, helped me out and then worked three keys to enter the little house.

"Uhuh," I said, noting security and safety were obviously paramount for the new resident country manager and his wife. And then I noticed the shuttered windows had no glass. Neither did they have even rudimentary clasps, but listed towards each other in a parody of alignment. "Oh God," I said on entering. "Nouvelle African chic."

The deep crimson, pseudo-leather sofa, I quickly learned, scorched the back of the legs before encouraging sweat to pool unpleasantly under the knees. Any attempt to rise became a challenge due to the suctioning grip of the plastic. The armchair was the same. The side tables were glass and chrome, the latter showed signs of rust where the condensation from countless beer bottles had rolled into the joints.

It was a dark little room, but the lighting was intense. A Rococo-style chandelier dominated the low ceiling with additional illumination coming from wall sconces. The dining table, overlooked by a menacing print of *The Last Supper*, was surrounded by four high-backed chairs whose seats were covered in a sunny yellow velour. Macabre tribal scenes adorned the other walls.

The air-conditioner fought a valiant battle with the humid whorls that crept invidiously through the shutters, along with flying bugs whose splodges dappled the sconce shades.

"It won't be for long," John promised, as he and Francisco unloaded the truck under Miss Meg's supervision. She specialised in getting her four legs under any two that happened to be in the way. "Three bedrooms, two bathrooms, almost the same as Houston. Have a look at the rest of the place."

"Hmmm. I have, it doesn't take long," I said, from the kitchen. Cooking, over the years, has become a relaxing pleasure for me. I do not need the latest Gaggenau appliances, but an oven would've been nice, instead there was a two ring electric hob. I opened one of the two small fridges. "Oh look, someone's left us some beer and water," I called. "That's kind." I opened the other. Nothing. "But we'll have to get some other supplies today."

"No problem. Let's just get a little organised and then we'll go into town," John said, swigging some water and leaning against the small stainless steel sink with one tap, cold, which sat in the middle of the counter whose cracked laminate was coming unglued. Above, precariously attached and listing on the walls, were cupboards held shut with teaspoons slotted through the handles. There was no shutter on the small square window, but the piece of fine mesh stapled over the hole would, I was sure, have been an effective bug screen had there not been a large tear in it.

"Okay, let's just unpack enough for tonight and for work for you tomorrow." I agreed, trying not to touch the mould spreading like bruised tentacles up the bedroom walls. The windows in the bedroom had glass, and rattled eerily as soon as the wind rose above a whisper but at least kept the room cool. The air-conditioner, an ancient machine snuffled and snorted like a rheumy old man with a fifty-fags-a-day cough. The closet was sturdy unless the door was carelessly tugged open, which sent a judder through its old frame and the hanging rail tipping off its precarious rest.

"The bed isn't too bad," John said, lying down amidst clothes already fallen off the wardrobe rail.

"I'm going to hang these here," I said, looping his silk ties over the curtain rail. There were no curtains so competition for space was slight.

Francisco had grudgingly handed over the keys of the pick-up and after a cursory attempt at tidying up and leaving the delights of the bathroom until later, we headed into the town for immediate supplies. Knowing Miss Meg would howl if left alone so soon in her new environs, she came too.

"I did warn you it was a little shambolic," John said, as he negotiated the highway, maneuvering past a gaggle of children wearing shorts and kicking a torn soccer ball.

"Are you okay to drive without a license?" I asked, visualising a bad start to our new posting if we got stopped or worse, had a prang.

"Yeah, I'm fine on my US one for a few days," he replied.

"Some of the older buildings could be lovely again," I said, as we passed the Town Hall, a Spanish colonial building with crumbling yellow walls, and a chipped and dry mosaic fountain at it's entrance. "They just need some paint and a bit of TLC."

"We'll go to the red shop first. I think *Hermanos Martinez* is the best stocked, but I can't remember where it is," John said, as he parked by the edge of an open drain, between a dumpster buzzing with flies, frantic for the rotting flesh inside, and a rusted green car fixed with parts pilfered from other vehicles.

"First?" I said, lowering the windows for Megan and trying not to step in the spilt and slimy overflow of trash.

"Yup, probably have to do the rounds to get everything," he said.

"Wow, wouldn't want to go short," I said, as pushing through the single swing door we were confronted with a wall of green beer bottles. The shop was dark and cool, with swept, though uneven, concrete floors that caught the wheels of the trolley and sent jolts up unsuspecting arms. High ceiling fans turned idly, swaying strips of sticky fly-encrusted paper. It was not the kind of supermarket I had got used to in America.

Tins stocked the rough unlined, wooden shelves. Tomatoes, peas, tuna, corned beef and *halal* luncheon meat, beans of various sorts and catering-size tins of olives. Loo paper, of the grease proof kind, and kitchen roll shared space with bleach and toothpaste but mostly the unvarnished shelves were bare.

"There must be a shipment due," reassured my husband. "Lots of wine though. We can discover *riojas.*"

"Nice for you, but I don't drink red wine," I reminded him, as he picked up his first bottle of *Campo Viejo.* "Let's get a rosé as well. Spain don't do whites do they?" I asked.

"Not really, no."

"Not a lot of fresh produce then," I said, eyeing a couple of droopy lettuces, edges a frilly brown, like an old-fashioned swimming cap.

"I think the market is quite good," John encouraged me. "A good deli though," he continued, peering through the smeared glass of the cabinet, protected from flies by flaps of once clear plastic attached to the back. "Look at all that cheese. And the salami looks okay. Let's just get some basics today. We'll do a proper shop tomorrow when we're not quite so tired."

"Alright, here goes." I said. "*Buenas tardes Señor.*"

"'*Tardes*," replied the surly faced man behind the counter, wiping his hands down his almost white jacket. He shoved *jambon* into a plastic bag for an African in a suit, black shirt and dark glasses.

"*Por favor, damme salami y queso*," I asked, pointing to a cheese that looked like Edam.

"*Quanto?*"

"Er," I pleaded to John. "How much do we want?"

"Just get a few slices for now."

"Oh great, and how exactly do I say that?" I asked, gesturing to the man already impatient with my fumbling attempts at Spanish.

Dog food could not be found so we settled on a tin of corned beef for Meg's first Malabo dinner.

"How much was that?" I asked John, handed a wad of notes to the Lebanese cashier, yellow smoke curling up his pockmarked face from a cigarette stuck to his cracked lips.

"About fifty dollars."

"For that! Damn. It's going to be expensive here," I said, as we waited for our goods to be bagged. The packer, a young man in a tattered Met's tee-shirt, was disappointed when we carried our own bags and I realised we should have tipped him.

"Well, it's an island. Everything has to be imported," I was reminded. "Booze is cheap though!"

"Oh that's alright then. Keep 'em drunk and happy," I replied, Meg wagging her welcome as we got back into the pick-up and headed home.

After our shopping spree and before I was treated to a night out on the town, our new home, I tried out the main bathroom while John showered in the little one. We might have had the luxury of two bathrooms, but we learnt very quickly lack of water pressure meant they could not be used simultaneously.

The shower hose and head did not attach to the wall and the head itself had a tendency to swivel at most inopportune times.

Bathing became part of my workout routine.

"Did you know the baths are three feet long and twenty-one inches wide?" I demanded, after one particularly trying session. "I measured them this morning."

Added to this, the hell of a power outage in the midst of ablutions made lingering in the bathroom not an option. The drainage was questionable. Large and very hairy tarantulas regularly had to be encouraged to roam elsewhere.

"Oh my God," I shrieked, having neglected to turn on the light when in need of a night-time pee, and about to perch. "John, come here!"

"What's the matter?" he grumbled, groggy from the rude awakening.

"There's a snake in the loo. Do something."

"Oh bloody hell, can't you just flush it? It's only little."

"No, I can't. It might come back."

We shared the same roof as our two neighbours and insulation between the homes was the merest slither of plywood. There was ample opportunity to share the sounds of day-to-day living and we became friends quickly. Friends do not tell tales. It was home but I did not consider five months 'temporary'.

When discussing the pros and cons of taking Miss Meg on our latest adventure, my primary argument had been that she loved us unconditionally and trusted nobody she hadn't been introduced to. It was during those five months in temporary accommodation her night-time role of guard dog was tested.

Meg's bed was in the steamy little living room with its latchless shutters and was not to her liking; given half a chance she would abandon her post. We would find her in the morning lying comfortably in the airstream at my side of the bed. Chastised, her tail would wag contritely, only for the pattern to be repeated when next the door showed nudgeability.

One night a guttural sound percolated through the miasma of a dreamless sleep. Struggling through the cotton wool of consciousness, I saw Megan's rump hunched and tense, her tail a taut straight line, trembling like a cat set to pounce.

"John?"

"Huh?" he responded manfully.

"Wake up!" I jabbed him.

"Wha'?" Meg's continuous growling penetrated the fog and he bolted up.

"A body. There," I whispered, pointing.

"Shit. Watch it." Struggling into shorts while pulling the light cord dangling by the door, he slid out of bed.

I watched.

"Oi, levantarse!" John said, standing above the prone shape.

"Is he dead?" I asked, from the safety of my pillows.

"No, of course not," he said, toeing the body's leg. With a slightly firmer foot he tried again. The body moved. Meg strained closer, breathing the same air.

"Get up!" John repeated.

The shape slowly stood, eyes never leaving the white teeth glinting millimeters away, to reveal a bare-chested youth of about nineteen in tatty shorts fastened with wire.

"Stay here!" my husband told me, hauling a tee-shirt on as he shoved the youth into the living room with Meg clipping his heels.

Arms already insiding out my kimono, I followed.

John, on the red *faux* leather armchair, was positioned

between the barefoot boy, now with out-turned pockets, and the front door. The shutters, gaping rudely, allowed moths and mosquitoes in with impunity. Man and dog glared at the intruder staring unblinkingly at the floor. Always good at waiting for explanations, my husband stayed silent and still.

I sidled through the arch into the kitchen ignoring John's scowl. Unsure what to do once there, I tugged open the only working drawer and removed two large, very blunt knives. There being no steel or sharpener, I started methodically, some might say maniacally, scraping the two knives. Why I will never know. I have a strong aversion to violence, besides which, blood would've spoiled my new, just-bought-for-Africa kimono.

Over the *szt, szt, szt* of blade on blade I heard the questions start.

"*Cómo se llama usted, joven?*" John asked the boy's name.

The reply was mumbled.

"*Dónde vives?*"

"*En Los Angeles,*" the boy replied.

Los Angeles, I knew from my wanderings, was near the Central Market. A warren of three-storey, crumbling, breeze-block buildings where electricity was as sporadic as in the rest of Malabo. It was not uncommon to see students clustered around the few working streetlights doing their homework. Water, when there was any, was pumped from standpipes in the middle of the dirt squares.

"*Porque es aquí?*"

Good question. I wanted to know why he was in my bedroom.

"Spik ingris liddle," the youth said, instead of answering the question.

"Why are you here?" John repeated.

"Nee yob. Me hered yu niu *jeffé* in Malabo."

"This is not how you get a job," said the new boss town.

I heard a smile in John's voice. With knives now not quite so blunt I slipped back into the interrogation room and ignoring my spouse's glare, sat at the dining table. The yellow velour electrified my kimono. The boy's eyes slid over to me, maybe to make sure I didn't have gleaming knives with me. Reassured, they returned to the floor, a swirl of bilious brown tile.

His explanation was halting, and heartbreaking. His father opposed the regime and was regularly beaten and thrown in jail, his mother died while giving birth to his sister who had surprisingly survived the odds. Now a teenager, the youth was her sole provider whenever his father was incarcerated. As in most small places, jobs were not readily available for someone whose affiliations were known.

"Write your name and address," John said, pushing pen and paper across the low ring-stained table between them. Miss Meg, whose snarling had eased to an occasional growl, revved up again.

"Shush," John petted her as the youth wrote.

John stood as did Meg, hackles a spiky ridge along her back, and said, "Now go home. If you return I will call the police. Do you understand?"

"Si, me unerstan', *señor. Gracias,"* the boy said, stuffing his pockets back in, and eyeing Miss Meg warily, edged around her.

"Do not come back here," Jay repeated, unlocking the three-keyed door.

"No *jeffé,* teng yu. *Señora, lo siento."* The youth apologised to me.

"What do we do now?" I asked, watching John relock the door and jiggle the shutters to an approximation of closed.

"Have a cup of tea," he said, as a flash of lightening heralded a torrent of equatorial rain.

"Did you believe him?" I asked over the roar.

"Yes I did. He could've taken your wallet and phone, which by the way you really shouldn't leave out here at night. Why the knives?"

"Didn't know what else to do," I replied, sipping tea with long-life milk.

"You're mad," he said with a hug. "And you Miss Meg are to sleep out here!"

The next morning I was amused to see my trainers had disappeared from the doorstep of our temporary home.

I suppose one of the biggest lessons I've learnt along the way is that things and people are not always what they at first seem. Sometimes we just have to take a leap and trust our instincts because things normally work out.

A home for me is completed when four legged creatures join the *tableaux*, though John and I have never had the menagerie I grew up with, and I've never had another monkey as a playmate. The overriding factor in not having a dog until we 'settled' in Houston the first time, was that I did not want to have to quarantine one.

Hardhearted as it sounds it is easier, for me at least, to leave a cat than a dog in the knowledge cats are so much more self-reliant. That is not to say I haven't loved our cats, which we've had wherever we have lived, and haven't shed buckets whenever we have had to leave them, but I was pretty sure once they had got over the hump at being relocated they forgot me, though we never forgot them.

Chatuchak Weekend Market in Bangkok, with Kate, was where I realised I was a pushover for both my daughter and bundles of fur, the latter against my better judgement.

"What shall we call them?" I asked Kate, as we eased the two kittens out of the box onto the floor once we got home.

"Fit and Fot," she answered immediately, looking at the marmalade spots on their white fur though being quite unable to pronounce 'sp'. Spoon became foon, and Fit and Fot were known as Spit and Spot to all but Kate.

The kittens provided much entertainment and having been checked out by the vet my concerns at buying from a market were allayed.

Kate, by then at the advanced age of three, was comfortable in her ability to feed and care for the kittens on her own, shades of me untethering Munnings.

"Mummy look," she said one Sunday morning, as she staggered into my bedroom clutching Spit.

"Oh my God, Kate what have you done?" I screeched, looking at the rainbow-hued kitten and levitating out of bed.

"Same like the wings, look. Pretty," she said, turning to give me a clear view of the fairy wings strapped to her back, which we had made the day before using food colouring.

"Where is the colouring now Kate? And Spot?" I asked, lifting Spit from her arms and heading downstairs.

"He runned away," she said. "And I feeded them too."

She had indeed fed the cats, spurning their normal kibble and instead giving them flour, Coco Pops and rice, most of which had also seen some food colouring. It took a while to clean up.

And then one evening, thankfully after Kate was in bed, Spit's tiny little stomach bloated and his mewls of pain had me sobbing as I held him. The vet wasn't answering, I couldn't contact John and so I fed him eyedropperfuls of brandy until he slipped into a coma and eventually died.

The next morning the same thing happened to Spot, but the vet was open this time.

I promised myself no more market animals. All our other cats fared better.

"What shall we call them?" I asked the kids, as we watched kittens scamper around the sitting room in Aberdeen.

"I am not standing at the door calling for Bing 'n' Ella," John rejected our first option, "It sounds like an Australian tin mining town."

The rest of the family thought the names rather clever, after Bing Crosby and Ella Fitzgerald. We settled on Boots and Ella, which I thought sounded like pasta.

And then we got Meg.

When we moved to the United States with the children we went with expectations it would be a long-term posting, and the promise of a much-longed for dog helped increase the excitement. A week after moving into our house Megan, or variations of that name, joined our family. That dog made me believe in serendipity. The last of the abandoned litter to be adopted, due, I was told, to her shyness and reluctance to go to anyone. I went to see her on my own so if she weren't suitable the kids would not be so disappointed. I sat on the floor and this bright-eyed little black and white Australian cattle dog mix pup climbed onto my lap and licked my face. She brought unquestionable joy to our lives.

We ended up with three other pets in Kingwood. Shadow joined us after John and I heard a mewling from the undergrowth when we were walking Meg late one evening. I took the dog home and by the time I'd returned with a saucer and some milk my hard-hearted husband was sitting in the damp with a tiny blur of grey fur on his lap, just starting to purr. Shadow and

Meg slept together from then on. Another stray cat, Millie, joined us a few years later.

"Mum," Kate sobbed down the phone.

"What is it sweetheart?" I asked, my mind instantly taking me to car crashes, Kate having just started driving.

"Oh Mum, I had to stop," she cried.

"Kate tell me what's happened. Where are you?"

"Just around the corner. I hate people Mum," she said.

"Stay there, I'll come to you."

"No I'm okay, I'll come home now. But I've got a puppy on my lap."

"Oh Kate! Okay, come home and we'll sort it out."

She had seen a well-dressed, bejewelled woman stop her SUV, open the back door and then deposit the puppy in the trees beside the road. The number of dogs we 'found' on our walks with Miss Meg put a whole new meaning to the tagline touted by Kingwood, 'the liveable forest'.

We kept the pup until we could find a good home for her but the others, about seven, all older and less appealing to adoptees, we had to take to the SPCA. Something of course their owners should have done.

But Miss Meg was special. I rarely lay down ultimatums as I find they have a tendency to backfire. This time I did. "If I go, the other bitch goes too," I told my long-suffering spouse, as we discussed the likelihood of a posting to Equatorial Guinea.

He nodded, resigned to travelling from America to Africa in the company of two recalcitrant females, both whining and howling at different stages of the journey.

Departure day dawned hellish hot and the check-in staff at the American Airlines counter did all they humanly could to make the transfer of an animal of dubious origins as difficult as possible. This despite the plethora of paperwork I had at hand. Passport, check; rabies certificate, check, though I thought that a bit rich considering our destination; bortadella certificate, check, though I wondered how many dogs would be on the same plane to a miniscule, despotic West African country. I was pretty sure I could count them on one finger.

Paperwork finally done we waved our black and white hybrid off. Her indignation at being caged precluded her from waving back. As she disappeared into the confines of the truck charged with delivering her to the plane, her whines changed to howls. It was not a happy start to twenty-four hours of intercontinental hell.

Houston to Dallas, the first stage of our trip was short. It was the next leg that worried me most. The transfer of said dog from one plane to another. What if they left her in the initial plane? What if they left her in the truck? What if she needed to pee? What if she ran away while peeing? What if they forgot to turn the air-conditioning on in the hold of the next plane? It was here John's forbearance was sorely tested as he attempted to pacify me.

I was distracted for a moment as I turned to glare at the large, sweaty and over-burdened woman following me up the aisle as she clipped my heels yet again with the sharp edge of her push-in-front carry on.

Being the shorter member of our partnership I was urged into the middle seat where I spent a couple of moments organising my affairs. Book, glasses, Hello! magazine, water. My patience was admirable. I waited until the vast majority of the travelling public were in situ and then urged my husband to flag down a stewardess.

"Do you mean a flight attendant?"

"You know exactly what I mean. Just grab one please."

It was here the real inadequacies of the flight staff came to the fore. Their ability to not see an initially politely raised hand, and later a frantically waving arm and hand as they slammed their way down the aisles, pushing and shoving bulging bags into the confines of the overhead lockers, was astounding.

"Do you think they are all myopic?" I muttered, as another turned on her heel as she neared our section.

"Just busy," John placated me.

"Rubbish. Not one of them has actually helped anyone with bags, or seats," I replied as my waving reached fever pitch. "Excuse me," I said, now standing.

"Yes?"

"Would you mind checking my dog has been loaded in the temperature-controlled hold please?" I asked, with a near perfect smile.

"All cargo is aboard," the woman, whose uniform strained across an ample rump, said. "Please sit down, we are about to close the doors and leave the jetway."

Now I knew that wasn't true because I could see stragglers still stumbling along the aisle on the long trek to the back of the aircraft. I smiled again.

"I'm sure it has, but would you please just double check for me, I am anxious."

"Ma'am, please sit. I have told you, all cargo is aboard," the bitch in blue replied. "Now please sit down."

I remained standing. "My dog is live cargo, not exactly the same as luggage is it? Now please just check for me."

"You have to sit."

"Not until you have checked," I countered.

John touched my arm tentatively. "She'll be okay you know."

"I just want to know she is actually on the plane. Look at them all, standing around doing bugger all. It is not a huge ask."

Another woman in blue, this one slightly less large and a little less aged, approached. "Ma'am, you really must sit down, we are about to start moving."

"I am not sitting down until you have confirmed my dog is aboard. Is it really that difficult to check for me?"

"S'right hun," said a voice behind me, "I'd wanna know too."

"Yeah," said another from across the aisle.

I smiled my gratitude at their understanding. John sat resigned. I stood defiant as I watched the hostess's jagged walk to the front of the plane scream irritation. Her passage was thwarted by a stocky man in khaki, and as they danced the tight-squeeze-tango I felt a pang for the passenger faced with a blue-clad behind.

The man continued his amble down the aisle. He checked a piece of wilted paper and approached. "Are you Miss Meg's mom?" he asked.

"Yes, that's me."

"Jes' wan'd to letya know, she's jes' fine. Mighty pretty dawg ya got there. Gave 'er another ice cube. She'll be fine."

"Oh thank you so much." If I could have reached him, I would have kissed him.

"No problem ma'am. Y'all 'ave a good flight now," he said, as he turned and made his way back along the plane.

I bounced into the hardness of the seat, buckled up and smiled at my husband.

"Thank God, now we can relax," he said, squeezing my hand.

"You happy now?" tossed the hostess, as she retreated to her seat ready for take off, and before her next arduous task of dispensing beef or chicken.

"Yes thank you," I replied sweetly.

After nearly three years in Africa the flight back to Houston was incident free, due in no small part to the fact we flew on a charter flight. And then suddenly it seemed our companion of almost fourteen years was dying. After ten days of subcutaneously injecting fluids four times a day to try and alleviate her kidney disease, it was getting increasingly difficult to find an area in the scruff of her neck in which to insert a needle. Due, the vet said, to her skin becoming saturated and sore.

Blood tests showed an alarming increase in numbers of the relevant areas, all bad news, and it was suggested the final injection be administered.

"No," I said, "We have to go for a walk."

I called John who said, "Not today, it's too soon." He was right.

We spent the weekend injecting when, and what, we could. Sometimes 250cc of sodium chloride took 25 minutes, sometimes 10. Either way it was horrid. Sometimes Miss Meg quivered, other times she lay still for the most part, occasionally lifting her head as if to check for herself the slowly descending trickle from the bag hanging above her head. As the needle was removed, she stood, shook and wagged her tail in forgiveness before moving to another part of the apartment, away from our probing.

In between the indignity she mostly slept, but when she woke she did what she had always done. Check up on me, coming to my desk and nudging my knee demanding attention in the form of neck rub or a tummy tickle. If John were around she would amble off to find him and demand the same administrations. They were always forthcoming. Her normal *modus operandi* would be then to have a quick drink before resuming her post on her daybed, having checked the borders of her domain.

After a month of eating the barest minimum, even with tidbits of cheese to tempt her, she stopped. We gave her an appetite stimulant, which made her ravenous but induced vomiting. I took her off it and then for some reason she started eating of her own accord. Always a finickity eater, she let it be known only chicken or mince, with a little couscous, were acceptable morsels. Dog food of any variety was spurned.

We had shared a bedroom in hotels across the breadth of the southern United States and when the sign said 'no dogs allowed' she graciously slept in the car. She watched the sunrise over the east end of the Grand Canyon with us and her junior charges, Kate and Edward. She drove with me from La Paz, Baja California to Houston, Texas, a road trip of five days and numerous stops by the *La Guardia* checking for drugs on the Mexican side of the border. As each case was tossed from the car and searched she would growl and strain at her leash warning the nervous and armed soldier not to even think of stepping near me.

She boated with us, rounded us up in numerous oceans and lakes swimming in ever decreasing circles as she coralled us, her family, into a manageable circle. The only thing she had ever fetched, despite years of trying, was a forbidden cricket ball in the middle of an inning but has wrestled, rolled and frolicked with the children for hours.

She had nurtured stray cats that wandered into her world, sharing a bed and a bowl with the scrappy little bundles of fur until a home could be found for them, but had chased every squirrel, possum or raccoon with the temerity to cross her path.

She pined when our children moved away to be grown ups. She sulked when the suitcases came out for a holiday she sensed she had no part of. Meg had been known to turn her back on her master as he attempted to pet her before leaving on a business trip. He was forgiven the instant he returned from a day or a month on the road, as we have all been.

Touch rugby was a normal Sunday outing for both her and John. He had not planned to take her that last Sunday. It was very hot and she was getting weaker, but she would not be left, tripping him up as he made his preparations to leave without her. She normally wandered the perimeter of the pitch while he and a dozen or so French, Dutch, British and Australian men raced around in the Houston humidity tossing an oval shaped ball up and down to their respective try lines. That day she lay and watched. She was proud of her role as official team mascot.

Meg had been my constant and utterly faithful friend, never telling tales of my foibles, never laughing at my idiosyncrasies. She featured in my stories. She danced with me and Tina Turner in my kitchen and stayed by my side as I recuperated from back surgery. She demanded attention and licked my tears, shed in private.

Megan loved this family unconditionally and she was a lesson in living life well. And we knew we had to find the strength to say, "Enough" when over the next few days her energy ebbed and her eyes dulled. We owed her that.

It was one of the few times I was glad Kate and Edward were not home. But I have never regretted having the pets we did, whether cats, terrapins, hamsters or Miss Meg. The joy they gave, the lessons they taught, the laughter they provoked, and the memories of homes around the world made the farewell tears a small price to pay.

It's not just places, people and pets that remind us where home is. Food, I think, also plays a part. We all have likes and dislikes; some dishes for comfort, some make us feel adventurous, some might even make us gag.

Food memories go back a long way, the first probably to the same sea voyage where I encountered the gully-gully man, which shows how long ago it was. That journey instantly invokes camels, olives and whisky. Camels because of their ungainly galumphing along the sandy desert, olives and whisky because each evening my mother would 'dress' for dinner and join the grown-up world as I dozed off in the top bunk of our little cabin. I would be brought back to sleepy consciousness by the gentle waft of whisky as she tiptoed back in a few hours later. If I woke fully I knew there would be a little bowl of olives, those big fat green ones with the pimento in the middle, sitting on the shelf by my bunk.

Thoughts of KL take me to the eight years Ah Moi ruled our kitchen; no one has ever been able to replicate her fluffy yellow omelettes, almost floating on the plate and yet stuffed full of cheese and bacon.

"Who's up for *satay* at Newton Circus?" Dad would ask some Sunday afternoons when we lived in Singapore.

"Me, me," Mum and I would answer, and we'd pile into the car and join the throng of Singaporeans, Malays, Tamils, Indians and European expats circling the huge roundabout looking for parking.

I loved watching the small charcoal braziers being fanned by wizened Malays hunkered back on their heels, sarongs firmly hitched up between their knees and *songkoks* askew on jet black hair, as they brushed oil and spices onto the chicken or beef or lamb threaded on bamboo sticks sizzling on the open flame.

"*Untuk anda* Missy," the man would say, as he offered me the tin plate filled with neatly laid out *satay.*

Mum's job was always to find, and then hoard, three plastic chairs around a rickety fold-up table, having already collected bowls of cooling cucumber needed to counteract the tangy peanut dip, and for her and Dad, with their hardy taste buds, shredded chilli in a vinegar sauce.

Sheep's eyes, spew and sinker fall into the gagging category.

Mum, Dad and I were the only foreigners and all eyes were on us as we attended the wedding reception of one of Dad's Chinese accountants not long before we left KL. I would have been about fourteen. We were seated at different tables, big round ones with lazy Susans centred on the crisp white cloths. Chopsticks, a bowl and spoon marked each place. A pile of thin pink paper serviettes and glasses of pink sugarcane juice, drizzling condensation into damp patches, provided the only colour.

Knowing we were in for a nine-course banquet I had paced myself. As a bevy of *cheongsam*-clad waitresses placed trays overflowing with a sheep's head, mouth stuffed with an apple and vegetables surrounding it in the midst of each table, I was ready.

"Miss Aphu, I give you," said Mr Goh, the groom's brother. He leant over and carefully, reverently, plucked the left eye out of the socket and with great dexterity placed the orb, a little shrivelled from boiling, squarely on my empty plate. It looked at me. I looked at it. "Eat, eat," he said.

It seemed like forever was in those seconds as we looked at each other, the dead eye and my eye. I picked up my chopsticks, regretting the hours spent using them in Ah Moi's kitchen. I was too good. Having been complimented earlier on my easy manipulation of the two pieces of lacquered bamboo, the eye could not now be accidentally dropped. With stomach contracting and throat gagging I picked it up and shoved it in my mouth and swallowed. Twice.

I smiled around the slimy sensation of eye meeting tongue. Delighted murmurs came from around the table.

"Oh Mr Goh, thank you, but perhaps your wife would like the honour," I said as I saw the other eye about to be planted on my plate by my generous table host.

I learnt two things that evening, I could eat one eye and diplomacy could save me from eating the other.

'Spew and sinker' was the regular Saturday lunchtime tradition at NEGS – forgive the vulgarity, but we were teenagers. In reality it was stew and steamed pudding; one served with congealed gravy, the other with a thick rubber coating on the custard worthy of its given name of 'fly's aerodrome', neither of which have been a favourite since that first weekend offering.

My culinary skills are varied, taking in a little of everywhere I have lived, but I think it fair to say the foods from my formative years make me feel most at home – they are certainly all things I now prepare, though my omelettes have never reached the delectable heights of those to come out of Ah Moi's kitchen.

"What," I asked Kate recently, "Foods make you think of home?"

"*Roti* and chicken curry," she instantly replied, surprising me yet again, which has pretty much been the case since she was born 28 years ago. If I were a betting woman I would have lost with my sure and easy answer of *quesadillas* and *fajitas*, she having spent her teenage years in Texas just north of the border down Mexico way. "It's the first thing I have whenever we go back," she explained. She has a right to her choice, it was what she was weaned on when we lived in Trinidad oh so many years ago, and she goes back regularly.

Edward never returned to Blundells without a boxful of flapjacks, his comfort food to make him feel at home at school. And he always expected chicken pie on his first night home, and still does. The tangy taste of *bitterballen met mayonnaise* is often what I yearn for after an evening out, a habit we picked up from that long ago Dutch period of our lives.

But it's not just the foods, it's the people who have served them, or who have invited us to share their meals, or who we've met along the road that have helped make us feel at home, wherever home happens to be at the time, like Faiz in Malacca who looked after the kids and I, and encouraged us to eat worms.

Occasionally though, and I think particularly when we are going through the sandwich generation part of life, trying to keep college children and aging parents on an even keel, feeling settled and at home anywhere can become a real issue.

"Where are you?" I asked Pat over the 'phone, struggling to hear her through the chatter around me.

"Edinburgh," she replied. "Decided to stop in and see Dad for a week on my way to Houston."

"How is he?" I asked, thinking of the sprightly roué who had graced many of our parties the first time we lived in Houston, a glass of whisky in hand as he regaled us with stories of his past in a lovely soft brogue.

"Getting old," she said. "And a bit grumbly."

"It's horrid isn't it? But wonderful that you can spend time with him now. When are you coming here?"

"End of the week. The kids will all be gathering for

Thanksgiving so we get to see them all at once. Jock's arriving on Saturday, direct from Dharan."

"Great, save some time for us before you head home!"

"God, Apple. I don't know where bloody home is. Saudi, Scotland or the States? I seem to spend equal amounts of time in all, and always want, or need, to be in the place I'm not, if you see what I mean."

"Yeah I do. It's not easy. I guess you just have to try and live in each moment."

Growing up, my mother despaired of me ever knowing anything about gardening. With four gardeners looking after the five acres surrounding our house in KL I really didn't see the need to be involved, though she spent hours each day tending her orchids. Rows and rows of purple vandas, yellow dendrobium, and dappled tiger orchids which once cut graced every corner of the house and often made their way, airfreight, to either England or Australia for family events. But as with many teenagers it is surprising how much I learnt from her, and orchids made up my wedding bouquet.

But gardening became a way for me to feel at home in every place. Holland was my first attempt, but apart from tulips, daffodils and mint, it was not an outstanding success. And if I couldn't grow tulips or daffodils in the land of bulbs, then I think I would've stopped then and there. Mint grows, I now know, anywhere and everywhere. Rampant mint was my downfall. It overtook the back garden.

"No one told me to contain it," I moaned to John, as he manfully tugged bucketfuls out on a rare day off.

Once I got back to the tropics I was in my element.

Trinidad might not have been the best place in the world, but the hibiscus, the ixora, and the jasmine all helped make me feel at ease. Our garden offered local tradesmen and friends a constant supply of Juliet avocadoes, too big and buxom to have the strong flavour of smaller varieties, but luscious nonetheless.

"Would you like to take some avocadoes?" I asked a particularly helpful electrician, who had finally fixed the washing machine.

"Oh yes, madam."

Later that day, pushing Kate in her stroller, I came across him selling them at a stall at the bottom of the road. He grinned and waved, not in the least sheepish.

"Wow Samuel, how many did you take?"

"Two sackful, is all," he replied. I had to laugh at his enterprise.

Not long after, making coffee one morning, I heard quiet. I had left Kate on the veranda chattering to her toys, and the cat, who had appeared one rainy night and then stayed. And then Kate wasn't there. The latch on the little gate was open, but the street gate was still thankfully closed. I dashed out into the garden, which fell steeply through the avocado and lime trees down to a jungle, fenced off but not entirely secure.

"Kate, Kate, where are you?" I called, trying not to sound panicked.

"Mummy, look," she snuffled, tottering back up the hill, nappy half off, clutching a lime in her fist, breathing in the tangy scent through the thumb she invariably sucked. Confident in her newfound ability to walk, she had taken herself off to explore. Her quest for limes became a daily occurrence. We would find limes discarded around the house when the aroma no longer pleased.

Our first move to Thailand was where I planted my first real garden; gardenias, hibiscus and a frangipani.

"Madam?" Es, our maid, asked tentatively.

"Yes."

"Madam," she said again, fussing with Kate's hair as I dug a hole.

"Yes," I repeated.

"Madam, not good," she finally said.

"What isn't Es?" I asked, wiping sweat from my top lip and stopping Kate tipping headlong into the hole, now ready for planting.

"Flower for temple," she said, looking at the fragile frangipani sapling soaking in a tub of warm water. "Bad here. Spilit no like."

"Oh Es, I'm sorry," I said, as I realised what a *farang faux pas* I had been about to make, but wishing she'd mentioned it before I finished digging the hole. "Would it be okay if I planted it over there?" I asked, pointing to the spirit temple on stilts in the corner of the garden, where Es prayed morning and evening as she wafted lit joss sticks before her closed eyes.

Gardening has been a source of happiness for me in every country ever since. Not just the physical aspect of digging and weeding and planting, but the company of gardeners we have employed, often a little uneasy at first at madam's willingness to get grubby. It is from them I have learnt secrets, not just of the soil, but also of their society.

Lord of the Ring's actor Viggo Mortenson, a TCK born in New York to an American mother and Danish father, spent much of his childhood in Venezuela, Argentina and Denmark and says, "Out of habit you assume that you have something in common with people no matter how different they seem." That ability to find common ground, to be engaged, is key in making a home, and being at home, anywhere in the world. Curiosity might have killed the cat, but it has opened many doors. Some I've only peeked around, but others I've flung open and jumped through. Not all have been successful, but I've learnt a lot and wherever I am, is home.

Take-Away Slice: It really isn't the buildings or the food, or the gardens that make a place home. It is the people who have made my life, occasionally more in retrospect, such fun and so privileged.

It is always about the people. Not only your loved ones who travel the globe with you, or other expatriates who have shared your dramas, high and low, but the people who are hosting you in their country. The people who have opened their customs and cultures to our curious eyes, who have welcomed us to their homes; it is they that make us feel at home wherever we go in the world.

Twelfth Slice:
R 'n' R – Repatriation and Retirement

Five days after Ava's birth, I awaited John's arrival at London Heathrow for a fleeting visit to view his first grandchild before he boarded a flight to Asia and the Antipodes. I wondered about all the hours I have spent in arrival halls all over the world, waiting for family and friends to start their holiday, waiting for John to return from some trip on the other side of the globe, or in the early days from for an upcountry rig. It has been, as Cilla Black, the British singer and TV personality, would say, 'a lorra lorra' hours.

A sign painted in blue and green, on a long roll of brown packing paper being held by two lads, maybe 11 and 14 saying, 'Welcome back Si and Lydia' caught my attention. Standing behind them making sporadic small talk were two sets of families, eyes darting to the doors swinging open to disgorge trolleys and weary travellers, all anxiously scanning the crowd for a familiar face, or a name on a placard.

A squeal erupted from one of the mothers as she spotted a girl, presumably Lydia. She rushed to the end of the barricade and wove her way through the baggage carts being pushed by a phalanx of men, women and children looking dazed and disoriented.

Lydia, wearing long cargo shorts and layers of different length tee-shirts with a tie-dyed muslin scarf tossed nonchalantly around her neck, looked mildly embarrassed at her mother's continued squeals. She shrugged off her rucksack and dropped it by her sneaker-encased feet, succumbing to a tight embrace. She glanced over her mother's shoulder at her travelling companion, and I assume, lover. A glance that asked, "What now?"

Si, meanwhile, had manfully shaken hands with his father and two brothers before bussing his mother's cheek. His attire, crimson and indigo-stripped baggy fisherman's trousers, topped by a red sleeveless tee, and shaggy starch-coloured hair testament to months of backpacking, gave away their chosen place of travel. Around his neck was a leather thong holding an amulet. Thailand had without doubt been the starting point for their return journey.

The couple, maybe in their late teens, and probably returned from a gap year spent travelling, were pleased to see their parents though appeared a little wary. I wondered if they were thinking how they would fit back into society's norms after a year of freedom from parental mores, how to say goodbye to a young lover after a year of constant closeness and how to yield to rules and expectations enforced by university.

The two younger brothers stood a little apart gazing at Si, a near stranger and yet strangely familiar. They didn't speak, but listened as their father quizzed his prodigal son, a boy when he left and now a man.

I felt sorry about the inevitable questions that would arise from the year of freedom and, as I shamelessly watched the scene unfold, it reminded me of repatriates.

Overseas freedoms and the anonymity of expatriate life – an anonymity that in a way allows reinvention with each new posting – wiped out at the return to the life maybe left many years earlier. The new reality hits in those first few moments of total disorientation in the arrivals hall.

It reminded me repatriation can occur at any age, not just at retirement, and my thoughts spiralled back to 1978 when John arrived back in England after two years as a VSO.

"Where've you been, 'aven't seen you around for while," said an old mate in the pub in Gloucester.

"I've in Papua New Guinea for the last two years, Jim, that's why," John replied, enjoying the taste of draught beer again.

"Really?   That explains it. Did you see the game at Kingsholm at the weekend?"

It was a difficult and in some ways lonely time for him, readjusting to the old life and realising it was not a life he wanted anymore. Fortunately he wanted me to share the new one, wherever it was in the world.

I wondered how I would feel if I knew my travelling days were over, if I knew I'd had my moment of freedom, that brief gap year of discovery, before I succumbed to the expectations of others.

Can I write about repatriation? I think so, because in effect we repatriated to the US when we left Equatorial Guinea. It might not have been our passport country, but we were returning to what we knew, albeit a different version.

Moving or relocating at the behest of a corporation is often on a promise. A stint in the office in Oslo will round out the experience gained in Oman, kind of hint. But returning to company headquarters from years abroad can be a frustratingly difficult time, a time when those dangled carrots do not end up in a stew but on the trash heap. Personnel change, companies are bought and sold, and living outside the loop can take an employee off the stove. The target has moved. John knew there was limited opportunity for him with the company that sent us to West Africa and opted to take early retirement. It was a strange time. Strangely liberating, and a little unnerving. The first day of that retirement we got back on a plane and ran away to Grenada for a couple of weeks. It was a good idea, breaking the routine of getting up and going to work.

"I'll start looking for another job when we get back," he said, as we had coffee overlooking the beckoning azure seas leading away to the Grenadines, vague mirage-like shapes in the distance.

"Why? It'll be the start of the silly season and the kids'll be back for Christmas. Wait a while," I said.

"Well, I'll have to put feelers out."

"No you don't. Take some time off, you're tired. Enjoy a break."

We bought a loft in Downtown Houston in an 'as is' state and spent many hours remodelling it ourselves, with the sometime help of patient and talented carpenters, and one tradesman I was not so keen on.

"I don't like him," I said, when John returned from showing him the door.

"He's fine. A bit rough. He's a man's man," he said.

"Oh really, a man's man? Well you can deal with him."

"Okay."

The day after the work started, John had to fly to England to see his ailing father.

The man's man sat on an upturned bucket on our terrace to have a smoko.

"What's that building with all the windows?" he asked.

"The county gaol," I replied, keeping Miss Meg's nose out of the open paint tin.

"I don't remember it having windows when I was in there," he mused. On seeing my horrified look he assured me he was now a regular Evangelical.

I did not feel reassured but told him the windows were all false, a sop to urban planning restrictions for building a gaol in the centre of town.

Our remodelling continued and for four months John was home. I had been a little concerned. In twenty-five years of marriage we had never had that length of time together in one period. I cried when he returned to work.

"Hi, Apple? It's Louise."

"Hi, how are you?"

"Great thanks. Look I wanted to ask you a favour,"

"Okay, you can ask, but I just might say no."

"Hope you won't. You might remember I am President of FAUSA. Would you consider speaking after dinner at the AGM next month? It'll be informal."

"Louise, I think I should be honoured, but I'm sorry, I'm not quite sure what FAUSA is."

"It's the US alumnae association of repatriated members of FAWCO."

"Oh," I said. "Would you mind if thought about it for a day or two?"

"No, of course not. As long as you say yes!"

Google quickly reminded me FAWCO, founded in 1931, was the Federation of American Women's Clubs Overseas with a network of 75 member clubs representing over 15,000 individuals throughout the world. A non-partisan, not-for-profit US corporation recognized as an NGO in 1995 with the Economic and Social Council of the UN granting it special consultative status in 1997. I also learned that over the years FAWCO has donated more than a million dollars in education awards and development grants globally.

The more I read the more I was surprised to be asked to speak, never having been a FAWCO member and as a life-long global nomad never having really repatriated. But I liked both the FAWCO and FAUSA mission statements, which promise support to both expatriate and repatriate American women respectively, while encouraging involvement in community projects and enhancing intercultural awareness.

Expatriates and repatriates experience equal doses of culture shock, the distinction is the latter often don't expect it. Forums are provided for the expatriate but not always for the repatriate, which is why lifelines like FAUSA are so valuable for American women returning to a country that may not have been 'home' for many years.

Over the years I have seen people struggle with repatriation and the issues it can provoke. Lifestyle changes can have many repercussions, from unsettled children to jobless spouses and hugely increased expenses, to just not feeling at home, at home. That missing link, support for repatriates, is one of the aspects of a global life that Families in Global Transition attempts to bridge, by educating those that bring us 'back'.

"Louise, hi!" I said a couple of days later. "I'd love to talk at the FAUSA AGM, thank you for asking me. It sounds like a wonderful organization."

Sometimes it seems as if 'home' has changed, or maybe it hasn't. Maybe it is we who have changed, grown to incorporate, often without realising, elements of our life abroad. The immediate family has coalesced into a tight unit, still with the everyday rattles of family living, but firm in its face to the outside world. New words, often foreign, have joined the family lexicon which members of the extended family back home have no notion of, and do not understand the reflective mood and quiet smiles those words might bring. They feel shut out, and indeed they are though not intentionally, just as we are not excluded intentionally from conversations revolving around the last family get-together. The one we missed because we were on the other side of the world enjoying a different kind of life, or maybe surviving in an alien environment dealing with new schools, new hospitals and so on, all in a foreign language with its own acronyms to confuse the unsuspecting expatriate.

But suddenly, it seems, you are 'home' for good. The initial excitement and anticipation of returning to our roots can quickly become a series of disappointments, of realisations; we don't actually want to be involved in every single family affair, we do care about what is happening in other countries, we don't care if a brother's garage door isn't working, we do care the rains have come early and fast in China.

It can be difficult to marry your old life, with your just-left life and your new life back home. And you didn't expect that.

It takes time to adapt, just as it took time to adjust to living in a new country. We might be back in the home country, but we are looking at it through a different cultural lens and have to allow the same adjustment period as when we expatriated. And we have to find something that anchors us, just as we did abroad.

All those skills we learnt in Gabon are equally viable in New Jersey and we have to remember we are that adaptable breed of men and women – the accompanying partner, the trailing spouse, one of the STARS and sometimes a chameleon, as we find the best way to fit in with our new, old life.

A few weeks later, after my talk, a light-hearted roadmap to living in Texas, some of the woman shared their experiences of returning home and how they had charted their new lives.

"We lived in the Middle East for twenty years," said a graying matron of indeterminate years, "Honey, it was hell moving back. Took me years to get used to having to bag my own groceries," she laughed.

"Where did you retire to?" I asked.

"The Texas Hill Country. My bones couldn't stand being back up north during winter."

"Is your husband from Texas?"

"No, we met at high school. But after dragging me around the world all his working life he was happy to let me choose where we'd end up. It was a good decision."

The evening strengthened my belief in organisations like FAUSA and FIGT, and in the resilience of the accompanying spouse wherever they go, home or abroad.

"There's always something to change." Words Max Gonzalez, owner of Catalina's, my favourite coffee house in Houston if not the world, said recently when I commented on the new layout of his counter.

Max's words and the tantalizing smells of Arabica from Brazil, Guatamala and PNG brought up fresh thoughts. Coffee does that to me.

Change can be hard to embrace sometimes and that's okay. To me embracing change comes from curiosity which can lead to adventures, and they come in all shapes and sizes; a child walking to school alone for the first time, college, first or fifth relocation whether to a new town or over an ocean. They are all adventures born of curiosity, tinged with a little angst and a dash of hope, and in my case lots of coffee. I think the sooner we can open up to that change and welcome the opportunities, the easier our lives become.

And repatriation is a big change. Repatriation and retirement effected at the same time is a helluva big change.

"Gosh Helena, I didn't realise you were leaving. It doesn't seem that long ago I was welcoming you to Houston," I said to the elegant woman looking morosely at the coffee urn at an International Connections of Houston meeting.

"Two years," she replied. "Mike's retiring. What the hell am I going to do in Plymouth? Mike can't wait to get a boat and piddle around on the water. I hate sailing."

"I thought Plymouth was quite nice," I commented. "There seemed to be quite a lot going on there. Theatre and stuff," I added lamely.

"Yeah I 'spose so. But all my family are in Essex and the kids are in London."

"You'll be closer in Devon than you are here."

"Yes I know. It'll be fine. I'm just not sure what I'll do." Helen shrugged.

"Exactly what you did here, and in Dubai, and Jakarta and all the other places you've lived," I said, pouring her another coffee and wishing I could add a swish of brandy to cheer her up. "Join a club, get out there. Treat it just like a new posting."

"Yes, but when you're an expat you're all in the same boat. It won't be the same there."

"No I know, but you will find people who you can connect to. It seems to me the West Country is full of old nomads like us. It must be the weather."

We talked some more and then went our separate ways, but Helena's unsettled thoughts stayed with me. Funny how some days we follow an unintentional trail, because when I got home I read a question on an online expatriate forum related to divorce after a restless repatriation. I do think, sadly, there is a correlation between marriage break ups in those who have been expatriates for a long time and the two R 'n' Rs – repatriation and retirement

My father was a classic example of both. After forty-five years abroad, in both the army and then working for trading companies, he retired 'home'. A word that his entire life had embodied England, but an England as he knew it in 1947, romanticised at that. A land of green and pleasant pastures, of warm beer, cricket on the village lawn and gentlemen politicians.

The reality is very different for many. The village might still be there but commonalities with the villagers are few, their interest in a life abroad cursory. But more importantly, the commonalities perceived to be in the marriage are not there either.

The 'virtual' conversation asked the question 'why do so many expatriate marriages end on assignment?' I was surprised, because in fifty or so years of expatriate life on the global trail, I have known remarkably few end in divorce. Living in a foreign country has its own stressors, but on the whole it tends to bring the family closer. Almost an 'us against the rest of the world' frame of mind, certainly in the early days of an assignment.

Reading the comments was interesting but offered no new magic elixir to manoeuvring within the labyrinth of marital disharmony, separation and divorce whether a nomadic or a settled marriage. If the desire to stray is there the availability is irrelevant.

We are the same people wherever we live, so I think we must use the same techniques to keep a marriage alive, to keep the lines open, to have independent thoughts and activities yet remain interested in, and interesting to, each other. In essence, to care enough to make it work, even with the inevitable blips that need to be negotiated in any marriage.

I've written about STARS retaining feelings of self-worth, about encouraging volunteer work or enterprise where viable, about supporting multiple moves and school choices and the myriad of things that surface on every relocation. We all know the adage 'if the wife ain't happy then nobody is!' Like all sayings there is an element of truth.

Sometimes that busy life of work, or supporting a spouse, or ferrying children, or volunteering, limits the actual time of 'together'. It is easy to get caught up in the whirl of expatriate society, the St George's Ball, or the museum opening or the Hash House Harriers. The list is endless. The bubbles floating out of the champagne flutes can easily capture us in a cycle of busyness that can do little to protect the precious bubble surrounding a marriage. The social gaiety can be contagious, the blemishes appearing surreptitiously as after an evening with the chocolate box.

The conversation with Helena triggered thoughts of my parents and of other people known, who when the realisation of empty nests and / or repatriation hits, so to does the realisation at the lack of community in the marriage.

Suddenly the independent yet co-dependent lives led as an expatriate couple are inexorably entwined in a bucolic idyll of sitting in the garden on a soft summer evening listening to the mourning doves, and if they're very lucky a cuckoo heralding the end of day. "This is bliss," they say, as they sip their gin and tonics and admire the hawthorn, but as the fingers of winter start creeping under the door, the closeness of the hearth seems suddenly too close. Or, maybe the longed for rhythm of life aboard a yacht gets lost in a litter of lines slithering over a deck as the close and constant proximity, and the gentle slap of waves on the hull, starts to grate after those first few free months.

The bubble wrap protecting the marriage has popped without you noticing in the scurry of expatriate life, and what is left is a flat sheet, dull with disinterest when there is no audience to participate in the marriage.

A busy important life abroad does not always transform well into retirement. The nurturing required is the same yet different, rather like looking after a garden in Asia and looking after a garden in Europe, the same principles but different watering habits. My parents' retirement, repatriation and subsequent separation shocked me when it happened. In retrospect they should have split up many years earlier, but it was the fabric of their expatriate society that kept them together, though apart.

Whenever parents separate it is hard and whilst I tried to be understanding and supportive to both at the time, I really wish, with those wonderful things called *age* and *distance* as my tutors, I'd told my father before he died I really did understand his decision to leave my mother.

Repatriation and retirement did not work out how they had initially planned it. As in most of my life, I hope I have learnt their lessons.

As expatriates we've all had so many new beginnings, but those final two, repatriation and retirement are probably, in many ways, the hardest.

And then it occurred to me that when R 'n' R is upon John and I, we must consider 'the now' as a new beginning, not the end of an exciting, exacting life.

New beginnings are like a new notebook or a blank computer screen. Exciting, but a little daunting. We're not quite sure what the year will bring, what will appear on that empty page – a new school or university, a new baby, a new job, a new country? It doesn't matter that you've done all the research possible, all eventualities can't be covered. Thank goodness. I don't think I would have done well if life had fallen into the boring box, if everything could be predicted, counted on.

John and I will have to remember we like new beginnings. They're exciting, challenging, sometimes a success, sometimes not. And from every new start, whether a year or a job, we have the chance to take what was good from the last year, the last posting, the last semester, the last relationship, and discard the dross.

We will have to remember we made mistakes in our old life, so will surely make some more, but as long as we learn from them they can never be considered a waste of time or energy, or caring.

Mum's words about treating every person met as a new friend come back to me and I realise what a wonderful lesson she taught me with those few simple words. That philosophy has stood me in good stead through twenty-six new beginnings in new locations, along with the readjustments made each and every time I returned to boarding school in Australia, from a holiday spent at home in either Malaysia or PNG.

Wherever I have lived has been home, whether a year in Trinidad and Tobago or seven long grey winters in Scotland, but there was always the lure, the tantalising promise of a move to another country, a new beginning.

That lure has gone as my husband has reached a stage in his career demanding we stay put. Fortunately, I love living in Houston, it is a city full of surprises, of diversity and energy and not just the pumping oil kind. It is a dynamic place thriving on change and yes, new beginnings.

But for a TCK who has spent her life roaming the globe it is a vast new arena to negotiate. I am learning the most important thing in staying put is not to stay static, but rather to produce static by continually looking for new paths to explore. But this time in the same place and not down some little Thai *soi* or a dusty Equatorial Guinean *avenida*.

A life spent relocating around the world is testing, scary sometimes but always exciting. The people make it so. For me now, I have to make sure the boundaries of life do not start to close, almost unwittingly, as the easy life of Houston engulfs me in malls, freeways and fast food.

It is a challenge, I think the hardest I have had to face. I can no longer dabble. Now my commitments, comments and actions will be all encompassing. I am here to stay. I cannot start again, having left behind in some other country an ill thought word spoken in haste, or an unintentional offence. I must remember I am not relocating. This is it, for the time being. And that is a novel concept for me.

Now the friends we must encompass, those people we are about to meet, will become our new beginnings. Our window to the world, although viewed from one place now, will always be open. So, no physical new beginnings. Rather a metaphysical one. That in itself is challenging and exciting. A new now.

Take-Away Slice: There isn't an expat alive who hasn't had 'no-to-change' days. Days of "What in God's name am I doing here?" For repatriates, questions like, "What the hell were we thinking, coming back here?" or "I think we've made a mistake retiring here."

If we can manage that change, actually thrive on it, relish meeting new people, some of whom will become friends, our thoughts, actions and words will be influenced in some way, whether through a different culture, custom or outlook. Becoming engaged in our final move is just as important as becoming engaged in our first. It probably all comes back to my mother's question, "Isn't it nice thinking everyone you meet will be a friend?"

Last Slice

I've talked about many people in this book; it is they who have made this journey so interesting. Some encounters, like the one early in our tenure in EG when a strange young man ended up on our bedroom floor, only became amusing after the event. Most though, have been illuminating and above all fun.

I wish I could thank everyone who has helped make this book. It is all our stories, with slight variations. Some names are real, and I thank you for your permission to use them. Some have been changed out of respect, or fear of retribution. Many will recognise elements of themselves, good and bad. I know I've made many mistakes along the way, but I comfort myself they were, mostly, unintentional.

I apologise to Kate and Edward for neither John nor I always being the best parents in the world. A low point in our parenting skills was probably on holiday in Tuscany many years ago, when we resented paying considerably more for their blood orange juice than our wine.

"Couldn't we just dilute wine for them?" John asked.

"No, I think that would come under abuse in the eyes of the law, even here," I replied, picking up my *chianti*, so similar in colour to their juice.

I sometimes find it hard to believe I was lucky enough to fall in with, and in love with, a man who has given me the dream life I didn't know I wanted. All I wish for my children, and Ava, is the same love and fun I have had.

We will always keep a base in Houston, the energy of the city suits us, but we are always open to new adventures and places. We know wherever we might go, we will hope for a good market with fresh produce, wine and no skinned monkeys are musts. As well as providing us with the staples in life it will, of course, always have the added benefit of being an early warning system to civil unrest, though I suppose the push of a cell phone button does it even quicker now, but with far less excitement or romance.

Some days I do find myself longing for the thrill of receiving a flimsy blue aerogramme, with the nod to Saint Exupéry's pioneer airmail deliveries in the Sahara, by having *par avion* stamped in the corner. Maybe like his *Le Petit Prince* we are all travelling the universe searching to understand life.

But if you are contemplating a life abroad, don't worry unduly about your family disintegrating as the miles add up along with the air miles; instead embrace the stories and memories that link you, rather than the miles that separate you. Just remember if you are new to the relocation business, in the sense you are the one doing the relocating, find yourself a Catalina's coffee house and meet new friends. Make yourself at home.

THE END

ABOUT THE AUTHOR

Apple Gidley started her expat life at a month old in Kano, Nigeria in the cooling embers of colonialism. Since those early days her itinerant lifestyle has included newly independent countries full of hope, nations we could all learn from and one or two we shouldn't. Picking up a husband and two children along the way, Apple has relocated 26 times through 12 countries. Her roles, as well as wife and mother, have included editing a regional magazine for an international charity, selling dive equipment and springing Distressed British Nationals from gaol among others. An Anglo-Australian now known to thousands as ExpatApple, thanks to her popular blog at the Daily Telegraph, she believes that to be a true global nomad we have to be actively engaged in wherever we call home, for the moment.

You can find her at www.my.telegraph.co.uk/applegidley
www.expatapple.com
www.twitter.com/ExpatApple

List of Photographs

First Slice   Apple and Munnings, Nigeria, circa 1963

Second Slice   Apple, Bangkok, 1988

Third Slice   Apple and friend, Nigeria, circa 1963

Fourth Slice   Dancers at Mount Hagen Show,
                   Papua New Guinea, 1977

Fifth Slice   Mak Peck Yoke, Apple, Ah Moi and Ebi,
                   Malaysia, 1973

Sixth Slice   Apple, NEGS, Australia, 1975

Seventh Slice   N'bili, Malabo, Equatorial Guinea, 2004

Eighth Slice   Airletters from Mum and John

Ninth Slice   Christmas Tree Skirt, Houston, 2010

Tenth Slice   Gigi and Ava, London, August 2011

Eleventh Slice   Miss Meg, Kingwood, Texas, 2001

Twelfth Slice   John, British Virgin Island, 2011

Last Slice   John and Ida Girling, and Apple, Nigeria,
                   June 1958
                   Ida and Apple, London, circa 1961
                   John, Apple, Kate, Edward and Miss Meg,
                   Kingwood, TX 1999
                   (courtesy of Theresa Kohlhauff)

Families in Global Transition

As a leader of a global network, FIGT promotes the positive value of worldwide transitions, and empowers the employee, the family unit, and those who serve them before, during and after international relocations by uniting theory and practice.

FIGT's global community is built by bringing together corporate, diplomatic, academic, the arts, military, missionary, and NGO sectors to share and develop leading edge research and concepts that address international relocation issues.

For information about FIGT, please contact:

Families in Global Transition
PO Box 3363, Warrenton, VA 20188
Email: execdirector@figt.org | Website: www.figt.org
Phone: (202) 360-4916 | Fax: (202) 962-3939

Expat
TEENS TALK

Peers, Parents and Professionals
offer support, advice and solutions
in response to Expat Life Challenges
as shared by Expat Teens

Dr. Lisa Pittman and Diana Smit

A Global Nomad's Journey From Hurt To Healing

Letters

NEVER SENT

RUTH E. VAN REKEN

MORE THAN **32,000** COPIES SOLD

SUNSHINE
SOUP

NOURISHING THE GLOBAL SOUL

Jo Parfitt

"An entertaining story,
told with wit and insight"
Paul Burston, author, The Gay Divorcee

PERKING
THE PANSIES

*Jack and Liam
move to Turkey*

JACK SCOTT

CPSIA information can be obtained
at www.ICGtesting.com
Printed in the USA
FFOW02n1705111113
2336FF